New Works in Accounting History

Richard P. Brief, *Series Editor*

Leonard N. Stern School of Business
New York University

A Garland Series

ACCOUNTING HISTORY FROM THE RENAISSANCE TO THE PRESENT

A Remembrance of Luca Pacioli

Edited by
T.A. Lee,
A. Bishop,
and
R.H. Parker

Garland Publishing, Inc.
New York and London 1996

Introductory material copyright © 1996 by T.A. Lee, A. Bishop, and R.H. Parker

Library of Congress Cataloging-in-Publication Data

Accounting history from the Renaissance to the present : a remembrance of Luca Pacioli / edited by T.A. Lee, A. Bishop, and R.H. Parker.

    p. cm. — (New works in accounting history)
    Includes bibliographical references (p.).
    ISBN 0-8153-2271-2 (alk. paper)
    1. Accounting—History. 3. Pacioli, Luca, d. ca. 1514. 3. Accountants—Biography. 4. Information technology. I. Lee, T.A. (Thomas Alexander) II. Bishop, Ashton C. III. Parker, R.H. (Robert Henry) IV. Series.
HF5605.A23   1996   95–51120
657'.09—dc20   CIP

All volumes printed on acid-free, 250-year-life paper.
Manufactured in the United States of America.

Design by Marisel Tavarez

CONTENTS

Chapter 3: A Recent History of Financial Reporting in the UK and US

71

Donna L. Street, James Madison University

Chapter 5: The Impact of Advancements in Manufacturing and Information Technology on Management Accounting Systems   143

Thomas Tyson, St. John Fisher College

Fenton F. Robb, Formerly, University of Edinburgh

PREFACE

In a unique sponsorship which also included The British Academy, The Institute of Chartered Accountants of Scotland and the Academy of Accounting Historians organised a one-day conference for an invited audience of accounting practitioners and historians. Over one hundred and fifty individuals from seventeen countries attended the conference which was held at the Royal College of Physicians in Edinburgh. It was part of a two-day Festival of Accounting organised by the Institute to explore the issue of the contemporary impact of information technology on the accountancy profession. It was therefore appropriate in such a context to include a programme centered on the history and influence of one of the most enduring accounting technologies, double-entry bookkeeping.

The conference was organised around a number of invited papers on selected topics directly and indirectly related to the emergence and development of double-entry bookkeeping. It was chaired by Ashton Bishop, President of the Academy of Accounting Historians, and introduced by Nigel Macdonald, President of The Institute of Chartered Accountants of Scotland. Each paper was presented in conjunction with a commentary by a discussant. A selection of the papers is presented in this text. Each has been researched by the author concerned, and amended in light of discussant and independent reviewer comments. As such, they provide a unique view of the history of accounting and accountants from the fifteenth century to the present time. Hopefully, therefore, this text will be useful to accountancy students and teachers interested in accounting history as part of the undergraduate and graduate curricula.

The text commences with Richard Macve's insights into Pacioli - his life, times, and contribution. It then proceeds to explore two main areas of accountancy development - financial accounting and reporting within the corporate sector, and cost and management accounting largely within the context of industrialisation. Dick Edwards and Dick Fleischman, respectively, research these areas from Pacioli's times to the 1960s. Donna Street and Tom Tyson take a more contemporary perspective of events and changes in the last three decades. The emergence and establishment of an institutionalised accountancy profession is researched by Tom Lee, and Fenton Robb explores the evolution of information technologies to the present time, particularly as they have impacted the profession.

In presenting these researched contributions, we do not wish to imply that it is a complete history of accounting and accountants. As with Richard Brown's (1905) text, it is a historical review and "state of play" of certain aspects of work which is generically described as accountancy, and of people homogeneously labeled as accountants. Because of the research interests of the invited authors, much of the material focuses on accounting (rather than, say, auditing or taxation), and the majority of the sources accessed are either British or American (ignoring, for example, financial accounting changes in Australasia and Continental Europe). To have covered a wider menu of topics and locations would have resulted in a project of massive proportions. We believe that, despite these limitations, the text provides a unique insight into the history of accounting and accountants.

In particular, the various contributions demonstrate to us the continuing usefulness of accounting history. They provide not only a unique celebration of a particular historical event in 1494, but also give the reader a sound contextual basis for studying contemporary issues affecting financial and management accounting, and the accountancy profession. In so doing, each chapter reveals the paradox of continuity and change which characterises the history of accounting and accountants - e.g. the use of complex numbers-based technologies to present and represent the economic actions and consequences of actions of firms. History is therefore not a matter of antiquarianism, of recording the "facts" of the past. Instead, it should be seen as a means of questioning the past in order to cope better with the present and the future. From this perspective, the contributions of this text should cause all accountants to take pride in the achievements of the past (particularly, the enduring value of a technology such as double-entry bookkeeping), whilst reminding them that there are past mistakes from which to learn and improve the quality of accounting services.

The text should also remind us that the history of accounting and accountants is not just a subject of potential interest and utility to accountants. Indeed, as the content of the various chapters testify, such a history is a window to a rich tapestry of related subject areas.

For example, accounting can be perceived as a technology, a profession, a university discipline, and a mechanism for social regulation and control. As such, it is worthy of study by students of education, government, information and systems, organisational behaviour, and sociology. In this sense, accounting ceases to be a separately identifiable discipline. Instead, it becomes a microcosm of economic, political and social life.

This text represents these themes, and does so in a way which is consistent with contemporary writing in history. The various contributions reflect the limitations of writing a history of accounting and accountants. It is subjective while attempting to reconstruct past "facts." It is observational and explanatory while remaining critical and questioning. It is neither a "new" nor an "old" history. It relies to a considerable extent on secondary sources yet, in each chapter, reveals original insights. Its major value is in its broad review of multiple events over considerable periods of time. We recognise these things as both strengths and weaknesses.

Many thanks must be offered to everyone associated with this project. First, the financial and non-financial support of the Scottish Institute and its Educational Trust, the Academy of Accounting Historians, and the British Academy is gratefully acknowledged. Without the whole-hearted efforts of the Institute particularly, the conference and the text would not have materialised. The unanimous vote for the project by the Institute's Council, and the infectious enthusiasm for it by its President, Nigel Macdonald, bear witness to the very unique contribution to the world of accountancy by Scottish Chartered Accountants. The success of the conference and the text also owes much to the sterling efforts of many employees of the Institute. Particular thanks go to Aileen Beattie, Ann Lamb, Isobel Webber, and Fiona Wright. Thanks must also go to the conference contributors and discussants - Dick Edwards, Dick Fleischman, Lyle Jacobsen, Moyra Kedslie, Tom Lee, Richard Macve, Michael Moss, Ken Most, Chris Nobes, Bob Parker, Fenton Robb, Ken Shackleton, Colin Storrar, Donna Street, Tom Tyson, Steve Walker, and Bernard Williams. Each individual not only responded to the deadline of the conference but also to several others connected with the production of this text.

A large part of Pacioli's legacy is captured in the contributions to this text. To say that his influence is alive and well almost five hundred years after his death is a remarkable statement of his impact.

We wish each reader of this text enjoyment from the history and the legacy.

Tom Lee (Tuscaloosa), **Ashton Bishop** (Harrisonburg), and **Bob Parker** (Exeter), 30 April 1995.

ACKNOWLEDGMENT

This book is published under the auspices of the
Scottish Committee on Accounting History of The
Institute of Chartered Accountants of Scotland and the
Academy of Accounting Historians

BIOGRAPHICAL NOTES
OF EDITORS AND AUTHORS

Ashton C. Bishop

Ashton Bishop is Ernst & Young Faculty Fellow and Professor of Accounting at James Madison University. He received BS and MS degrees from Virginia Commonwealth University, and his doctorate from Oklahoma State University. He was the 1994 President of the Academy of Accounting Historians, having previously served as its Secretary and as Manuscript Editor of the *Accounting Historians Journal*. He has also served as the Manuscript Editor of the *Journal of Accounting Education*. In addition to authoring journal articles, Dr Bishop has compiled and edited several books of readings. He currently serves on the Editorial Board of the *Journal of International Accounting, Auditing and Taxation*. His teaching interest is in management accounting.

John Richard Edwards

Dick Edwards is a professor at the University of Wales College of Cardiff and is Director of the Business History Research Unit of the Cardiff Business School. He was educated in Wales before serving his accounting apprenticeship in the London office of Cooper Brothers & Company. After qualifying as a member of The Institute of Chartered Accountants in England and Wales and of the Institute of Taxation, he gained a postgraduate degree in economics. He has taught at the New York Graduate Business School in 1982 and at Newcastle University

(Australia) in 1992. Professor Edwards' areas of lecturing expertise are advanced financial accounting, taxation, and accounting history. His research is directed primarily towards exploring the origin and development of accounting practices, and the conventions and concepts on which these practices are based. He has published extensively in academic journals, and is the author of *A History of Financial Accounting* (Routledge). Professor Edwards is the founding editor of the international research journal, *Accounting, Business & Financial History*, and a Trustee of the Academy of Accounting Historians.

Richard K. Fleischman

Dick Fleischman is currently the KPMG Peat Marwick Accounting Professor in International Business at John Carroll University in Cleveland, Ohio. He holds a BA (History) from Harvard College, and an MA and PhD (History) from the State University of New York at Buffalo. He also has an MBA degree with an accounting emphasis from SUNY-Buffalo. Dr Fleischman taught history at the University of Hawaii from 1969 to 1981, and accounting at John Carroll from 1983 to the present. He is the immediate past Chair of the Department of Accountancy, serving from 1986 to 1994. Dr Fleischman's research interests combine his history and accounting backgrounds, featuring published work in *The Accounting Review*, *Accounting and Business Research*, *Journal of Accountancy*, *Accounting Historians Journal*, *Economic History Review*, and *Accounting, Business & Financial History*. The majority of these articles have dealt with UK Industrial Revolution cost accounting and US municipal accounting during the Progressive era. Dr Fleishman is on the editorial boards of *Accounting, Business & Financial History* and *Accounting, Auditing & Accountability Journal*.

Thomas A. Lee

Tom Lee has been the Hugh Culverhouse Endowed Chair of Accountancy at the University of Alabama since 1990. Previously, he held Chairs at the Universities of Liverpool (1973-6) and Edinburgh (1976-90). He was Head of the Department of Accounting and Business Method at Edinburgh from 1976 to 1988. Dr Lee has been a visiting professor at the Universities of Maryland, Utah, and Edinburgh. He is currently a visiting professor at Deakin University in Australia. After serving a five-year apprenticeship and qualifying as a member of The Institute of Chartered Accountant of Scotland (ICAS) in 1964 (winning the ICAS Gold Medal and other national prizes), Dr Lee was employed as an auditor with a Big Six firm until entering academe in 1966. He holds two research-based degrees from the University of Strathclyde (MSc and DLitt). Continuously active with his professional body, ICAS, he has served on its education and research committees as well as its governing Council, and was seconded as Director of Accounting and Auditing Research between 1983 and 1984. Dr Lee's research and teaching interests cover the areas of financial accounting (particularly theory), auditing, and accounting history. He has authored over thirty books and monographs, and more than one hundred and fifty articles in academic and professional journals and various literature collections. Approximately one third of these publications are in the area of accounting history. Dr Lee currently serves as Convenor of the Scottish Committee on Accounting History, a Trustee of the Academy of Accounting Historians, associate editor (history and education) for *The British Accounting Review*, and is on the editorial boards of *Accounting and Business Research* and *Accounting, Auditing & Accountability Journal*.

Richard H. Macve

Richard Macve is the Julian Hodge Professor of Accounting and Head of the Department of Accounting and Finance at the University of Wales, Aberystwyth. He was a coopted member of the Council of

The Institute of Chartered Accountants in England and Wales from 1986 to 1993 and, in 1994, he was appointed as an academic advisor to its Research Board. He is a member of the Accounting Standards Board's Academic Panel, and of the Board of the UK Centre for Economic and Environmental Development. Professor Macve was educated at Chigwell School, New College, Oxford, and the London School of Economics. He qualified as a Chartered Accountant in the London office of Peat Marwick Mitchell & Company, winning prizes at all three levels of his professional examinations. His main research interests are in accounting for insurance, accounting history, and environmental accounting and reporting. Recent books include *Marking to Market* (with J. Jackson) (ICAEW, 1991), *Business, Accountancy, and the Environment* (with A. Carey) (ICAEW, 1992), *A Survey of Lloyd's Syndicate Accounts* (with D. Gwilliam) (Prentice Hall/ICAEW, 1993), and *Accounting Principles for Life Insurance: A True and Fair View?* (with J. Horton) (ICAEW, 1995). Publications on accounting history include "Some Glosses on `Greek and Roman Accounting'," *History of Political Thought* (1985), (with K. Hoskin) "Accounting and the Examination: A Genealogy of Disciplinary Power," *Accounting, Organisations and Society* (1986), (with M. Ezzamel and K. Hoskin) "Managing It All By Numbers," *Accounting and Business Research* (1990), (with K. Hoskin) "Reappraising the Genesis of Managerialism: A Reexamination of the Role of Accounting at the Springfield Armoury," *Accounting, and Auditing & Accountability Journal* (1994), and (with R. Fleischman and K. Hoskin), "Boulton and Watt: The Crux of Alternative Accounting Histories?," *Accounting and Business Research* (1995).

Robert H. Parker

Bob Parker is Professor of Accounting at the University of Exeter, and a Professorial Research Fellow of The Institute of Chartered Accountants of Scotland. He has long-standing research interests in accounting history and international accounting, and has published extensively in both areas. His most recent publications include (with B. S. Yamey) *Accounting History: Some British Contributions* (Clarendon Press, Oxford), (with C. Nobes) *An International View of True and Fair* (Routledge), and (with T. Cooke) *Corporate Financial*

Reporting in the West Pacific Rim (Routledge). The fourth edition of his text with Chris Nobes, *Comparative International Accounting* was published in 1995 by Prentice Hall. From 1975 to 1993, Professor Parker was the Editor of *Accounting and Business Research*. He is a member of the editorial board of *Accounting and Business Research*, *Accounting Historians Journal*, and *Accounting, Business and Financial History*. He was the first Convenor of the Scottish Committee on Accounting History. Many of Professor Parker's articles on accounting history were collected in his *Papers on Accounting History* (Garland, 1984). He has been a visiting professor at the Universities of New South Wales and Sydney, and at the European Institute of Business Administration in France.

Fenton F. Robb

Born and educated in Scotland, Fenton Robb served in the Royal Navy and graduated in economics (MA, 1949) from the University of Edinburgh. He gained a widely varied business experience with P A Management Consultants and, later, as an associated company director with Rowntree. This experience included industrial production, sales, marketing, managerial services, and senior management. In 1979, having studied under Gordon Pask and Professor Frank George, Dr Robb graduated PhD (Cybernetics) from Brunel University. He joined the British gas industry in 1962, serving in marketing, management services, and general management. He retired as the Deputy Chairman of Scottish Gas in 1985. On the recommendation of Professor T. A. Lee, Dr Robb was appointed as Professor of Management Information Systems and Control in the Department of Accounting and Business Method at the University of Edinburgh. Since then, in addition to teaching honours and postgraduate students, he has contributed over sixty articles to refereed journals on accounting, information systems, systems theory, and philosophy. He received an award for his " outstanding scholarly contribution" from the International Institute for Advanced Studies in Systems Research and Cybernetics in 1993. Since retirement from Edinburgh University in 1992, Dr Robb has continued his research.

Donna L. Street

Donna Street received a BBA from East Tennessee State University, and a MAcc and PhD from the University of Tennessee prior to joining the faculty of James Madison University. She is currently an Associate Professor and KPMG Peat Marwick Faculty Fellow. Her teaching interests are financial accounting and accounting theory. She has published articles addressing accounting education and financial reporting topics, and serves on the editorial board of *Advances in Accounting*. She is a member of the Academy of Accounting Historians and serves on the National Council of Beta Alpha Psi.

Thomas Tyson

Tom Tyson is an associate professor of accounting at St John Fisher College in Rochester, New York. He is a Certified Management Accountant and an Enrolled Agent of the Internal Revenue Service. Dr Tyson obtained an MBA from New Mexico State University, an MEd from the University of Pittsburgh, and a PhD in accounting from Georgia State University. He has published over twenty five articles in a variety of academic and professional journals including *Accounting, Auditing & Accountability Journal, The Journal of Business Ethics*, the *Accounting Historians Journal*, and *Management Accounting*. Two of his five previous *Management Accounting* articles received Certificate of Merit awards. Dr Tyson's current research interests include cost accounting history, business ethics, and gender issues.

INTRODUCTION

Nigel Macdonald, Chartered Accountant and Former President of The Institute of Chartered Accountants of Scotland

Celebrating anniversaries without an underlying purpose is, at best, mere nostalgia and, at worst, pointless. There was, however, real purpose in the Seminar which this book summarises, and which was held in Edinburgh in 1994 in the five hundredth year since the publication of Luca Pacioli's *Summa de Arithmetica, Geometria, Proportioni et Proportionalita.* The purpose was simple but relevant to every accountant. It was to revisit some fundamentals that lay behind Pacioli's decision to write his *Summa,* and see whether the accounting framework in which we work today has overlooked basic issues because of its continued focus on development of the existing financial accounting model.

So we tried to look at Pacioli's legacy from several different perspectives, deliberately choosing to do so in ways that addressed considerations that his work reflected. We looked again at the nature and characteristics of the bridge between academic analysis and insight on the one hand and practical application on the other. We also looked at the dominant influences in the evolution of accountancy for managing stewardship and for reporting of that stewardship. By doing so, we attempted to identify influences that had been less pressing and so had been ignored or overlooked. We also considered how changing technology had affected the way we manage the accountancy process. The presentations, and the discussion that followed, were both fascinating and stimulating.

It was fitting that the Seminar was managed and initiated by The Institute of Chartered Accountants of Scotland, the oldest professional accountancy body in the world. The seminar formed part of a Festival of Accounting presented jointly with The Nederlands Instituut van Registeraccountants, a body respected throughout the world for its training and professional standing. I hope that this text will prove a valuable reminder of the Seminar and Pacioli's legacy.

1

1 PACIOLI'S LEGACY

Richard H. Macve
University of Wales, Aberystwyth *

*I would like to record my debt of gratitude to Geoffrey de Ste. Croix for first interesting me in accounting's history; Basil Yamey for inculcating a measured scepticism about almost every assertion that has been made about double-entry; and Keith Hoskin for the insights I have gained through working with him on accounting's history over the last decade. I am also grateful to Michael Moss and an anonymous reviewer for their constructive comments on a previous draft of this paper.

INTRODUCTION

The date in Pacioli's life accountants remember and celebrate is not his birth or death (both of which are disputed)[1] but 1494 - the date of publication five hundred years ago of his *Summa de Arithmetica, Geometria, Proportioni et Proportionalita*. Although venerated as the "Father of Accounting," his treatise on bookkeeping, the *Particularis de Computis et Scripturis* (henceforward the *De Scripturis*), is just one section of the *Summa*. Moreover, Pacioli did not invent double-entry. Rather, as he explained in the first chapter of the *De Scripturis*, he was expounding "the Venetian method which certainly among the others is much recommended and which can be used as a guide to all others" (von Gebsattel, 1994, p.42).   Indeed the structure of the section outlines a different method for preparing the trial balance and closing the ledger in one of its chapters from that given in the conclusion. This suggests that the conclusion came from a separate piece of writing, and that some earlier works were brought together to construct the *De Scripturis* which, in later periods, became a single treatise on double-entry (Durham, 1992, p.50; and Hernandez Esteve, 1994).

3

PACIOLI'S *DE SCRIPTURIS*: WHAT IT WAS NOT AND WHAT IT WAS

Every subject has its classic text - i.e. a text which is so well-known and taken for granted that it is often rare to find someone who has actually read it. Recall the game "Humiliation" in David Lodge's *Changing Places* (1975) where, to win the game, the American tenure-track Assistant Professor of English confesses that he has never read *Hamlet*. In other words, as Homer to the study of classics, so Plato and Aristotle to philosophy and, more recently, Shakespeare to English literature, Smith to economics and Darwin to biology. Yet the demands of modern curricula often preclude direct study of these works of genius. And the minutiae of scholarly dispute may be more concerned with challenging their authorship or date than with critical appraisal of their contribution.

For accounting, the classic text is Pacioli's *De Scripturis* (his publisher's running title). Like many classic texts, its authorship is in dispute. As copies survive for inspection, there is no doubt that a book, including the first printed text explaining double-entry bookkeeping, was published in 1494 (and reprinted in 1523) with Pacioli's name on it (*Frater Luca de Burgo Sancti Sepulcri* [Antinori, 1959, p.3]). However, scholars have disputed the extent to which it may have been plagiarised from manuscripts of other authors already in circulation (although no such manuscripts have been found) (Yamey, 1967; and 1994a, p.24).[2] On the other hand, there is also the intriguing possibility that Pacioli may also have authored a later "Marie-Celeste" work (*La Scuola Perfetta dei Mercanti* etc. of 1504) - although, if it existed, it may have comprised no more than relevant extracts, possibly pirated, from the *Summa* circulating as a manual on bookkeeping (Yamey, 1974a; and Taylor, 1956, p.179). Fortunately, it does not matter very much, given that Pacioli never claimed to have invented double-entry bookkeeping. The historical significance of his work primarily lies in its incorporation into a book of mathematics and its treatment by a mathematician such as Pacioli.

The stated objective of the treatise was practical. Addressed to the merchant subjects of the Duke of Urbino, it would "give them sufficient and adequate rules for the proper keeping of all their accounts and books" (von Gebsattel, 1994, p.41). But its practical usefulness as a means of instruction has been criticised for three major deficiencies (e.g. Yamey, 1975a, p.xvii; and 1978, p.17):

> There was no integrated model set of account-books and entries; there was inadequate guidance for the identification of the debit and credit aspects of the various types of transaction likely to be encountered in practice; and there was a confusing exposition of the procedure for balancing and closing the ledger.

To these deficiencies one can add three further criticisms of the range of Pacioli's treatment. First, while much of the work stresses detailed procedures for laying out books and accounts (including, for example, pre-numbering of pages and notarisation, in Chapters VI and VII), and processes for writing up and checking the accuracy of books of account, he (or his printers) let the merchant down on minor but important points of detail. Thus, Pacioli describes a mechanism for setting out journal entries utilising double lines between the two parts. But his illustrative example fails to include lines of this kind. Again, after posting journal entries to the ledger, he suggests cancellation through each half of the entry in turn with oblique lines. But the illustrative entry does not show such lines (Crivelli, 1924, p.85; and Yamey, 1976). His explanation in Chapter XIII of how to index the ledger is also obscure. Pacioli's treatise is in this regard reminiscent of those modern manuals provided to assist users of computer packages (such as word processing or spreadsheets) which always seem to omit the crucial instruction or indicate the wrong key to be pressed. These matters are often trivial and self evident to the compiler, but time-wasting, confusing and annoying to the user!

In the second place, Pacioli's description is only at the level of an introductory textbook, and does not reflect the state of the art already achieved by the larger Italian businesses (in particular, the merchant-bankers) (De Roover, 1956, pp.173-4). As De Roover illustrates, while Pacioli's classification of the three principal books needed (i.e. the waste-book, journal and ledger) covers the logical categories, it does not reflect the usage of either multiple divisions of the ledger (with or without control and reciprocal control accounts) or the journal/cash book. Nor does his treatise cover practices such as the use of "Nostro" and "Vostro" accounts, the role of internal audit (e.g. in relation to bankers' doubtful debts), and the introduction of accounting conventions (i.e. depreciation, contingency reserves, adjustments for prepayments, and elements of cost accounting), examples of which are to be found in practice about one hundred years before (albeit mainly outside Venice). In the third place, and at the other end of the scale, "one looks in vain in the Tractatus for a theory of double entry or for a unifying analytical principle" (Yamey, 1978, p.6).

What would the modern accountant make of the *De Scripturis*? The major omissions, as compared with a modern accounting textbook, have already been noted. Perhaps more surprising are the accounting conventions which are adopted and, indeed, taken for granted. Some of these remain areas of controversy in modern accounting (Yamey, 1977). Take, for example, the entity concept. Classical scholars have criticised the "primitive" nature of ancient Greek and Roman accounting (which definitely did not have double-entry bookkeeping [de Ste. Croix, 1956; and Macve, 1985]) for failing to segregate personal and business affairs. But Pacioli's exposition begins by requiring a listing or inventory of all the merchant's assets and liabilities "in good order... all of my moveable and immovable assets and debts receivable and payable, being my wordly possessions as of this day" (von Gebsattel, 1994, p.43). The majority of illustrations of journal entries (in Chapter XII) are for the purpose of entering the initial inventory into the books. Only in the case of partnership enterprises (Compagnia) (Chapter XXI), a shop operated separately from the merchant's house (Chapter XXIII), and voyages (Chapter XXVI) does Pacioli envisage creating distinct systems of accounts with their separate "capital" (Cavedal). Strict segregation of business and personal accounts is a much more modern idea (e.g. Yamey, 1981, p.134).

Unlike accounts in the ancient world, where the inventories of items were maintained solely in quantitative, physical terms (Macve, 1985), Pacioli's inventory has an additional dimension (i.e. monetarisation into a common unit of account or numeraire). In this way, it is possible to summarise total capital in one monetary amount, as becomes clear when the capital account is transferred from an old to a new ledger "so that your total inventory appears at once (or, at a glance)" (von Gebsattel, 1994, p.86).[3] Monetarisation into a single currency system solves the problems of non-monetary assets (e.g. furniture, jewels, etc.), and the coinage in circulation of different currencies. This monetarisation is purely for accounting purposes, as

Pacioli acknowledges in Chapter XII that the merchant may actually wish to obtain proceeds of sale in currencies other than the accounting numeraire.[4]

But monetary measurement requires not only a common unit of measurement but also a valuation basis. Here Pacioli does not hesitate in recommending a choice on the criteria of what he regards as most useful and most likely to have desirable behavioural and economic consequences (von Gebsattel, 1994, p.54):

> ...distinguish clearly each item... assigning the usual value to each. Set the price higher (`fatter') rather than lower (`leaner'), so that if you believe it is worth 20, attribute 24 etc. so that you can more easily obtain a profit.

His bias towards overestimating the "usual value" suggests target pricing, not historical costing, is where he starts from.[5]

As Yamey (e.g. 1949; and 1964) points out, the calculation of profit and loss in early account books is more a by-product of the accounting requirement to balance the ledger than a prime objective and output of the system. This is one reason for Yamey's doubts about double-entry having had any significant role in the development of capitalism. Pacioli treats profit and loss primarily in this way and, while he comments favourably on the practice among the major merchants of balancing annually, he also treats balancing as a task dictated by the practical needs of transferring from a full ledger to a new one (in Chapter XXXII).

However, although it may be only implicit in the procedures described, and even if it is not explained as analytically as a modern university professor might aim to do, the theorem, if not the theory, of double-entry accounting is clearly understood by Pacioli. That is, that it provides articulation between stocks and flows, and is a record of changes in the owner's capital (an abstract concept distinct from the actual collection of assets owned and liabilities owed) and thereby forms a complete, closed system.

Thus, right from the beginning of Pacioli's explanation of ledger entries (in Chapter XIV), the reasons for entering the opening inventory into a ledger in double-entry form, debiting assets and crediting capital, and having one entry in the journal with two in the ledger (so that the sum of the debits equals the sum of the credits), are explained in terms that "And from this the trial balance is derived, which is made when the ledger is closed" (von Gebsattel, 1994, p.32).[6] Perhaps this explains Pacioli's concentration on the opening inventory and setting up the logical system, rather than on the analysis of transactions and careful and consistent exposition of the closing procedures. It is axiomatic, having set up the system according to the basic rule, that following the rule thereafter will maintain it in balance and produce the inevitable end result. To a mathematician with a Neo-Platonic and mystical interest in the "perfect forms" that contain the quintessence of the cosmos (Yamey, 1994a, p.12), that perhaps seemed sufficient, both as a theorem and as a clear guide to practice.

WHO WAS PACIOLI? HIS LIFE AND TIMES

By far the best way to gain a feel for the kind of person Pacioli was, and learn the conventionally accepted facts of his life,[7] is to watch the Pacioli Society's excellent video (Pacioli Society, 1990).[8] In a more traditional medium, there is Taylor's book (summarised in Taylor, 1956; and Nobes, 1979) which portrays his humble origins and early life in Sansepolcro, including his early business training as an apprentice while living with Folco de Belfolci, and his early religious teaching from the Franciscan friars. Pacioli made the acquaintance of the artist Piero della Francesca, preeminently the artist of and writer on perspective, and Sansepolcro's more famous son, who gained him access to the library of Frederico the Count of Urbino (with whose son, Guidobaldo, he was later to be painted [according to the usual identification] in the well known portrait by Jacopo de Barbari). He spent a period as tutor in Venice to the three sons of the rich merchant, Antonio de Rompiasi, where he continued his study of mathematics under Domenigo Bragadino, and wrote his first manscript on mathematics at the age of about twenty five in 1470 (which he dedicated to Rompiasi's sons). After Venice, and through his association with Piero della Francesca, Pacioli went to Rome and lived for a while with Leon Battista Alberti, the painter, poet, philosopher, musician and architect and author of books on sculpture and architecture as well as of the first manual on perspective and the first vernacular (i.e. non-Latin) grammar.

After taking his vows to join the religious order of the Franciscans Minor, Pacioli went in 1475 to teach at the University of Perugia for six years, where he wrote his second manuscript dedicated to the "Youth of Perugia." For a while, he travelled both outside and inside Italy (e.g. he wrote his third manuscript at Zara in Dalmatia in 1481), until required by the Head of his Order to return from Florence to teach at the University of Perugia in 1486, by which time he was calling himself "Magister." However, Pacioli soon resumed his travels, including Rome, Naples, Padua, Assisi and Urbino (Crivelli, 1924, pp.8-9). Between 1481 and 1494, he published a fourth manuscript, of which no details are known.

Pacioli's *Summa* of 1494 aimed to redress the poor state of mathematical teaching which he attributed to poor methods and lack of available subject matter (Taylor, 1956, p.179). He gathered material from a variety of sources. His primary source was the work of Leonardo of Pisa (c.1200). But he also drew on such lively examples as military games and exercises gleaned from discussions with his uncle, Benedetto Baiardo, who had been an infantry captain-general with a variety of armies (Taylor, 1956, p.177).

After publication of the *Summa*, Pacioli was invited to Milan to teach mathematics at the Court of Duke Lodovico Maria Sforza where his associates included Leonardo da Vinci, who provided illustrations for Pacioli's manuscript *De Divina Proportione* (finished in November 1497 and later printed in Venice in 1509). Fleeing the French capture of Milan in 1499, Pacioli and Leonardo left for Venice via Mantua. Although no copy survives, tradition has attributed to Pacioli at that time a book on games such as chess (Taylor, 1956, p.181). They then moved to Florence. Pacioli taught in the Universities of Pisa, Bologna and Florence, and also gave lectures in Perugia, Rome and Venice. As noted above, authorship of *La Scuola Perfetta* of 1504 has been attributed to Pacioli. In 1508 in Venice, Pacioli gave an important lecture on "Proportion and Proportionality" by reference to the Fifth Book of Euclid, emphasising the relationship of proportion to religion, medicine, architecture, printing, sculpture, music, law and grammar, as well as all the liberal arts (Taylor, 1956, p.181).[9] In 1509, Pacioli's book on Euclid was published in Venice along with his *De Divina Proportione*,[10] which included not only Leonardo da Vinci's illustrations but also the first printed vernacular version of Piero della Francesca's Latin manuscript on perspective (Eisenstein, 1979, p.551).[11] In 1510, he was recalled to be head of the Franciscan convent in Sansepolcro and, in 1514, was summoned by the new Pope Leo X to teach mathematics at the Academy in Rome. This is the last known fact of his life, and he was probably around seventy years old. Indeed it is not certain whether he actually went to Rome.

Pacioli fits the modern image of a Renaissance man not only in his mastery of wide ranging knowledge, but also as an exemplar of the adage "it's not what you know but whom you know." During Pacioli's lifetime, with printing only just invented, these two conditions were often necessarily and largely equivalent. Thus, he became a close friend of Giuliano della Rovere, whose uncle, Francesco, was Pope Sixtus IV (1471-1484), patron of the Sistine Chapel. Guiliano was to become Pope Julius II (1503-1513). Pacioli stayed at Guiliano's palace in Rome in 1489 and, as Pope Julius II, Guiliano granted him a Bull in 1508 giving him authority to hold property in exemption from the Rule of the Franciscans Minor requiring the Brothers to live "in obedience, without property, and in chastity" (Taylor, 1956, pp.179 and 182).

So much for the traditional picture of Pacioli. Whatever the precise details of his life, at first sight the most remarkable fact about the author of the first printed work on commercial bookkeeping (printed in the Italian vernacular) is that he was not a merchant. While he clearly had contact with commercial business experience, it would appear to have been mostly at second hand and its depth is not known. Pacioli was primarily a teacher. But not merely a commercial tutor, rather a religious and university teacher, friend of leading intellectuals and artists (who mainly wrote in manuscript and in Latin for the benefit of the educated elite) as well as of Dukes and Popes.

But Pacioli clearly was no ivory tower mathematician. He was concerned with the application of mathematics to practical problems.[12] It can be assumed he would have approved heartily of the Pacioli Society adopting video as the medium for teaching about his life, work and influence. He exploited state of the art technology (printing), and used the most accessible and user friendly media of communication - i.e. the Italian vernacular (rather than Latin) and arabic numerals (rather than the Roman). Pacioli's objective was perhaps not far removed from those of the better MBA courses today. These include assisting business managers and students to structure their experience by means of intellectual articulation of relevant principles and practices, and integration with mainstream academic disciplines -

thereby enabling them to better analyse the nature of the practical problems they will face and decide how to deal with them rationally.

PACIOLI'S INHERITANCE

Two major preconditions were required for Pacioli to include a section on commercial bookkeeping as well as aspects of commercial arithmetic in his *Summa*. First, use of the double-entry system had developed in commercial practice (as he did not invent it) and, second, he perceived it to be appropriate to publish a book that "linked double-entry book-keeping and business arithmetic with Pythagorean harmonies and the music of the spheres" (Eisenstein, 1979, p.548).

This is not the place to retrace arguments over how double-entry bookkeeping might have evolved from earlier practice. Frustratingly, the few example entries appended to the *De Scripturis* (reproduced in Thompson, 1991, p.591) show ledger accounts of an intermediary acting as a banker. They involve only personal accounts, and not the real and nominal accounts which are the hallmarks of the system.[13] Theoretical views linking its evolution to developments in agency bookkeeping, for example, have been rehearsed by Yamey (1947) nearly fifty years ago and, as far as can be determined, there is nothing in more recent research to alter his conclusion (p.272):

> And so the probings into the origin of double-entry bookkeeping lead from one speculation to another. The true story is likely to remain as much of a mystery as double-entry itself must be to the uninitiated.[14]

Examples can be seen, however, of double-entry systems evolving in individual businesses. For example, de Roover (1956, pp.139-41) describes the records of Francesco di Marco Datini (ca. 1335-1410), a famous and wealthy merchant banker of Prato in Tuscany. These show, first, in a ledger of 1367-72, the prevailing Tuscan practice of ledger accounts split with debit entries in the front (up to folio 150) and credit entries in the rear (folios 151 to the end on folio 300). This is the transitional form between "paragraph form" (where credits normally appear below the related debits on the same page), and the "bilateral form" where debits and credits for the same account are put in opposite columns either on the same page or on opposite pages (as in the "Venetian Method").[15] A later ledger of Datini (1383-6) shows the bilateral form for personal accounts, while merchandise expense and profit and loss accounts continue in paragraph form. But the ledger is clearly in double-entry if it is accepted that the separate cash book was part of the system.[16]

Thus, whether practice evolved independently in different places and was transmitted through business intercourse, or by teachers and their methods of instruction, there was no shortage of material and experience for Pacioli to base his exposition on. He was writing about a system that, in its basic structure, first appeared about two hundred years before his publication. In other words, in 1994, the celebration is not of the quincentenary but the septuacentenary of the supposed invention of double-entry bookkeeping.

The second precondition to publication was that such material (which would not now be found in a mathematics syllabus - even a business mathematics syllabus) was perceived as appropriate for a mathematical *Summa* - i.e. everything you ever wanted to know about arithmetic, geometry, proportion and proportionality. This requires some understanding of the way a medieval university organised knowledge, and of the way in which the procedures of knowledge dissemination (i.e. of teaching and learning) had been changing. Recent work has given further insights and also helped understanding of the context in which a new way of writing accounts could have emerged. There are a number of threads that can be traced.

ARABIC NUMERALS

One feature of Pacioli's *Summa* is its use of arabic numerals (in the *De Scripturis*, Pacioli only uses Roman numerals for the dates in the account books). It has been suggested (e.g. de Ste. Croix, 1956) that the introduction of arabic numerals with their "place" value to the West, and traditionally associated with the work of al-Khwarizmi in the early ninth century (Durham, 1992, p.36), led naturally to the use of columns of figures, and then to the opposing columns of debits and credits in a ledger account.

In this regard, the work of Leonardo of Pisa ("Fibonacci"), author of the *Liber Abbaci*, which promoted the use of arabic numerals in 1202, was seen as a significant influence on commercial practice. It used many commercial examples, and was published at a time when the numerals acquired their modern forms and almost three hundred years before Pacioli's *Summa*, for which it was a major source. But any connection must now be seen as problematic. The belief that Leonardo stated he had learned from Arab merchants the new arithmetical technique of "algorism" (which he was promoting as superior to use of the abacus) has been shown to be a misunderstanding, and credit for the new "arithmetical mentality" cannot go to the merchants (Murray, 1978, pp.192-4).

Leonardo's role, if any, is thus unclear. His work was apparently not widely read even in academic circles in his own time and, while there are sporadic, mostly Pisan instances of use of arabic numerals within account books in the fourteenth century (approximately one hundred and fifty years before Pacioli), how they might have been influenced, if at all, by Leonardo of Pisa's work is unknown (Durham, 1992, p.43). Moreover, if it was the superiority of arabic notation and its association with algorism that had caused the changes in commercial practice, Roman numerals would have been replaced before Leonardo of Pisa.

Thus, a direct influence of arabic numerals on commercial practice seems unlikely. Account books, including double-entry books, continued to be written in Roman numerals, and arabic numerals did not spread significantly in accounting contexts until the latter part of the fifteenth century (i.e. around Pacioli's time). They spread from Italy to the rest of Europe in the sixteenth century (Durham, 1992, pp.39 and 45). Of greater significance is the influence of arabic numerals on mathematics in the university context. Here, handbooks were produced in the twelfth century showing how to use arabic numerals in the new pen-and-paper system of algorism (Evans, 1977). Thus, Pacioli may be seen as promoting the use of arabic numerals on the basis of their academic superiority, and trying to influence business practice to change from its cultural conservatism, and its attachment to Roman numerals and the abacus.

WRITING AND RE-WRITING

Consideration of arabic numerals therefore leads to a wider question of the relationship between academic learning and business developments. A major feature of the emergence of Europe from the "Dark Ages" is the focus on new ways of writing and interpreting texts in the newly established teaching institutions, the universities. In particular, emerging in both academic and commercial spheres, new patterns of "doubling" based on writing may be seen. By the eleventh century (four hundred years before Pacioli), layouts of texts exhibit new techniques such as alphabetical ordering, subject indexing, and marginal indexing symbols. By 1200, such systematic ordering and gridding of texts was endemic in the academic world (Hoskin and Macve, 1986, p.108). During the twelfth and thirteenth centuries, further innovations in the layout of pages of texts (e.g. of the Bible) to provide systematic internal and external division, indexation, cross-referencing and commentary, were creating a new visually-oriented layout for book and page. The basic elements for writing words and numbers (i.e. the letters of the alphabet and arabic numerals) were deployed in an alphanumeric system - with the alphabet used for indexation, and different letter sizes used to stratify text; and arabic numerals superseding Roman numerals and letters for use in page numbering (foliation) and line numbering (Rouse & Rouse, 1979, pp.27-34; and Hoskin and Macve, 1986, p.111).[17]

Such techniques made reading into silent reading (Saenger, 1982) and, by re-writing them, scholarly work into an examination of and commentary on texts. The book became a mirror - i.e. a reflexive work or an interconnected series of works. By writing the same thing twice, commentary became a way of saying something new (Hoskin and Macve, 1986, p.121-2, citing Foucault, 1981). The new textuality was to be given a vital impetus by the invention of printing in the middle of the fifteenth century. This brought both a further visual ordering of layout and a new approach to books as a depersonalised and, through the cheapness of paper, more widely accessible source of knowledge (Thompson, 1991, pp.588-94).

The importance of the new universities, however, was not just in relation to knowledge. They also created powerful new social elites - the "Magistri" or Masters (Pacioli was a Master) who had passed the formal examinations first introduced in Paris and Bologna in the twelfth century, and which gave new dimensions to learning (i.e. success and failure). The new graduates used the techniques by which they had learned (e.g. archiving, cross-referencing and examination) as techniques of power in the service of the Court or the Church (an extreme example was the Inquisition) (Hoskin and Macve, 1986, pp.111-12). In the English context, Clanchy (1975, pp.685-6; and 1979, p.68) notes of these "modern men" that, by the mid-thirteenth century, "the great majority of clerks and accountants were trained at universities." Thus, Thomas á Becket, destined to argue fatally with his King as to who was the more powerful, began his career after study at Paris as a clerk-accountant ("clericus et rationalis") in London in the 1140s.

Thus, an interrelationship of power and knowledge emerged. New knowledge and skills learned in educational institutions created new potentional for achievement, and became the means of access to power. Those individuals who thereby became newly powerful promoted and privileged the use of knowledge and skills they had learned. Extending from the traditional arenas of power such as the Court and the Church, the new power-knowledge relation was also to colonise, through men such as Pacioli, the new European arena of power in which Italy was leading the way (i.e. banking and commerce).

The new learning spread beyond a new textuality and new approaches to numeration and computation. For example, developments in art and architecture also portrayed new concerns with visual presentation - i.e. with a focus on proportion and symmetry (another "doubling"), and on the role of perspective in transforming painting into a more "realistic" representation of reality. As already mentioned, Leon Battista Alberti, Pacioli's early patron, was the author of the first manual on geometrical perspective, and Sansepolcro was the birthplace of Piero della Francesca, whose work on perspective Pacioli was to popularise through his *De Divina Proportione*, assisted by the illustrations of Leonardo da Vinci. Pacioli related art and writing through his interest in designs of geometrically perfect proportional letter forms for printing (Eisenstein, 1979, p.540).

Whatever the linkages may have been, alongside changes in the world of learning were important new developments in the writing of the economic and commercial world. Of these, the most significant new re-writing was that of money into new forms. This included the development of the bill of exchange involving, in its early form, the "doubled" writing of two bills in order to create bilateral written exchanges, from which was to later develop the "double writing" of endorsement and then, by discounting on one bill, the creation of paper money (Hoskin & Macve, 1986, pp.116-20). In parallel with these changes[18] was the new writing of debit and credit entries in account books, which was to lead to double-entry accounting.

To explore these interrelationships fully requires the knowledge and skill of a medieval scholar, which this writer is not. But, without going to the extremes of Zeitgeist pilloried by Lopez (1962) (who cites a student's examination answer which claimed: "Double-entry book-keeping in the Medici Bank goaded Michelangelo to conceive and accomplish the Medici Chapel; contemplation of the Medici Chapel in turn spurred the bankers to a more muscular management of credit") (quoted by Yamey, 1981, p.135), it can be seen that important developments in learning, teaching and art, alongside those in commerce, created conditions in which there could emerge a new, disciplined form of ordered, self-referential, alphanumerical texts, constituting an interrelated system of books for business accounts. Such a system, in turn, would seem to a university teacher to be a legitimate topic for exposition, and one to which he could apply his knowledge in popularising and promoting its practical application.

BUT WHY IN A *SUMMA* ON MATHEMATICS?

The new universities were also realigning the divisions of knowledge - i.e. its disciplines. Durham (1992) has recently argued that, traditionally, arithmetical reckoning through use of the abacus had been associated in schools not with the mathematical syllabus (the *quadrivium*), but with that part of the curriculum concerned with language skills, including rhetoric and logic (the *trivium*) in its section on grammar (equivalent, therefore, to literacy and numeracy). The teaching of accounting and auditing was traditionally associated with grammar and related legalistic studies, especially the *ars dictaminis* or art of business communication which was taught in the "grammar" schools linked to the universities (in England, at Oxford University, and in Continental Europe, at the older Italian universities such as Bologna and Padua). At Bologna, the greatest *dictator*, Boncompagno, claimed his subject "was worthy to be an eighth liberal art" (Hoskin and Macve, 1986, p.116). Thus, traditionally, accounting had not been linked with mathematical studies (Durham, 1992, p.46).

In the fourteenth century, however, changes in the university curriculum rejected medievalism, emphasised the nobility of (Greek and Roman) classical literature and learning, and presented arabic numerals in mathematics as representing the wisdom of the East. By the late fifteenth century, grammatical studies, emerging from the old *trivium*, were turning towards "literature" and "humanities," and accounting was cut adrift from its traditional base in grammar and law. At the same time, the *quadrivium* was developing into "mathematics," so that commercial reckoning was again left to go its own way.

In this context, Pacioli's enterprise was a bold one - to attempt a new and accessible synthesis of the range of mathematical knowledge, incorporating traditional elements (e.g. based on Boethius's *de Institutione Arithmetica* originating a thousand years before in the late fifth to early sixth centuries), and new topics such as algebra and accounting. He was attempting an ecumenical reconciliation between the Aristotelians and schoolmen on the one hand, and the Platonists and humanists on the other. But the bookkeeping and the other commercial topics he included were hardly applications of mathematics. Even the arithmetic involved was, for the most part, little more than elementary addition and subtraction. Thus, Pacioli was an exception, and unable to forge lasting links between mathematics and accounting, a subject traditionally associated with grammar, rhetoric and law (Durham, 1992, pp.47-51).

DIVINE PROPORTION

Pacioli's project was, however, more than one of mathematics. He was also the author of *De Divina Proportione*. Mathematics and proportion, the new basis of art and architecture, were perceived in combination as the purest illustration of the divine order of things. As Thompson (1991) has concluded, the end of the fifteenth century marked the pinnacle of the Church's power before the devastation of the Reformation and the new secularisation of knowledge. In the medieval scheme, the role of the merchant was problematic, typically being categorised as covetous, and always in danger of running foul of the Church's prohibition on usury (Letwin, 1963, p.87). Indeed, Aho (1985) has argued that Pacioli's work, by commending the ethics of the Christian businessman (to whom he gives much uplifting spiritual advice in the course of the *De Scripturis*, not least to invoke the Name of God at the beginning of his account books [Yamey, 1974b]), emphasising the "just balance" of business activity exemplified in the double-entry form of accounts, and highlighting double-entry's aesthetic pedigree in a realm of geometric and proportionate equivalences, was essentially employing classic rhetorical devices in order to justify commercial activity. But this appears to put the motivation back to front. Instead, it would appear that Pacioli, in explaining the balanced order of things as sanctified by God, needed to find a way to colonise and fit the new arena of power (banking and commerce) into the divine structure of society (which had hitherto been represented by the Church and the Court),[19] and into a neo-Platonist scheme where all true knowledge was at a deep level accessible only to the privileged elite (Plato's "philosopher-kings").

PACIOLI'S LEGACY

In considering Pacioli's legacy, we need to consider both his contribution and the significance of the double-entry system that he was presenting. While Pacioli's attempted new synthesis of mathematical knowledge in the *Summa* appears to have been unsuccessful, his influence as a mathematician on succeeding generations was considerable. Thus, portions of the *Summa* appear to have been excerpted and paraphrased by Bishop Tunstall in his *De Arte Supputandi* (1522) and Girolamo Cardano in his *Ars Magna* (1545), both of which were the chief arithmetic texts that replaced Boethius in sixteenth century college courses (e.g. at Oxford by 1549 [Eisenstein, 1979, p.548 fn. 78]). In his work on Euclid, John Dee's preface to the first printed English translation of Euclid in 1570 shows he was familiar with Pacioli's similar attempt to bring Euclid to "unlatined people" (Eisenstein, 1979, pp.540-1).

The section of the *Summa* on bookkeeping, the *De Scripturis*, was also to have a major influence (although with somewhat patchy recognition - Yamey, 1980, p.82) on the later treatises which began to appear throughout Europe. By 1550, there were several texts. For example, Manzoni's treatise in Italian, *Quaderno doppio...*, appeared in Venice in 1540, as "an improved version of Pacioli's treatise supported by a useful set of illustrative accounts" (Yamey, 1975a, p.xvii). Jan Ympyn's treatise, *A notable and very excellente woorke...*, appeared in Dutch (Flemish) and in French in Antwerp in 1543, and in English in 1547. Hugh Oldcastle's, *A Profitable Treatyce...*, (which lacked the addition of illustrative accounts) also appeared in English in London in 1543. Both of the latter texts were close to that of Pacioli.[20] By 1549, Schweicker's (flawed) exposition, *Zwifalch Buchhalten*, appeared in German in Nuremberg, based on Manzoni and, hence, indirectly on Pacioli (Yamey, 1975a, p.xvii).[21]

However, when the list of later authors through to the end of the eighteenth century is considered, it does not provide a clear line of worthy successors to the Franciscan Doctor of Divinity, mathematician and university professor. Many of the authors were schoolmasters or teachers who gave lessons in bookkeeping, often in addition to other subjects such as commercial arithmetic, mathematics and foreign languages. Many of these teachers also practised as bookkeepers and kept accounts for merchants, or were otherwise practically involved in commercial matters. But, apart from teachers who also participated in business affairs, a number of authors were more fully engaged in trade, either on their own account or as employees of merchants.[22] A number were primarily book-keepers who may have taught as well (Yamey 1975a, p.xxii). Some showed wider interests. Thus, Simon Stevin (1548-1620) was a "universal man" (i.e. mathematician, natural philosopher, physicist, engineer and teacher, counsellor and friend of Prince Maurice of Nassau). Yet others were medical or religious men, engineers, etc. (Yamey, 1975a, p.xxii; and 1980, p.84). Overall, therefore, the *De Scripturis* and its influence became detached from the rest of the *Summa*, and went its own way outside the major arenas of learning. It is also not clear by how much Pacioli influenced writers on accounting rather than accounting itself. Later developments in technique often appear to have passed writers by (Yamey, 1980, p.91; and Thompson, 1991, p.588).

And what of double-entry itself? Should we be grateful for Pacioli's influence as a popularist, teacher and preacher in aiding its transmission to others (to which the secretive guild mentality of merchants might have been less inclined [Eisenstein, 1979]) and, thence, to the modern business world? Here the anomaly has long been observed that, while knowledge of double-entry was available in treatise form from around 1500, it is not until the nineteenth century that it is clear that it had been widely adopted in Europe and the US (Yamey, 1981, pp.129-30).[23]

ROLE OF DOUBLE-ENTRY BOOKKEEPING

Goethe has Werner say of double-entry bookkeeping that "It is among the finest inventions of the human mind" (*Wilhelm Meisters Lehrjahre*, I.10).[24] But Werner is an anti-hero. As to double-entry's usefulness, the most familiar products of the system today are the profit and loss statement and balance sheet - statements that purport to report the income and capital of a business. Such is the embedded tradition of double-entry in modern accounting theory and practice that it is perceived, by those who develop conceptual frameworks to explain, justify and attempt to reform current practice, as a natural step to argue that the users of accounting statements who need relevant information to guide their decisions, require a profit statement and balance sheet (supplemented nowadays by a cash flow statement), and that the articulation of these statements is fundamental to the nature of accounting (e.g. Solomons, 1989a and 1989b; contrast with Macve, 1989a and 1989b).

The attempted harmonisation of European accounting through European Union Directives has also been most successful in the arena of imposing standard layouts and formats for the two traditional statements. But, of course, the use of the double-entry system is neither necessary nor sufficient for calculating business income, although it may often be very convenient (Yamey, 1964; and Macve, 1985). Income can be calculated for a period without any transactions records, by taking an opening and closing "inventory" - i.e. a valuation of assets and liabilities. The change in net assets for the period (after adjusting for any new capital subscribed during the period, and any withdrawals of funds by the owner for consumption) represents the income of the period. An Italian example of 1347 of this technique for the partnership of Bugarro and Delle Brache has been described by Yamey (1989). At the other extreme, all changes in all assets and liabilities can be entered in double-entry transactions records, thus enabling the system to provide a profit statement and balance sheet without any need for taking an inventory.

Thus, given Pacioli's initial inventory, a bookkeeper can either proceed directly to the taking of a closing inventory, indirectly by the double-entry system or, as in normal practice, utilise various mixtures of both approaches. The system provides a list of "expected" closing balances of assets and liabilities, against which an independent check can be made by means of a physical inspection of the actual assets and liabilities at the end of the period. Indeed, it is the fact that much of the information in the system is redundant that is one of its most valuable features. It provides some independent corroboration of the accuracy and completeness of the closing inventory. It is the re-writing that gives the added meaning.

Not only is double-entry not necessary (though highly convenient) for the calculation of income, it is not sufficient. Determining income requires decisions on how assets are to be valued, and how much of the change in their value is to be treated as income. The double-entry method imposes no restriction on these choices, and the history of accounting shows that a variety of valuation methods has been employed in preparing accounts.

It may be that double-entry is valued for its inbuilt checks which help to indicate when errors have occurred. But, as Yamey (e.g. 1974b) has pointed out, there are plenty of errors to be found in extant double-entry ledgers which have often been written off without investigation. The system has perhaps been valued because it was a small extension of the interrelated cash and personal accounts that an economy trading on credit needed to keep; or because it was often convenient (though not essential) for keeping track of the shares of the partners in business adventures; or because it enabled the recording of absolutely every transaction, as well as the "housekeeping" work in balancing the books etc. to be reduced to a rule of one simple form. In addition, it made possible the division of labour between several clerks who could each do their part (e.g. all the debits or all the credits, or a particular block of accounts) without any need to understand the whole picture while, at the same time, automatically producing a comprehensive picture as the joint output of their several labours.

Whatever its virtues in the eyes of those who adopted and developed it, the history of double-entry bookkeeping, together with the arguments mentioned above, make it extremely unlikely that it can be regarded as having been crucial to the development of entrepreneurial capitalism (the so-called "Sombart" thesis). Nor can it be argued that double-entry supplied the means whereby sedentary merchants could control the honesty and efficiency of their distant agents, factors or partners in the new international trading businesses (Yamey, 1975b). In the modern times of "managerial capitalism," however, double-entry has acquired a significant role in facilitating the co-ordination and control of large commercial organisations and, in recent years, its single "rule" has proved to be ideal for programming computers to perform.

OUR INHERITANCE

Pacioli's immediate legacy is therefore like buried treasure awaiting rediscovery. It was not until the beginning of the nineteenth century that a significant change in the role of double-entry accounting appeared. To take sides in a current debate over when and where accountability of the modern kind emerged (i.e. exercising managerial as well as financial control [e.g. Fleischman and Tyson, 1993; and Hoskin and Macve, 1994]), it can be argued that the scene must shift from Europe to the US. In both arenas, important elements in the development of accountancy were present, including the consequences of the industrial revolution, the growth of the joint-stock corporation, and the development of an accountancy profession. And, while Europe, and particularly the UK, led the way in many of these changes, the presence of technological and institutional conditions of possibility for change was not the crucial factor.

As in Pacioli's time, the key element can be seen to be changes in educational practices - i.e. in ways of learning to learn; in examination to measure human performance (for the first time graded by marks as units of account); and in the writing of organisational structures and rules. In turn, these new methods of knowledge production became embedded in new relations of power as graduates of the new kind increasingly occupied strategic positions in the development of industrial business practice.

Such changes can be seen in the US at the West Point Military Academy (then one of America's elite university institutions), beginning in 1817. Through the agency of West Point's engineering graduates came the revolutionary effect on business practice of a new means of accountability for human performance through establishing norms and measuring deviations. Accountability was extended from the individuals "memorialised" in early account books to the masses of workers and managers who became the "statistics" in the exploding nineteenth century populations. And, while the seminal institutions are not private businesses, nor even using double-entry accounting (Ezzamel et al, 1990), the impetus of this powerful new discourse colonised and transformed the available accounting technology, and secured its universal dominance within a hundred years. In contrast, the preceding three hundred years since Pacioli had only seen slow and sporadic advances.

The nineteenth century also saw the adoption of double-entry as the core of the body of knowledge of professional accountants and auditors, in part assisted by the State. For example, the model articles and specimen accounts in Table A of the Companies Act 1856 provided for a balance sheet prepared from double-entry books (Edey and Panitpakdi, 1956, p.362). The requirements of new legislation, perhaps assisted by professional auditors, encouraged the adoption of double-entry by institutions, such as Oxford colleges, which had successfully managed their extensive wealth since long before Pacioli in blessed ignorance of his accounting system (Jones, 1992).

The nineteenth century would also see the beginning of the rehabilitation of double-entry into the intellectual scheme of things. Particularly in Continental Europe and also in America, authors formulated and debated different theoretical approaches to explaining the internal coherence of double-entry accounts and the logic of the system (Yamey, 1975a, p.xxiv). With the development of graduate business schools in US universities, accountancy was taught there from the 1880s. It became the chief component of the course at the New York University graduate school which opened in 1896, the same year that Lawrence Dicksee, one of UK accountancy's great exponents, was one of the first to qualify as a chartered accountant in London by means of examination (Hoskin and Macve, 1986, p.133).

De Roover (1956, p.114) comments, in the introduction to his painstaking survey of surviving accounting records from 1157 to 1494 (the three hundred years before Pacioli), that "the new approach to accounting history"... "places greater emphasis on accounting as a tool of management and control," while "the older writers" (e.g. Besta in 1909) "attached much importance to the matter of form and procedure". De Roover further states that "while I fully sympathise with this new approach to accounting history, I also believe that form and procedure are not completely devoid of significance and should not be entirely overlooked."

In the last decade, there have been yet newer accounting histories stressing alternative theoretical foundations, and deploying new social and critical theories to understanding the development of accounting's modern role (Miller et al, 1991). But, as the history of double-entry and of the work of its first and most famous exponent shows, it is precisely in the interrelationships of new practices and, in particular, new ways of learning and writing ("form and procedure") that one sees the emergence of new ways of knowing about and understanding the world (new discourses), with immense consequences for changing relations of power in the "real" world outside the cloister walls.

The power of new knowledge techniques such as double-entry therefore goes beyond a simple economic justification and requires an institutional focus. As Yamey (e.g. 1975b) has argued, the traditional views of the economic necessity of double-entry either as a basis for capitalist entrepreneurship, or as an instrument for administrating the far-flung international business outlets of the sedentary merchant, do not stand up to historical analysis. But its exponents believed in its importance. Thus, Pacioli argues in his first chapter that, of the three things which are "necessary for those who wish to trade with due diligence," the first is the availability of money and other assets (*substantia*); the second is to be "a good reckoner and a quick calculator"[25] (and so in the preceding parts of the *Summa*, Pacioli "presented rules and canons relating to each arithmetical operation"); while the third is "that all transactions are recorded in good order so that information may be had quickly concerning debits and credits which are the basis of trade" (von Gebsattel, 1994, p.42).[26]

At first sight, Pacioli's *De Scripturis* seems a universe away from the latest jargon-filled book on strategic international marketing, suitable for today's (if not 1494's) aspiring businessman. But for the successful exploitation of "substance" (the first of his three necessities for carrying on business), Pacioli's imposition of rule and order through systematic double-entry bookkeeping may be more significant than it is now fashionable to suppose. It is at the beginning of the line of those disciplinary systems which modern man has now internalised - "the systems that quietly order us about" (Foucault, quoted by Megill, 1979, p.493). Moreover, while Pacioli did not invent double-entry, he was the first published exponent of the system and, by writing it down, he articulated and made visible in printed form the rationale of the procedures of business practice. By intellectualising it, he gave the mass of detail a simplicity and reproducibility, so that the knowledge could be transmitted and refined into a basic idea that non-accountants can now be taught to appreciate in just a few minutes. For that we should be grateful.

NOTES

1. It is generally assumed he was born in Borgo San Sepolcro (Sansepolcro) in Tuscany in 1445, and died in the Franciscan monastery there in 1517 (perhaps on June 19th). But this evidence is not complete (Nakanishi, 1979).

2. There was an Italian manuscript, written by Benedetto Cotrugli in Naples in 1458 and later published in printed form in Venice in 1573 (*Della mercatura et del mercante perfetto*) which, albeit briefly and obscurely, appears to refer to the double-entry system, although it could not have been the source of Pacioli's detailed exposition (Yamey, 1967, pp.73-4; and 1994b).

3. *perche prima volta tutto tuo inventario apare* (transcriptions of the original Italian of the *De Scripturis* are taken from Antinori [1959] and Yamey [1994a]). While the effect is clear, Pacioli's exposition of the procedure for balancing and transferring the capital account is "a perplexing muddle" (Yamey, 1994a, pp.162-3).

4. De Roover (1956, pp.137-8, 146 and 150-1) draws attention to the difficulties of handling multiple currencies circulating at rapidly fluctuating exchange rates, and has argued that this inhibited adoption of the double-entry system for manufacturing activities, or led to its apparently breaking down and being abandoned by some banks. See also Crivelli (1924, p.86) and Volmer (1994, pp.10-11) for discussion of the various moneys in circulation in Venice.

5. *E fallo grasso più presto che magro, cioè se ti pare che vaglino 20 e tu dì 24 etc. aciò che meglio te habia reuscire el guadagno.* In Chapter XXXVII, he recommends that items entered should not be of a value less than ten ducats "since items of little value are not entered in the ledger" (von Gebsattel, 1994, p.91).

Comun pregio, translated here as "usual value," may in the present context "have meant the current market price or value" (Yamey, 1994a, p.118). Volmer (1994, p.8) observes that Pacioli's advice to make the prices higher rather than lower "means that next to a prudent profit calculation, current (high) values are useful to estimate the value of the firm and the owner's equity." But this is attempting to strain too much modern meaning out of text which cannot support such an interpretation (see Yamey, 1994a, pp.118-19 for other interpretations).

It may be noted that, presumably because the Venetian system dealt primarily with accounting for ventures (whereby the sale proceeds are credited to the account of each merchandise, so that the profit and loss on the venture is only determined when the venture is concluded [Chapter XXXVII]), Pacioli gives no advice on how to value stock in hand when the ledger is balanced (Yamey 1994a, p.150).

6. *E di qua nasci poi al bilancio che del Libro si fa nel suo saldo*. For the nature of Pacioli's trial balance, see Yamey (1994a, pp.123-4). Later mathematicians were to explain more fully the mathematical principles by which the balance is maintained (ibid).

7. I have not attempted to weigh the evidence for the record reported in this section although much of it is attributed to autobiographical remarks in the *Summa* (Taylor, 1956, p.184). The details are presumably less important than the overall picture.

8. The two major weaknesses of the video are that it leaves an impression that Pacioli was the inventor of double-entry, and it attributes a Sombartian significance to double-entry as a key element in Europe's subsequent unprecedented economic growth.

9. Erasmus and Durer were in Venice at the time and may have attended the lecture. It has been argued that Erasmus' criticisms in his *Praise of Folly* (1509/10) of mathematical showmen and of religious men who toadied to merchants were aimed at Pacioli (Fennell, 1994, pp.17-19).

10. These two books, together with the 1494 and 1523 editions of the *Summa*, comprise the known corpus of his printed works.

11. Somewhat surprisingly, given his acknowledgement of other sources, Pacioli failed to acknowledge unpublished manuscripts by Piero della Francesca as the source of certain material in the *Summa* and the *De Divina Proportione* (Volmer, 1994, pp.5-7; and Yamey, 1994a, pp.18-20 and 24).

12. Pacioli originally planned to divide the material in the *Summa* into treatments of arithmetic and algebra; various subjects of commercial interest (including, for example, bills of exchange and

barter); book-keeping and accounts; weights and measures and exchange rates; and pure and especially applied geometry. In the event, the *Summa* is in two parts, the first of which includes the first four subject areas of the plan, with the second, third and fourth subjects (the business subjects) constituting the ninth *distinctio* within which the eleventh *Tractatus* (of twelve) is the *De Scripturis* (Yamey, 1994a, pp.15-16).

Thus, material of mercantile interest was not limited to the *De Scripturis*, and one explanation of the mysterious *Scuola Perfetta* (if it existed) is that it was a compendium of the various parts of the *Summa* directly relevant to commercial affairs (Yamey, 1974a).

13. Specimen entries in some chapters do refer to nominal accounts (e.g. *spesi de mercantia* (expenses or charges of merchandise) and *spesi di casa* (household expenses) in Chapter XXII), and real accounts (e.g. the various goods accounts in Chapters XVIII and XX).

14. Bryer (1993) has argued that double-entry reflects, not the economic spirit and needs of capitalism as stated by Sombart (see discussion below and Yamey [1949 and 1964]), but the socialisation of capital and the creation of the merchant bourgeoisie in Northern Italy. Bryer stresses the role of the new partnerships (*compagnia*) and the loan arrangements for foreign ventures (*commenda*). However, Pacioli's exposition of double-entry bookkeeping focusses on the individual merchant's pursuit of profit, and partnerships and voyages only receive a chapter each (Chapters XXI and XXVI). They apparently receive special mention primarily because of the need to keep separate sets of books to the main accounts which deal with the merchant's own business and personal wealth.

15. As De Roover (1956) shows, there were two separate, albeit related developments - i.e. the layout of the accounts (paragraph, "front and back" and bilateral forms), and the method of accounting (whether or not double-entry). He gives examples of records that have survived from Tuscany, where it is now generally accepted that there was double-entry without bilateral form from around the beginning of the fourteenth century (approximately two hundred years before the *Summa*). Conversely, accounts were kept in Northern Italy (e.g. in Genoa from 1313) in bilateral form (*ad usum banchi* or *ad modum banchi*) before they were kept in double-entry (which first appeared in Genoa in 1340, although probably going back there to 1327 [de Roover, 1956, p.131]). In Florence the bilateral form (called *alla*

Veneziana) appeared by 1382 (p.139). The method described by Pacioli combined double-entry with the "Venetian" bilateral form in the manner that became universal for hand-written ledgers using "T" accounts.

16. Precisely when the Datini ledgers exhibit double-entry depends on the criteria for defining the system. Melis argued that virtually all the surviving Datini ledgers were in double-entry (i.e. there was full duality of entries). De Roover considered the 1367-72 ledger to be single-entry and, as he also required the cash book to be integrated with the ledger, he hesitated to accept that the 1383-6 ledger was in double-entry. "The argument, therefore, is not decisive" (De Roover, 1956, p.141). By the 1390s, De Roover further argued, the double-entry system was applied in most of the Datini branches abroad and at his main office in Florence, although Zerbi would not accept even these were in double-entry (p.141).

17. The 1305 statutes of the University of Padua required book-sellers to put their prices in "plain letters, not by means of ciphers" so as to be visible on the outside of the book - which is normally interpreted as a reference to the book-sellers' practice of using the "new" arabic numerals with which they were familiar from the foliation of their books (Durham, 1992, pp.44-5).

18. The connection between bills of exchange and double-entry bookkeeping is suggested in the historical preface to Kelly's popular treatise *The Elements of Book-keeping* (1801), which also mentions insurance (Yamey, 1980, p.87).

19. For the corresponding religious interpretation of Jacopo de Barbari's 1495 portrait of Pacioli, see Thompson, 1991, pp.582-4. Pacioli also appears (as St. Peter the Martyr) in Piero della Francesca's altarpiece "*Madonna col Bambino...*," which portrays Frederico da Montefeltro, Duke of Urbino, in full armour and kneeling before the heavenly assembly (Nobes, 1979, p. 66).

20. Yamey (1975c) discusses the role of Juan Paulo di Bianchi, cited by Ympyn, and concludes that, first, it was di Bianchi's adaptation of Pacioli's *De Scripturis* (including material on bills of exchange from elsewhere in the *Summa*) that Ympyn translated into Dutch, adding an illustrative set of account-books and, second, Ympyn was not himself familiar with Pacioli's book.

21. Non-Paciolian works of the period in German were published in Nuremberg by Schreiber (?1521) and Gottlieb (1531) (Yamey, 1975a; and 1989).

22. Including Colinson, author of the first book published in Scotland, *Idea rationaria...*, in 1683. See also Volmer, 1994, pp.14-15.

23. While the use of double-entry has been found in many business ledgers dating from earlier periods, it cannot be argued to have been universally adopted. In Chapter Two of this text, Edwards reports examples of sophisticated double-entry records in British industrial companies in the late seventeenth and eighteenth centuries. But, given the dominance of owner-managers until the nineteenth and twentieth centuries, it is not surprising that a wide range of records may be found. Hudson (1977, p.445) notes that in the textile industry in the West Riding "it was in the 1830s-1840s that some concerns... adopted double-entry systems of accounting." For businessmen who generally preferred to do their own accounting, the double-entry method appeared tedious and "the appeal of single-entry theories such as those of Jones and Cronhelm had a certain logic in the West Riding" (p.442).

Yamey (1949, p.105) cites Charles Hutton's book-keeping text of 1811 which observes that single-entry bookkeeping "is used in almost every shop," while a German author reports a similar state of affairs in Germany: "many merchants preferred single-entry, which they could manage without outside assistance". The irregular closing of the sixteenth, seventeenth and eighteenth centuries examples of double-entry books cited by Yamey (1964, pp.124-5) shows they were clearly not being kept in order to provide regular periodic reports of profitability and capital, while examples of major joint-stock companies that did not have full double-entry systems include the Dutch East India Company, the Sun Fire Insurance Office of London (until 1890), the Whitin Machine Company in the US (until 1918), and the Capital and Counties Bank in England (until the merger with Lloyds in 1918). Lemarchand (1994) analyses the historical influences that led to certain kinds of major French companies in the eighteenth century (including mines, some of the metallurgical companies, and others such as the Saint-Gobain glass and Sevres porcelain manufactories) retaining charge and discharge accounting. Saint-Gobain, for example, adopted double-entry in 1820 and "its use became widespread during the first half of the nineteenth century" (p.140).

24. *Welche Vorteile gewährt die doppelte Buchhaltung dem Kaufmanne! Es ist eine der schönsten Erfindungen des menschlichen Geistes, und ein jeder gute Haushalter sollte sie in seiner Wirtschaft einführen.*

25. Crivelli (1924) translates *buon ragioneri e prompto computista* as "good accountant and sharp book-keeper." But this second requirement is better considered as a requirement for the merchant to be quick and accurate at arithmetic (the third requirement being for good bookkeeping) (Yamey, 1994c, p.60).

26. *La 3a e ultima cosa oportuna si è che con bello ordine tutte sue facende debitamente disponga, a ciò con brevità possa de ciascuna haver notitia quanto a lor debito e anche credito, chè circa altro non s'atende el trafico.*

2 FINANCIAL ACCOUNTING PRACTICE 1600-1970: CONTINUITY AND CHANGE

John Richard Edwards
Cardiff Business School
University of Wales College of Cardiff *

*I wish to thank participants at the Festival of Accounting in 1994 for helpful comments - particularly Richard Macve and Stephen Walker. I am also grateful to Harold Edey, Michael Jones, Bob Parker, Stephen Zeff and the anonymous referees for their criticisms of an earlier draft of this chapter.

INTRODUCTION

A survey of financial reporting practice over the selected period from 1600 to 1970 requires a view to be taken on precisely what is meant by the term "financial accounting."[1]   This is not a straightforward matter. For example, does it include the records as well as the financial statements prepared on the basis of those records, and does it include statements prepared for internal use as well as for external use?

According to Parker (1991, p.120), financial accounting today is:

> That part of accounting which is concerned mainly with external reporting to shareholders, government and other users of accounting outside the enterprise. It emphasises the stewardship rather than the control or decision-making aspects of accounting and is heavily constrained by legal regulations ...

This characterisation of financial accounting as information intended primarily for people outside the business is a little narrow in view of the targeted time-span for this chapter, as is Parker's emphasis on stewardship at the expense of decision making and resource allocation. It can be argued, for instance, that the profit and loss account and balance sheet were devised (pre-external reporting) in order to provide information relevant to decision making. It might also be suspected that it is the accountancy profession which has, in the past, stressed stewardship to simplify the auditor's job and limit his perceived responsibilities. The true role of financial accounting might also have been obscured by the fact that accruals accounting developed out of stewardship-oriented cash accounting, and because of the historical orientation of the financial statements prepared. This raises the final question concerning the scope of this chapter. Is financial accounting forward looking or only backward looking?

The approach adopted is to assume that financial accounting consists of statements prepared to summarise the overall financial progress (and position) of an enterprise for a past time period, whether prepared for owners, managers, creditors or any other interested party. The discussion will make some reference to the underlying records due to their implications for the form of the financial statement prepared. The principal orientation of the chapter will be UK accounting practice with certain corresponding or contrasting developments elsewhere also identified. There is space to do little more than chronicle major developments in financial accounting practice and refer to some of the major ideas and actions designed to shape these developments. Finally, the *transfer* of ideas and practices between countries is not explicitly addressed.[2]

CHARGE AND DISCHARGE VS DOUBLE-ENTRY BOOKKEEPING

In medieval times in Britain and elsewhere (e.g. in France [Lemarchand, 1994]), the method of accounting employed by significant economic entities (i.e. landed estates, local authorities, and religious and educational organisations) was charge and discharge. In due course, all large-scale organisations moved over to the system of double-entry bookkeeping which emerged as an alternative method for recording transactions in the Italian city states in the thirteenth century (Lee, 1977).[3] The significance of this transition, for the purpose of this analysis, is the implications of the system of record-keeping in use for the form and content of periodic financial accounts.

Charge and discharge accounting usually gave rise to the preparation of a cash statement typically designed to enable the steward to inform the lord of the manor how resources entrusted to him (the charge) had been applied (the discharge). The system had its origin in the need to report to a higher authority. In contrast, identified attributes of double-entry bookkeeping are that the records are more comprehensive and orderly; duality of records provides a convenient check on the accuracy and completeness of the ledger; and, most important in the context of this chapter, the records contain, in convenient form, the material needed to prepare the profit and loss account and balance sheet (Yamey, 1956, p.7).

The main, though not invariable difference between these two systems is, therefore, the application of the accruals concept to the recording of "business" transactions. In this context, it is important to remember that what might today be considered the most significant of the advantages of double-entry bookkeeping (i.e. the preparation of the profit and loss account and balance sheet) was not, it seems, the reason for its initial development. Instead, it was a potential subsequently exploited (Yamey, 1956, pp.8-9). It is important to remember this fact, particularly when attempts are made to develop further applications for the system. As Baxter (1981, p.5) warned the 1980 Congress of Accounting Historians:

> (We) will not (then) be surprised if accounting seems to falter when called upon to perform new and different tasks - such as predicting future income, and aiding investors to make decisions. If we have such ambitions for accounting, may we not be like a farmer who demands that his faithful old cart-horse learn the violin?

EARLY PROFIT AND LOSS ACCOUNTS AND BALANCE SHEETS

Where the system of double-entry bookkeeping is in use today, there is an expectation of a sequence of accounting events which involves closing the books, extracting a trial balance, and then preparing a profit and loss account and balance sheet. In earlier times, the common practice was to close the nominal accounts to a profit and loss account (variously described) within the ledger, transfer the balance to the capital account, and then prepare a balance account or balance sheet (sometimes inside and sometimes outside the ledger). It has been argued, by Yamey (1977, p.23), that little use is likely to have been made of the resulting "profit" figures for performance assessment and resource allocation - an examination of bank records for the period 1500-1800 producing the conclusion that the profit and loss account served principally as "a weeding-out process, in which the detailed and unwanted information in the ledger was removed."

UK businessmen had begun to prepare a balance sheet *outside* the ledger by the seventeenth century (in Italy, the practice occurred at least three hundred years earlier) and, according to Chatfield (1977, p.69), it "was by far the most important financial statement," and the one emphasised by early UK writers. Preoccupation with the balance sheet stems from the fact that it was more useful in answering traditional stewardship questions, which had their roots long before the introduction of double-entry, such as the manager's honesty and ability to account for resources entrusted to him. Even where interest extended to the financial state of business operations, attention was usually confined to assets, liabilities and capital. Expenses and revenues were considered merely incidental in an agricultural environment where the rate of change was gradual.

The quality of financial records and accounts was not always as low, and its purpose not invariably as restricted, as is sometimes imagined. For example, the annual accounts of two firms of charcoal ironmakers, carrying on business near Sheffield between 1690 and 1785, show considerable sophistication (Edwards and Boyns, 1992). Features include the use of transfer prices and allocation procedures for joint costs in order to identify profits and losses at the level of the department as well as for the firm as a whole. Further documentation of carefully prepared financial statements for use by Welsh industrialists in the eighteenth century has been presented by Jones (1985). In these records there is clear evidence of the application of the fundamental accounting concepts - i.e. going concern, accruals, consistency and prudence (which received formal recognition by the UK Accounting Standards Steering Committee in 1971 [ASSC, 1971]).

FINANCIAL REPORTING

Published financial statements, which may be seen as a subset of double-entry-based financial accounting, date from the need to raise capital from the general public and the consequent separation of ownership from management. In the UK, chartered companies date from the sixteenth century, and the most famous early example is the East India company established in 1600. Its accounting practices have been the subject of detailed research which has shown that the officers were required to "deliver up a perfect Ballance of all the said accompts unto the Company [shareholders], by the last day of June yearely" (Baladouni, 1986, p.20), and that the "wrong way round" balance sheet presentation, widely employed in the UK until the Companies Act 1981 took effect, was used in the first surviving "Ballance of the Estate" (balance sheet) published in 1641 (Baladouni, 1986, p.27).

An important stimulus for the creation of the *chartered* company was the need to provide a convenient vehicle for conducting overseas trade in circumstances where monopoly powers, conferred by the Crown, were an important condition for success. The use of the *statutory* company to undertake trading activities grew out of the canal construction movement of the second half of the eighteenth century, and reached a high-point in the second quarter of the nineteenth century with the advent of the railways and public utilities. By 1849, railways had to a great degree superseded all other modes of long-distance transport. There were approximately five thousand miles of line in operation at a cost exceeding two hundred million pounds (BPP, 1849, x, pp.471-2). Again monopoly powers were required, this time conferred by Parliament for the compulsory purchase of the land. The private statutes required to bestow these and other characteristics, including limited liability, contained increasingly onerous accountability requirements (Pollins, 1956, pp.336-9; and Edwards, 1986, Vol.1, pp.2-28).

There were early signs that the railways, as well as revolutionising transport, would prove to be enormously profitable for investors. The emergence of the capital-intensive railway companies required capital for business investment on an unprecedented scale, and this had major implications for the development of a formal capital market. The London Stock Exchange, which had previously dealt principally in government stocks, began to deal with corporate securities on a significant scale in the mid-1830s, while additional exchanges were set up in a number of provincial cities over the next ten years. The mid-1840s saw a period of intense speculation in railway shares (called the "railway mania"), and this gave unscrupulous or overoptimistic businessmen the opportunity to exploit gullible investors. It appears that the main body of shareholders were easily deluded by favourable reports in an atmosphere which the Chairman of the London and North Western Railway described as "that calm and dreamy state which, while they are getting large dividends, they are so apt to fall into" (Railway Times, 1849, p.834). This condition did not last long. With dividend expectations unfulfilled, disquiet with the management and financial practices of railway companies quickly grew. There followed a series of investigations by shareholder auditors (the "amateur" audit was commonplace at this time) who called in public accountants to provide the necessary financial expertise. Their investigations confirmed suspicions of "cooked" accounts. The leading accounting firm of the time, which owed much of its initial reputation to the successful investigation of railway companies, was Quilter, Ball & Co.

The most famous revelations concerned the activities of George Hudson, "the Railway King" at the Eastern Counties Railway. Quilter, Ball & Co.'s report revealed £318,144 wrongly omitted from the debit of the revenue account (comprising revenue items incorrectly debited to capital, the omission of amounts owing, and bad debts not written off); £35,315 wrongly credited to the revenue account; and interest charged to capital instead of revenue amounting to £84,591. Investor confidence plummeted and, between 1845 and 1848, the share prices of the twelve leading railway companies fell, on average, by sixty four percent (Edwards, 1989a, p.167). There were demands for regulation, and a government Select Committee was appointed and reported in 1849. The government's plan to introduce standardised reporting requirements was successfully countered through resistance from top railway management, and through efforts made to improve the reporting package led by the London and North Western Railway (Edwards, 1985). In other words, the industry "put its house in order."

Concerns with lack of general business regulation did lead, however, to important changes around this time. Businessmen required capital to exploit their ideas and this was in generous supply. It was difficult and expensive to obtain incorporation by Royal Charter or Act of Parliament, and businessmen began to operate on the basis of a joint stock in the absence of any formal organisation for the protection of investors and the general public. Failure was commonplace and sometimes the result of fraud. The government's response was the appointment of the Select Committee on Joint Stock Companies 1844, chaired by William Gladstone, which outlined "The Modes of Deception Adopted" by companies in its report. The Committee's far-sighted recommendations led to the creation of the joint stock company formed by the simple expedient of registering under the Joint Stock Companies Act 1844. This provided a cheap and easy means for creating the organisational entity which, following the introduction of limited liability in 1855, grew into the publicly financed business enterprise today dominant in most industries.

To obtain a flavour of contemporary financial reporting practices, it is of interest to examine, briefly, the published accounts of an early limited liability company. The Staveley Coal and Iron Company Ltd, incorporated in 1863, was a major supplier of coal and cast iron pipes in the late nineteenth century and beyond. The statements (directors' report omitted) for 1868 (reproduced as Figure 1) are fairly typical of the time. They may look a little quaint by today's standards, but they compare favourably, in terms of form and content, with the statements published by UK companies generally until the Companies Act 1929 took effect. Moreover, an examination of the company's underlying records[4] shows that the four fundamental accounting concepts were applied for the purpose of preparing the company's accounts. Stock of goods "worked and unworked" was valued at cost or below. Expenditure on fixed assets was capitalised at cost. The depreciation charge was designed to recover the cost of fixed assets over their expected useful life. Revenue was recognised in accordance with the realisation concept. And amounts owing to "sundry persons" were accrued as liabilities.

Figure 1

It is particularly requested that this Balance

THE STAVELEY COAL AND

DR.   *BALANCE SHEET, year*

LIABILITIES.

To Capital—			
1,250 Vendors' Shares, having £80 paid thereon £100,000 0 0			
4,750 Ordinary Shares, having £60 paid thereon 285,000 0 0			
3,100 New Shares, having £10 paid thereon 31,000 0 0			
		416,000 0 0	
,, Balance of Purchase or consideration money due to John Barrow, Esq., with			
interest thereon, and on Vendors' Shares		99,062 10 6	
,, Payment in advance of Calls		200 0 0	
		515,262 10 6	
,, Railway Tolls, Royalties, and Rents due from the Company		35,205 13 0	
,, Accounts owing to Sundry Persons		14,624 8 7	
,, Special Suspense Account, as per last Balance Sheet 23,788 14 0			
Less Expenditure on Special Account during the year 4,057 17 11			
		19,730 16 1	
,, Insurance Fund, to June 30th, 1867 .... 3,100 0 0			
,, Ditto to June 30th, 1868 .... 1,000 0 0			
,, Interest on £3,100 for one year, at £5 per cent. 155 0 0			
		4,255 0 0	
,, Schools and Charities, as per last Balance Sheet 980 0 0			
Less Gifts during the year .. ..: 45 0 0			
		935 0 0	
,, Balance of Profit from last year 552 13 10			
,, Profit this year 65,040 10 0			
	65,593 3 10		
Less Interim Dividends paid on the 4th February, at £4 on			
the Old Shares, and 13s. 4d. on the New Shares, and on the			
29th of June, at £2. 10s. on the Old Shares, and 8s. 4d. on			
the New Shares 42,358 6 8			
		23,234 17 2	
		£613,248 5 4	

PROPOSED APPROPRIATION OF PROFIT.

To Dividend on 6,000 Old Shares, at £3. 10s., making £10 for		
the year £21,000 0 0		
,, Dividend on 3,100 New Shares, at 11s. 8d., making		
£1. 13s. 4d. for the year 1,808 6 8		
	£22,808 6 8	
,, Balance carried forward to next year's account 426 10 6		
	£23,234 17 2	

Sheet be considered private and confidential.

IRON COMPANY LIMITED.

ending 30*th June*, 1868. **CR.**

ASSETS.

By Collieries, Properties, Ironstone Mines, and Iron Works, as per last year's statement £477,393 2 6		
Less Coal got during the Year 43 4 0		
	477,349 18 6	
,, Depreciation to June 30th, 1867 .... 30,782 10 0		
,, ,, for the year ending June 30th, 1868 .... 10,000 0 0	40,782 10 0	
	436,567 8 6	
,, Amount expended on Capital Account during the year	25,598 7 10	
		462,165 16 4
,, Stock of Materials, Worked and Unworked, on hand		57,851 4 6
,, Sundry Debtors for Coal, Castings, &c.		73,468 2 7
,, Shares held by the Company		8,673 9 8
,, Mineral Royalties, Purchased and Unworked		5,121 7 8
,, Cash on hand, and Balance in Bank		5,968 4 7
		£613,248 5 4

SUMMARY OF RESERVES AND DEPRECIATION ACCOUNT.

Special Suspense Account £19,730 16 1		
Insurance Account 4,255 0 0		
	23,985 16 1	
Depreciation deducted from value of Property for 5 years	40,782 10 0	
	£64,768 6 1	

64, CROSS STREET, MANCHESTER,
August 17, 1868.

TO THE SHAREHOLDERS OF THE STAVELEY COAL AND IRON COMPANY LIMITED.

GENTLEMEN,
We beg to report that we have examined the Balance Sheet and Accounts of your Company for the year ended June 30th last, and have certified the same to be correct.

We are, yours obediently

CHADWICKS, ADAMSON, COLLIER, & Co.
AUDITORS.

Yamey (1960) has pointed to the latter part of the nineteenth century as crucial to understanding the development of accounting conventions. It certainly seems likely that the dominant position of conservatism in financial reporting owes much to the situation which then prevailed - i.e. falling prices, fluctuations in economic conditions between boom and slump, widespread fraud, and the position of creditors as primary users of financial statements. It may be argued, however, that the development of the quoted company during this time period had more problematic implications for financial reporting. During a period which witnessed an increase in the number of parties interested in the form and content of financial reports (in a period of industrial unrest, employees and, possibly, government, as well as shareholders and creditors), the seeds of the movement towards concealment and distortion can be seen. Before examining this matter further, it is illuminating to consider the main concerns with financial reporting practices expressed in the contemporary accounting literature.

ACCOUNTING THINKERS: SOME CONTRIBUTIONS

In view of the UK's primary role in the development of capital markets, financial reporting, and professional accountancy bodies (Parker, 1986), it is perfectly natural that it should also be the country in which were written and published early substantial contributions to the literature on auditing and accounting. The leading late-nineteenth-century auditing texts were Pixley's *Auditors: Their Duties and Responsibilities* and Dicksee's *Auditing: A Practical Manual for Auditors*. Despite the title, Dicksee's "first, and also his most important, book ... is most of all distinguished for a real attempt (in Chapter 5) to work out an acceptable and rational basis for asset valuation, depreciation, and income" (Kitchen and Parker, 1994a, p.211). Dicksee's *Auditing* ran to fourteen editions during his lifetime (he died 1932) and, together with his many other works including *Advanced Accounting* (1903), "an important book, associated with his university courses at Birmingham and London" (Kitchen and Parker, 1994a, p.218), he must have exerted an enormous influence on practitioners and the thousands of students who used this material as preparation for professional examinations.[5] Indeed, one claim is that Dicksee "provided a literature for accounting single-handed" (Kitchen and Parker, 1994a, p.218).

The impact of Dicksee's *Auditing* was not merely local, but part of "a body of knowledge which [Britain] then exported to the rest of the English-speaking world" (Defliese, 1981, p.106). More specifically (pp.106-7):

> Robert H. Montgomery, founder of the firm which became the American segment of Coopers & Lybrand, published, with permission, an American version of Britain's Dicksee's Auditing in 1905, the first such book in America.

And Kitchen and Parker (1994a, p.211) have remarked that:

> It has been said that Montgomery's adaption of Dicksee's text to American needs in 1905 marked the beginning of American literature in accounting.

Later, in 1912, Montgomery published his own *Auditing Theory and Practice* but, by this time, Hatfield's (1909) major work, *Modern Accounting: Its Principles and Some of Its Problems*, had appeared. Hatfield believed that the greatest challenge facing the "`science' of accounting was the lack of uniformity in accounting principles, and the accompanying latitude in terminology" (Mills, 1994, p.297).

Dicksee, Hatfield and other writers in the English language around this time accepted the basic historical cost model, and their major efforts were directed towards the identification and encouragement of what they saw as best practice. Concerns with the need for conservatism and the strict application of the realisation principle feature prominently in their writings. The emphasis, particularly in their early writings, was on the balance sheet, with a primary focus on the valuation of assets and liabilities, with the profit and loss account of secondary importance. The extent to which these writers influenced contemporary financial reporting practice would be worthy of investigation. However, their hey-day coincided, in the UK at least, with a period (the late nineteenth and early twentieth century) for which there is evidence to suggest that quoted companies, turning more and more to the stock exchange for finance, published less information rather than more (Edwards, 1981; and Edwards and Boyns, 1994). Also, there is little evidence to suggest that measurement procedures (e.g. depreciation) showed any improvement over this time period (Edwards, 1981).

It is not suggested that these writers were responsible for any observed decline in accounting standards. Indeed, the evidence is that they were increasingly critical of accounting practice as the twentieth century progressed. For example, Dicksee attacked the growing use of secret reserves in the 1920s, and the tendency of companies to group together a number of items under a single heading in the balance sheet (Kitchen and Parker, 1994a, pp.220-1; see also Dicksee, 1927). These criticisms were echoed by F. R. M. de Paula (Professor of Accountancy and Business Methods at the London School of Economics, 1926-9), and the prominent economist Josiah Stamp (Kitchen and Parker, 1994a, pp.229-32). There is need to move to continental Europe, however, to find a contemporary literature which contained major reexaminations of the application and/or validity of the traditional accounting model.

Eugen Schmalenbach, businessman and academic, published his major work, *Dynamische Bilanz* (Dynamic Accounting) in 1920.[6] According to Tweedie and Whittington (1984, p.21):

> The essential purpose of Schmalenbach's dynamic accounting was to shift the emphasis of accounting from the balance sheet, a static statement, to dynamic statements of changes in position, such as the profit and loss account. He rejected the "dualist" view that it was possible to produce an articulated balance sheet and profit and loss account which would produce both a balance sheet which would serve the "statist's" objective of giving a realistic snapshot of the entity's current assets, liabilities and net worth and the "dynamist's" objective of measuring accurately the performance of an entity resulting from its transactions for the period. When these two objectives conflicted, Schmalenbach asserted that the dynamic objective should be paramount because it was only by an accurate appraisal of the earnings that the business as a whole

could be valued, this value being the capitalised
value of the prospective earnings stream.

Schmalenbach therefore accepted the traditional historical cost
framework, but advocated a different orientation (Tweedie and
Whittington, 1984, p.21):

> placing emphasis on the accuracy of the allocations
> to the profit and loss account, and regarding the
> balance sheet as a mere accrual sheet, recording
> sunk costs not yet allocated to profit and loss, rather
> than as a serious attempt to value the assets of the
> business.

According to Canziani (1994, pp.151-2), conditions of economic
instability, epitomised by high levels of inflation, led Gino Zappa to
reach similar conclusions in Italy, during the 1920s, concerning the
respective roles of the balance sheet and profit and loss account. A
little later in Finland, Martti Saario emphasised an "expenditure-
revenue theory" in the successful endeavour to supersede the balance
sheet equation by influencing both the content of the educational
curicula and Finnish legislation (Lukka and Pihlanto, 1994, p.69).
According to Canziani (1994, p.161), Saario achieved for Finland
what Zappa did for Italy and Schmalenbach for Germany.

There emerged during the inter-war period even more
fundamental criticisms of contemporary accounting practice. These
contained a common concern with the lack of correspondence between
financial statements prepared in accordance with the historical cost
framework and so-called economic reality. It is again in continental
Europe, worried by the impact of hyper-inflation, that an embryonic
literature is found which deals with the need to take account of
changing price levels. Achievements during the inter-war period are
summarised by Tweedie and Whittington (1984, p.34) as follows:

> Germany and France [particularly W. Mahlberg] in
> the 1920s had provided the basic work on the CPP
> model, and Germany and The Netherlands
> (particularly Fritz Schmidt and Theo. Limperg) had
> provided the CCA model.

According to Tweedie and Whittington (1984, p.34) it was the American, Henry W. Sweeney who:

> clarified the techniques of CPP for the benefit of an English-speaking audience and had shown the possibility of combining current valuation of assets, based on specific prices, with general purchasing power adjustment of capital, based on a general index.

Sweeney's magnum opus entitled *Stabilised Accounting* was published in 1936.

In the UK, these ideas received little attention prior to the post-Second World War periods of high inflation, and it was not until the 1970s that determined attempts were made to give them practical effect in published company financial statements. In the Netherlands, some of these ideas received practical application much earlier. Limperg, for example, was instrumental in the development of a literature advocating the use of values in the late 1920s and 1930s (Camfferman and Zeff, 1994, p.117), though the writings of Schmidt were already well-known in the Netherlands, and there is some uncertainty and controversy concerning the extent to which Limperg built on Schmidt's ideas (Camfferman and Zeff, 1994, pp.120-1; see also Clarke and Dean, 1992). Limperg's achievements are distinguished from those of many other accounting theorists in the sense that his ideas not only received attention from the academic community, but were also adopted by a number of companies in the 1950's and 1960's, notably Philips Electrical Industries whose practices were the subject of acclaim by Gynther (1966, pp.223-40; see also Brink, 1992).[7]

Turning to the US, concern with the lack of reality in company accounts was the subject of Kenneth MacNeal's *Truth in Accounting* published in 1939 (MacNeal, 1939). MacNeal's forthright, arguably outspoken, criticisms of conventional practice made use of three "fables" to highlight the weaknesses and criticisms of the primacy attached to realisation and conservatism in financial reporting. One of MacNeal's major achievements was that his criticisms did not go unnoticed. However, according to Zeff (1982c, p.540):

In view of the strength of MacNeal's convictions,
and the almost sanctimonious tone of the argument,
it is perhaps not surprising that MacNeal's academic
and professional critics were quick to find fault.

It may be that academics did not favour an incursion from someone
outside their community. Certainly, they did not like his language.
And he did not like theirs (Zeff, 1982c, p.543):

MacNeal was stung by the ferocity of the published
criticism" and "withdrew from the literature two
years after he had entered, a disappointed man.

MacNeal's criticisms stemmed from the not unreasonable
conviction that accounting information should meet the expectations
of the ordinary small investor. More specifically (Zeff, 1982c, p.535):

A balance sheet and a profit and loss statement
purport to state values. In order to fulfil their
purpose, they must state values according to
economic concepts, commonly called economic
values, because these are the only values that anyone
knows how to state.

Equally, MacNeal (Zeff, 1982c, p.539) believed that the profit and
loss account should reflect both realised and unrealised profits and
losses on the grounds that they represented changes in the wealth of
the shareholder.

TRIALS AND TRIBULATIONS[8]

There has been much popular criticism of financial reports in
recent years (Griffiths 1986; and Smith, 1992), with attention drawn
to the widespread use of window dressing, off-balance sheet finance
and schemes of cosmetic accounting, each of considerable legal
complexity and designed to mislead external user groups. This is
nothing new as it derives from a lack of congruence between the
message which preparers and users of financial reports wish such

documents to convey. It was in the 1920s that certain events in the US and UK increased public awareness of this fact.

In the US, the stock market abuses of the 1920s which culminated in the Great Crash, "together with inadequate accounting tenets and disclosures ... pointed to the need for reform" (Defliese, 1981, p.107). A particularly stern critic was the Harvard University economist, Professor William Z. Ripley. "In three articles in *The Atlantic Monthly* and a book, *Main Street and Wall Street"*, Ripley accused "large corporations of, inter alia, deceptive and misleading financial reporting practices" (Zeff, 1984, p.208; see also Previts and Merino, 1979, pp.231-7).

Turning to the UK, the level of disclosure in the financial statements of companies was undoubtedly on the decline in the 1920s. It may well be that this development was designed to conceal declining profitability. It might also, or alternatively, have been part of a general move to lower levels of disclosure as shareholdings became more widely dispersed, and the gap between ownership and management grew. Certainly, contemporary legal regulations did not help a great deal. According to Sidney Pears of Cooper Brothers (Pears, 1929, p.150) the directors:

> were within their legal rights (under the Companies
> Act 1908) in showing capital, creditors and the
> balance of profit and loss ... on the one side, and
> sundry fixed assets, debts etc. on the other side.

Criticism of actual practice contained in evidence presented to the Company Law Amendment Committee 1926, included complaints from the Society of Incorporated Accountants and Auditors of "an increasing tendency for the information given in balance sheets to be attenuated" (BPP, 1925, Appendix FF, p.lxxxiii). Concealment was in some cases accompanied by distortion. Methods of deception around this time were rather less subtle than those seen today, however, and are thought to have consisted mainly of the movement of reported profit between different years using secret reserves or the mis-allocation of capital expenditure write-offs.

It seems that, initially, these procedures proved acceptable to users of financial statements. For example, secret reserves were described as "one of the cornerstones of modern company finance" during the inter-war period (Samuel, 1933, p.269). More specifically, they enabled companies to disclose a steady, upward trend of reported profits, and provided a financial cushion against a downturn in the trade cycle. The downside, demonstrated in the *Royal Mail* case of 1931, was that such reserves were sometimes used to persuade investors that a company, on the verge of ruin, remained profitable and deserved continued financial support. The Chairman (Lord Kylsant) and the auditor (Harold Moreland of Price, Waterhouse & Co.) were accused of circulating a balance sheet considered to be false and fraudulent. The published accounts for 1926 contained a profit figure described as follows:

Balance for the year, including dividends
on shares in allied and other companies,
adjustment of taxation reserves, less
depreciation of fleet, etc.   £439,212. 12. 1

Investigations showed that the company had in fact suffered an operating loss of about three hundred thousand pounds, which was concealed by making an undisclosed transfer of approximately seven hundred and fifty thousand pounds from tax provisions surplus to requirements which had been built up during the First World War. The prosecution failed on the grounds that the caption used, although misleading, was technically correct at a time when there was no statutory requirement to disclose transfers to and from reserves; the key words being "adjustment of taxation reserves". Mr Justice Wright's charge to the jury, however, contained severe explicit criticism of the company's reporting practices, and implied criticism of the external audit function. The disclosures in this case produced a furious reaction from shareholders and the financial press and, as usual, when "fingers are burned", there was a strong demand for regulation to stamp out abuse.

Raising Standards: Initial Response

To Tribulations ...

Criticisms voiced in the US by Ripley found a sympathetic listener in the person of George O. May, senior partner of Price, Waterhouse &

Co.   Although disagreeing with some of Ripley's more extreme notions, May expressed doubt whether "auditors have done their full duty" in ensuring that stockholders were properly informed and urged them to "assume larger responsibilities" (quoted in Carey, 1969a, p.244).   Price, Waterhouse were appointed in 1927 to be accounting adviser to the New York Stock Exchange, and were represented by May who "acquired the freedom of time and of action which permitted him to lead the profession in some urgently needed reforms" (Carey, 1969a, p.244).

In recognition of the need for more effective monitoring of financial reporting by listed companies, the New York Stock Exchange also appointed J. M. B. Hoxsey to the new full-time post of Executive Assistant to its Committee on Stock List.   According to Carey (1969a, p.245):

> May cultivated his acquaintance. Hoxsey was wholly
> in accord with May's objective to make financial
> statements of listed companies as informative and
> reliable as possible, and consulted May informally on
> technical questions.

In 1930, Hoxsey proposed that the American Institute of Accountants and the Stock Exchange cooperate on improving corporate financial reporting procedures.   A committee was established with May its chairman.   In 1932, May also became Chairman of the American Institute's newly established Committee on the Development of Accounting Principles (Carey, 1969a, p.249).

In 1933, the New York Stock Exchange announced its requirement for companies seeking listing to be subject to an independent audit, and the Securities and Exchange Act of the following year established the Securities and Exchange Commission (SEC) to administer the requirement for companies to file the accounts periodically issued by listed companies (Zeff, 1984, pp.208-9).   The SEC was invested with the power to prescribe accounting methods but, instead, gave the accountancy profession the opportunity to take the initiative in this matter.   Carman G. Blough was appointed as the SEC's first Chief Accountant, and between 1935 and 1938 urged "the accounting profession to narrow the range of diversity in accounting practices" (Zeff, 1984, p.209).   In the late 1930s, May advised the American Institute to increase the resources and thereby the capability of the Committee on Accounting Procedure (CAP) (Previts and Merino, 1979, p.260).[9] The Institute complied with this request and, in 1939, in response to a suggestion made by the CAP, authorised the CAP to issue pronouncements on accounting and establish a research department. The first four *Accounting Research Bulletins* were issued later that year (Zeff, 1984, p.210).

The American Accounting Association (AAA), founded by academic accountants in 1916 and initially called the American Association of University Instructors in Accounting, was also active producing in 1936 a pamphlet entitled *A Tentative Statement of Accounting Principles Underlying Corporate Financial Statements*. This employed deductive reasoning in an endeavour to develop accounting principles (Zeff, 1984, p.209). According to Carey (1970, pp.11-12), the cumulative effect of Blough's criticisms:

> in conjunction with the earlier challenge of the American Accounting Association, made it clear that if the Institute wished to maintain a position of leadership it would have to do more than it had done so far to promulgate authoritative accounting principles.

The work of the CAP and successor bodies and the AAA has been chronicled by Zeff (1984; see also Carey, 1969b and 1970; and Previts and Merino, 1979). An important development was the publication of Paton and Littleton's (1940) monograph entitled *An Introduction to Corporate Accounting Standards* which elaborated the earlier *Tentative Statement* of the AAA. According to Zeff (1982c, p.541), this publication "was to become the definitive explication (and, in large measure, defence) of conventional financial accounting." According to Previts and Robinson (1994, p.313):

> If a single document can be attributed to have influenced a generation of academics to consider the primacy of the matching principle, an income determination process and earning power, *An Introduction to Corporate Accounting Standards* would have to be the most prominent candidate.

The emphasis on the income statement has been described by Paton as "something of a departure from accounting tradition" (quoted by Previts and Robinson, 1994, p.313). But, in other respects, it reinforced much of existing practice in an endeavour to obtain acceptance among practitioners (p.314). It is seen to have had a substantial impact on the subsequent development of accounting standards in the US (pp.313-14).

... and Trials

The impact of the Great Crash on financial reporting in the US was to some extent mirrored in the UK by the *Royal Mail* case which encouraged the accountancy profession to consider whether it might not play a more active role than hitherto in helping improve the informative value of published financial statements. The possibility of close regulation had been a matter of regular debate from the mid-nineteenth-century onwards, and detailed disclosure requirements were in fact introduced for certain categories of company - i.e. railways, public utilities, and certain financial institutions. The possibility of more widespread enforcement was discussed by a government committee in 1877, where one of the witnesses, Sir George Jessell, Master of the Rolls, highlighted a fundamental flaw in the case for standardisation made by the prominent accountant and company promoter, David Chadwick M.P., and others. Standardisation is manifested in three ways - which balances to be disclosed, how to present them, and the valuation procedures to be used. Contemporary proposals focused on the first two areas which, Jessell insisted (in an exchange with Chadwick), did not get to the root of the problem and, moreover, gave an impression of reliability which was illusory and, possibly, misleading. In stating that "It is not sufficient to put it in form; it is the substance" (BPP, 1877, x, 2242), Jessell may be regarded as one of the architects of the notion of "substance over form" in accounting.

The nature of regulation became a recurring theme among committees subsequently appointed to enquire into the possible reform of company law. By the time of the *Royal Mail* case, the conclusion embodied in the Companies Act 1929 was that the appropriate way forward was based on the concept of minimum disclosure. This specified a range of information which was required from all companies in order to achieve a *minimum* level of accountability. But it left the market to decide how much additional information should be disclosed in particular cases. This approach may be contrasted with the contemporary position in Germany where standardised formats were receiving growing attention. The breakthrough there came in 1927 with Schmalenbach's *Der Kontenrahmen* (The Standard Chart of Accounts) which "has influenced theory and practice of accounting in Germany to the present day" (Potthoff and Sieben, 1994).

Following the *Royal Mail* case, two of the leading professional accounting bodies (The Institute of Chartered Accountants in England and Wales [ICAEW] and the Society of Incorporated Accountants and Auditors) were in disagreement concerning the best way forward. The case had resulted in the acquittal of the defendants, presumably on the grounds that the wording used provided a technically correct although, some would say, not a fair indication of the company's financial performance. The Society favoured stronger legislation designed to help the professional accountant force management to report fairly, while the ICAEW emphasised the need for professional accountants to recognise a higher ethical obligation - i.e. to focus on the economic substance rather than pure legal form of transactions.

The government appears to have been persuaded by the case put forward by leading chartered accountants and, although it monitored major areas of concern with financial reporting practices through the early 1930s (Bircher, 1988), it left the accountancy profession to put its house in order. The response of the profession and industry proved effective with important leadership provided by the Dunlop Rubber Company which, under the influence of its financial controller, F. R. M. de Paula, made major innovations in the financial statements published for 1931 and 1933 (reproduced in Kitchen and Parker, 1980, pp.99-107). These statements blazed a trail for UK companies in the same way that the United States Steel Company's statements of 1902 (reproduced in Brief, 1986, pp.15-53) had pointed the way forward for US companies some thirty one years earlier. This may be seen as an early illustration of how the UK, although it "pioneered modern financial reporting" (Baskin, 1988, p.228), soon lost ground to the US.

UK accountants did play a part in bringing about early improvements in the US, however, which tends to suggest that features within the respective business environments other than the role of the individual were crucial in triggering accounting change. For example, Arthur Lowes Dickinson took charge of Price, Waterhouse & Co.'s US operations in 1901 and, "working with W. J. Filbert, controller of U.S.

Steel, developed consolidated theory based on the entity premise"
(Previts and Merino, 1979, p.177). Together with other UK and US
accountants, Dickinson worked hard to disseminate knowledge
concerning the theory and practice of consolidated financial statements
in a series of lectures delivered and through books and articles
published between 1904 and 1912 (Walker, 1978, pp.148-52; and
Edwards and Webb, 1984, p.35).

According to Dickinson (1924), there were just two major
differences between the financial reporting practices of UK and US
companies, and these underline the importance of the lead provided by
United States Steel. The differences were found among the accounting
practices of steel companies, where the comprehensive financial
reporting practices introduced by the United States Steel Corporation
had been followed by "other steel companies .... and to some extent by
other large manufacturing companies" (Dickinson, 1924, p.475); and
in the publication of consolidated statements where "American
companies are much in advance" of their UK counterparts (p.477).

Further light is thrown on the forces encouraging accounting
change in the US by Sir Gilbert Garnsey, a London-based partner in
Price Waterhouse (Garnsey, 1923, p.54). He drew attention to
institutional support for the preparation of consolidated statements
provided by the New York Stock Exchange, which "laid special stress
on the necessity of filing consolidated balance sheets", and the Federal
Reserve Board, which took the view that applications for credit should
be supported by a consolidated statement. Legal recognition of the
consolidation principle was first contained in the federal tax
legislation, which required consolidated returns of net income and
invested capital beginning in 1917. Garnsey (1923, p.54) and
Dickinson (1924, p.477) agreed that the preparation of consolidated
accounts was almost universal practice, while Dickinson further stated
that this had been the situation "for more than fifteen years past"
(p.477).

The contemporary paternalistic attitude of UK company directors
towards financial reporting is, by way of contrast, well illustrated by
the following extract from a letter to *The Times*, dated 3 June 1925,
and written by the Chairman of Lever Brothers, Francis D'Arcy
Cooper (a chartered accountant and previously a partner in Cooper
Brothers & Co.):

> If directors considered that the publication of an amalgamated balance sheet was in the interests of their shareholders, they would no doubt publish it.

The following comment made by Garnsey (1931, p.103) six years later is perhaps more consistent with the available evidence:

> Perhaps the real opposition to any but the most essential changes in the form of the published accounts often comes from boards of directors who are not all imbued with the desire to give shareholders as much information as possible.

Indeed, the Company Law Amendment Committee 1926 agreed that one of the main reasons for structuring business activity through subsidiary companies in the early decades of the twentieth century was to avoid "disclosure of matters relating to what in substance is the business of the parent company" (BPP, 1926, ix, para.87).

To an extent, there are good reasons for the slower development of financial reporting practices in the UK, both generally and in relation to consolidated financial statements. The accountancy profession was established earlier on in the UK. Professional bodies were formed in the third quarter of the nineteenth century whereas, in the US, the process of professionalisation began to develop only around 1900. The result of this factor, and others, was that, in the UK, there was traditionally a much greater reliance on the protection provided by the external audit (a statutory requirement for all companies from 1900), and the right of members to ask questions at the annual general meeting. In the US, a more demanding public, without the protection of a statutory audit, appear to have insisted upon information as the basis for an independent judgment.

PROFESSIONAL INITIATIVES IN UK

Following the *Royal Mail* case, the failure of the professional accountancy bodies to take the initiative in issuing guidance for members was a disappointment to at least some practising accountants. With the importance of ethical responsibilities emphasised in the professional press, however, there was a voluntary movement towards realism rather than legalism as the basis for financial reports. Direct intervention was not long delayed. Following further press criticism in the early 1940s (Zeff, 1972, p.10), the ICAEW assumed a much closer responsibility for reporting procedures, with the establishment of the Taxation and Financial Relations Committee (TFRC) in 1942 (renamed the Taxation and Research Committee in 1949, and the Technical Advisory Committee in 1964, still operating at local level).

The remit of the TFRC was "to consider matters affecting taxation and the financial relationship of the business community with the Inland Revenue or other government departments." This wording reflected a decision to give greater recognition to the needs of the growing number of ICAEW members engaged in industry whose interests had previously been almost entirely ignored. Arrangements were made for the election of non-practising members to Council, with F. R. M. de Paula becoming the first in 1943. According to a member of the ICAEW closely associated with its technical activities at the time (quoted by Zeff, 1972, p.9):

> The establishment of the new committee made possible for the first time the close collaboration of practising and non-practising members of the Institute and this was in itself sufficient to bring a new spirit into the Institute's affairs.

The initial membership of the TFRC was set at twenty seven, of which eight including de Paula held commercial and industrial appointments. According to Kitchen and Parker (1994b, p.225)[10], de Paula was:

> the main progenitor of the ICAEW's important Recommendations on Accounting Principles which began to appear under his Vice-Chairmanship and Chairmanship of the ICAEW's Taxation and Financial Relations Committee early in the 1940s (and which brought to fruition a sufficient revolution in professional attitudes to transform within a few

years both accounting practice and legislation on financial reporting).

However, according to Zeff (1972, p.10):

> The procedure through which a proposed Recommendation had to pass was cumbersome indeed, owing to the Council's desire that it be exposed to a broad range of comment. The object of a Recommendation was to offer guidance to members on `best practice'.

The "fire-fighting" exercise had begun in earnest. The TFRC immediately tackled the most pressing problems, including reserves and provisions (*Recommendation 6* in 1943), group accounts (*Recommendation 7* in 1944), depreciation (*Recommendation 9* in 1945) and stock (*Recommendation 10* in 1945). The last of these statements was hailed by the TFRC's chairman as "the most revolutionary of any of the recommendations issued to date by the Council" (Zeff, 1972, p.16). The important point seems to be that it emphasised the need to apply the chosen procedure consistently over time in order to discourage companies from switching between accounting methods in order to distort the trend of reported profits.

The impact of initiatives taken by individual accountants and the accountancy profession was not lost on the Company Law Amendment Committee (CLAC) which reported in 1945 (BPP, 1945, iv, para.97):

> The recent tendency has been to give more information and this tendency has been fortified by the valuable recommendations published from time to time by the responsible accountancy bodies as to the form in which accounts should be drawn up and the information which they should contain.

In framing its recommendations on accounting, which formed the basis for the accounting content of the Companies Act 1948, the CLAC drew heavily on the ICAEW's submission which was, in turn, founded on the *Recommendations* previously issued. The CLAC's recognition of their prime importance in bringing about improvements in financial reporting procedures, and the government's willingness to provide a back-up system in the form of statutory support for *Recommendations* which had proved successful, undoubtedly helped improve the status of both the *Recommendations* and the ICAEW itself. These events therefore mark a period when leadership in the development of financial reporting practices was firmly in the hands of the accountancy profession.

The series of *Recommendations* proved acceptable to the business community, and are thought to have significantly improved reporting practices (Zeff, 1972, p.23). Widespread compliance was partly due to the consultation process, and partly because companies were allowed to choose from a range of approved practices - i.e. flexibility was the price paid for acceptance.

In the UK, the Companies Act 1948 may be seen to reflect a change of atmosphere in favour of the US model. Whereas financial confidentiality was considered desirable in the 1920s, the watchword instead became fullest practicable disclosure. The decision to appoint an accountant from the younger school (Russell Kettle) to the CLAC in 1943 (rather than someone like Plender who, as the doyen of accountants in the inter-war period, had been influential in persuading the government to adopt a light touch in the aftermath of the *Royal Mail* case) is indicative of the government's conviction of the need for more radical regulatory requirements in financial reporting.

The Companies Act 1948 significantly increased the level of corporate accountability, though continuing to base new measures on the concept of minimum disclosure. This may be contrasted with contemporary developments elsewhere in Europe. For example, in France (Colasse and Durand, 1994, p.49):

> The economic crisis and subsequent political turmoil of the 1930s had inclined many, if not most, influential people to believe that "technique et machinisme" had killed liberalism. A new breed of politicians, economists and civil servants were well aware of the "solutions" worked out in Italy, the Soviet Union and Roosevelt's America, solutions based on nationwide statistics, economic research, cost and price controls, and national economic plans.

French resources in this field were far from satisfactory. There were too many small companies unable to produce accurate figures and large ones were commonly accused of hiding theirs.

In an endeavour to improve the position, plans were introduced in 1942 and 1947 (i.e. the *Plan Comptable Général* or General Accounting Plan) which had much in common with the charts used to help regulate the German economy (Standish, 1990). These "plans" were designed to: produce reliable financial reports, make cost control easier, and facilitate the creation of professional statistics for consolidated into nationwide statistics. A different ethos persisted in the UK until 1981.

PERMISSIVE PROFIT MEASURES

The 1950s saw criticism of accounting practice again reaching the public domain, though it was some time before it had any noticeable impact in the UK. In the US, Leonard Spacek, managing partner of Arthur Andersen & Co., "began to command attention in the popular press with his attacks on financial reporting practices" (Previts and Merino, 1979, pp.285-6). Spacek berated the American Institute of Certified Public Accountants' (AICPA) committees (including the CAP) for yielding "to industry pressures on matters of accounting principle and auditing procedure" (Zeff, 1984, p.211). These actions, together with his description of the CAP's pronouncements as "generally accepted and antiquated accounting procedures," did nothing to endear him to the accounting establishment (Zeff, 1984, p.211; see also Carey, 1970, pp.74-7). An internal investigation conducted for the AICPA not surprisingly found Spacek's allegations to be groundless. But continuing concern and criticism pointed to the need for institutional changes which included the replacement of the CAP by the Accounting Principles Board.

Criticisms from the academic community were most vociferously expressed by Australia's Raymond Chambers. According to Gaffikin (1994, p.3), lectures presented by Chambers in the early 1950s:

signalled his intention not to simply accept the
sacred cows of accounting but to seek some logical
justification for accounting action. He argued that
conservatism had no place in accounting, it cannot
be theoretically justified and flies in the face of many
other basic principles of accounting ... And he also
argued that accounting is a fact-finding function, a
belief that persisted throughout his subsequent work.

A possible difference between Chambers and some other academic
writers around this time was that Chambers not only advocated
particular procedures (principally, continuously contemporary
accounting or CoCoA) but engaged in outspoken criticisms of existing
practices. He estimated that, even assuming compliance with the
existing *Recommendations*, it was possible to come up with "a million
sets of mutually exclusive rules, each (apparently) giving a true and
fair view of the company's state of affairs and its profits" (Chambers,
1965, p.15). Chambers further concluded that "where there are so
many possible rules there are in effect no rules."

The message was clear enough but there was no immediate
evidence that the policy makers were listening. This soon changed. In
the UK, the liberalism of the 1960s has been blamed for a range of
social problems which have become more evident in the last five or ten
years. Reaction to permissive profit measures came rather more
quickly. According to Tweedie (1981, pp.169-70), financial reporting
had evolved, by the late 1960s, into:

a system which attempted within the compass of two
basic statements to meet several (often conflicting)
objectives at once - to measure efficiency, to protect
creditors, to control assets, to aid management
decision making, to inform shareholders of
management's stewardship of their investment and
so on.

With the benefit of hindsight, it might be asked how the system
survived so long without closer regulation. Certain *causes célèbres*,
small in number but significant in the extent to which they affected the
public's perception of accounting, played a crucial part. According to
Wise (1982, p.80) "The erosion of the unquestioning attitude towards

accountants in the UK set in with the collapse of the Rolls Razor company in 1964." This company was launched by the former washing machine salesman, John Bloom, who began to import cheap machines and sell them door to door, later diversifying into vacuum cleaners, dishwashing machines and refrigerators. Prominent features of his business tactics were cut-rate prices and high pressure advertising. Widespread concern with Rolls Razor's financial affairs followed revelations in a BBC television programme which the Department of Trade Inspectors (Morris Finer QC and Henry Benson of Cooper Brothers) initially suspected might have been responsible for precipitating the failure of the company. However, further investigation revealed that (Benson, 1989, p.143):

> the business was rotten through and through and the more we looked into it the worse it became. The management was weak and inefficient, the company was under-capitalised, the accounts were unreliable, some of the stock valuations were suspect, and production problems had developed with the machinery and equipment incorporated in the washing machines which resulted in rejects and claims by dissatisfied customers which were continually increasing.

The collapse of Rolls Razor occurred shortly after it had published its annual report for 1964. It was soon noticed that the report had contained no indication of impending problems, and this touched off a spate of publicity about the shortcomings of the accountancy profession and its failure to ensure that published financial statements provided a fair indication of the true condition of the enterprise (Wise, 1982, p.81).

A few years later the accountancy profession was embarrassed by revelations concerning profit forecasts issued by the directors of target companies in the endeavour to resist takeover bids. In October 1967, GEC (General Electric Company) made a takeover bid for the shares of AEI (Associated Electrical Industries). The directors of AEI issued a profit forecast of ten million pounds as part of the defensive strategy. The takeover bid was nevertheless successful, and when AEI's financial statements for 1967 were published in April 1968, they revealed a loss of four and one half million pounds. A report subsequently prepared by GEC's joint auditors, Deloitte, Plender, Griffiths & Co. and Price Waterhouse & Co., commissioned by the GEC's Chairman, Lord Aldington, pointed out that "the appraisals of stocks, contracts and a number of other matters involve the exercise of judgement; they are not matters of precision" (quoted in *The Accountant*, 10 August 1968, p.167). More specifically, the investigation showed that the turn around of £14.5 million was mainly caused by the new management team making conservative accounting estimates and assumptions when valuing AEI's assets, with approximately £9.5 million attributed to matters of judgment and £5 million to matters of fact. The general public, buoyed on by the media, was surprised and shocked to discover that accountancy was not a precise science, and that the level of reported profit was subject to substantial variation depending on judgments reached concerning the values of assets and liabilities.

Intense public concern surfaced a third time in the Autumn of 1969 when Leasco withdrew its proposed offer for Pergamon, a company in which the Maxwell family held a major interest. A 1969 editorial in *Accountancy* observed (p.722):

> When doubt is cast on the "quantum and quality" of profits which a company has published, and on which independent accountants have reported, there is cause for concern by the public and the accountancy profession.
>
> There appears to be credibility gap between the view which the accountancy profession has of itself and its practices and the view which the public has of it... The accountancy profession cannot afford to ignore this gap in understanding. One way to bridge it would be for the profession to find means of ensuring that recognised best standards are clearly seen to be the sole yardstick by which financial statements are judged, and that departures therefrom are fully disclosed.

Following withdrawal of the bid for Pergamon, but mindful of a possible renewal of interest in view of the fact that Leasco had purchased thirty eight per cent of Pergamon's issued share capital, the board of Pergamon appointed Price Waterhouse to carry out an investigation. The accountancy firm's report did not recommend "any changes in the general accounting principles adopted by the group," but it did recommend "very material changes in the way in which those principles have been applied" (quoted in Holmes, 1970, p.699). It further concluded that figures previously published in respect of the year to 31 December 1968 should be amended as follows - that profit before taxation be reduced by seventy six per cent from £2.1 million to £0.5 million, and net assets revised downwards by thirty six per cent from £7 million to £4.5 million (Holmes, 1970, p.702). These findings did nothing to allay growing public concern.

What Tweedie (1981, p.170) has described as "inherent defects in the reporting system in the United Kingdom" had by this time been the subject of comment in a letter of complaint from the Chairman of Courtaulds, Frank Kearton, to the President of the ICAEW in 1968 "questioning the need for a multitude of generally accepted accounting principles" (Holmes, 1970, p.702; see also Stamp and Marley, 1970, p.69). The time was ripe for a further broadside, and it was not long in coming.

At the time the Pergamon affair made banner headlines, the Professor of Accounting and Business Method at the University of Edinburgh, Edward Stamp, was paying a short visit to the US. It is interesting to note a close parallel between the circumstances surrounding Stamp's initial involvement in an accounting controversy, and that of MacNeal thirty-one years earlier. In the autumn of 1938, the editors of *Fortune* had learnt of MacNeal's forthcoming book, and commissioned him to write an article critical of the accountancy profession in the wake of the McKesson & Robbins scandal of 1938 (Zeff, 1982c, p.543).[11] In 1969, Stamp received a telephone call from the editorial writer for the financial section of *The Times*, who had read an academic article written by Stamp critical of accounting and the accountancy profession, and inviting him to comment on the Pergamon affair. According to Stamp (1981, p.234):

> Having by then had nearly two years' experience of dealing with the moguls of the British accounting profession I was quite sure that nothing I could say or write would have the slightest effect upon their attitudes. I had of course reckoned without the

peculiar and penetrating impact of The Times on the
British Establishment.

There is no doubt that the accountancy profession was shaken by
Stamp's criticisms in *The Times* of 11 September, 1969, and it is
interesting to note that this might reflect the medium of the message in
view of the fact that the criticisms, when previously expressed in an
academic journal (Stamp, 1969), in common with those of Chambers a
few years earlier, had passed relatively unnoticed.

Possibly the key event in this episode, however, was the decision
of the President of the ICAEW, Ronald Leach (then senior partner of
Peat, Marwick, Mitchell & Co.), to enter into a public debate by
publishing a reply eleven days later in *The Times* (Leach, 1969).
According to Stamp (1981, p.235) this action was:

> against strong advice from the more traditional
> members of the profession's Establishment who
> thought, quite rightly, that for him to reply to my
> (Stamp's) criticisms would only serve to grant them
> wider currency.

The accountancy profession has been accused of a failure to
present both sides of the argument (Stamp and Marley, 1970, pp.166-
7). Certainly, neither Kearton's nor Stamp's letters were reproduced in
either of the two major contemporary accounting journals,
Accountancy and *The Accountant*. And it is interesting to note that
this contrasts with practice in the late nineteenth century, when *The
Accountant* appears to have missed no opportunity to publish and
attempt to answer critical comment directed at the new profession
(Chandler and Edwards, 1994, pp.xix-xx). But, even in 1969, the
November issue (p.800) of the ICAEW's journal, *Accountancy*,
contained a considered editorial which included the following
comments:

> The proper reaction to Professor Stamp, and those
> like him (and as the universities and business
> schools produce more non-accountant business
> graduates, there are certain to be more like him), the
> right reaction is not "backs to the wall" but
> acceptance of criticisms as a spur.

For accountancy has not solved all its problems. On the financial reporting front alone there are three key areas which need, and are receiving, a good deal of further thought: the problem of comparability; the computation of earnings per share; and the accounting treatment of trade associate companies.

According to Mumford (1994, p.280), "Stamp happened to be the right person in the right place to translate public concern into action." Probably the same could be said of Leach (1981, p.4) who, writing twelve years later, observed:

I was the unfortunate President of the English Institute at the time and was besieged by members demanding action from the Council to stem the mounting criticism of the profession in the press.

It also seems that in the case of Leach, Stamp was preaching to at least the partly converted, since the former has commented (Leach, 1981, p.4) that *Recommendations on Accounting Principles* "were in no way mandatory and not much help to the auditor in persuading his client to accept best accounting practice."[12]

Indeed, Stamp (1981, p.235) soon revised his view of at least one of the "dinosaurs" which he had previously believed were in charge of Moorgate Place:

Ronnie Leach was just as keen as I was to see an adequate set of accounting standards developed in Britain... Patience, persuasion, diplomacy, and a willingness to compromise, combined with a steady belief in the need for reform, were the qualities required to rally support for what was in fact a radical change of policy at that time. Sir Ronald Leach possesses all of these qualities in abundance.

In December 1969, the *Statement of Intent on Accounting Standards in the 1970s* was published (ICAEW, 1969). As stated in *Accountancy* (1970, p.2), this expressed the intention to "narrow the areas of difference and variety in accounting practice" in order to improve (in the words of the President's covering letter) "the comparability and usefulness of financial statements."[13]

RECURRENT THEMES

The expression "there is no new thing," although hackneyed, has much to commend it. It can certainly be applied to financial reporting where a number of problems have proved incredibly resilient (Lee, 1979). In this final section of the chapter, an attempt will be made to articulate two recurrent themes - i.e. the intractable problem of valuation, and the conflicting priorities of preparers and users of financial reports.

The second half of the nineteenth century was a period of major developments in financial reporting. The enlightened form of the accounting requirements contained in the Joint Stock Companies Act 1844 (the publication of an audited balance sheet) is widely acknowledged.[14] Compulsory disclosure was discontinued in 1856, but the accounting requirements recommended thereafter were even more adventurous.[15] Presumably in response to market pressures, the level of voluntary disclosure appears, initially, to have been quite impressive. This did not last long. For the early part of the twentieth century, it is possible to make, with the benefit of hindsight, the following criticisms of UK financial reporting practices - failure to publish profit statements; published balance sheets which suffered from excessive summarisation (sometimes one heading to cover all the items on the asset side of the balance sheet); obscure terminology; the creation of group structures to conceal the true financial position; and the use of secret reserves and valuation procedures (e.g. variations in the depreciation charge) to help smooth the trend of reported profit.

It is a measure of the achievement of accountants and businessmen that broadly satisfactory solutions have been worked out for most of these problems. But other problems recognised in those early days have proved far more enduring - e.g. accounting for intangibles, uncertainty, and changing prices. The correct conclusion may be that they are not capable of a permanent solution. The lesson would seem to be not to become over-anxious if the search for a definitive answer proves unfruitful. In many cases the best that can be done is to devise procedures which work reasonably well in the present circumstances - i.e. learning how to live with problems, while not giving up the attempt to devise improved methods.

In addition to the difficult problems of estimation and valuation inherent in the publication of financial statements, the accountant has also to contend with the determination of some managers, at least, to use financial reporting as a means of deception. This, again, is not a new problem, with the history of financial reporting in the UK marked by stormy periods followed by interludes of relative calm. The publication of misleading information during the time of the "railway mania" (discussed above), may have been the first major public outcry concerning the informational content of published financial statements. The plan to introduce regulations was dropped, but problems elsewhere led to the creation and regulation of the joint stock registered company in 1844. It was not until the second half of the 1860s that substantial dissatisfaction was again voiced concerning financial reporting practices: "Directors were often tempted to disregard all moral and legal obligations to make things look more pleasant to their proprietors" (Editorial in *The Times* of 27 August 1866).

The major financial crisis of 1866, particularly the failure of Watson Overend & Co. (a firm of railway contractors) which had placed a lot of railway shares on the market) led to the appointment of the 1867 Royal Commission on Railways which emphasised the importance of having a uniform or standardised system of accounts. The Regulation of Railways Act 1868 contained fifteen financial and statistical statements designed to improve comparability and provide shareholders with a means to "see at a glance what was the exact financial position of each company" (Hansard, Vol.190, Col.1955). In the endeavour to ensure effectiveness and acceptance "*some most eminent accountants*" were consulted on the matter and the forms were drawn up with the railway companies "consent and approval" (BPP, 1910, lvi, minute 10169).

Eleven years later, following the failure of the City of Glasgow Bank, investigations revealed the publication of "imaginary" and audited balance sheets, and resulted in the introduction of a statutory audit for banks in 1879. There then followed a period of about fifty years when, despite the economy moving between slump and boom, and companies between prosperity and failure, financial reporting remained free from widespread major criticism. Was this therefore a golden age? The period of calm may not be entirely unrelated to the efforts of chartered accountants who, in the absence of any statutory requirement, were appointed auditors of many quoted companies by 1900.

It can be speculated that, during the second half of the period from 1880 to 1930, professional accountants became more preoccupied with their legal responsibilities rather than their duty to ensure that shareholders were properly informed. Why might this have happened? One possibility is that the second generation of chartered accountants, qualifying through examination on the basis of texts such as Dicksee's *Auditing*, first published 1892, and Spicer and Pegler's *Practical Auditing* (1911), gave undue status to judicial and statutory pronouncements which formed such a high proportion of each of these volumes. Perhaps these preoccupations were exploited by managers in the 1920s. The 1920s was a period when, following the re-organisation of industry to meet war-time requirements, there existed considerable excess capacity in basic industries such as iron, steel, coal and shipping. Operating results were deteriorating at a time when finance was required for survival, re-organisation and rationalisation. This caused companies to publish less information in the endeavour to obscure the true financial situation (Edwards, 1981), while a means for concealing operating losses was available in the form of undisclosed reserves previously created and augmented by provisions to meet war-time taxation which, as a result of successful negotiations, often turned out to be massively in excess of requirements. It has been shown that these reserves provided, for some companies such as the P & O Group (Napier, 1991), the financial cushion for survival until trading conditions improved. Elsewhere, such as at the Royal Mail Group, pockets were not so deep.

Problems in accounting practice also surfaced in the US at about the same time, though for different reasons. The US, by way of contrast, "experienced a wave of prosperity, which, except for a brief recession in 1920, mounted steadily until the stock market crash in 1929" (Carey, 1969b, p.241). The period has been described by Samuel Eliot Morison as "the greatest orgy of speculation and overoptimism since the South Sea Bubble of 1720" (quoted by Carey). The two countries initially reacted to their problems in different ways. In the US, there was immediately a move towards closer regulation which has gained pace to the present day. The UK has followed a similar path, but more slowly. Steps were taken to allay criticism, firstly on a voluntary basis but, subsequently, with the support of professional and statutory regulations.

It was therefore the shock effect of the financial scandals which, as in previous times, proved a necessary pre-condition for convincing accountants and businessmen of the need for action. It seems fairly clear that the identification of weaknesses in accounting practice, whether by academics or businessmen, is not in itself a sufficient condition for accounting change. There needs to be a broad-based, possibly public concern with the prevailing state of affairs and criticism, for it to be effective, and it must be expressed simply and through the popular press. It also seems, however, that there was a general lack of critical comment in the UK literature at least up to the Second World War. The need for a reorientation of accounting reports, articulated for example in Germany by Schmalenbach in 1919, was only given broad *recognition* in the UK as the result of revelations in the *Royal Mail* case.

It was not until the late 1960s in the UK that financial reporting practices were again the subject of perceived abuse and public criticism. Since then, there has been the development of a wide range of sophisticated procedures designed to transmit a message which management wants user groups to believe, rather than to portray what has actually happened. There have also been determined, but increasingly unsuccessful, attempts made by the accountancy profession to reduce the range of options available when valuing assets and measuring profit. *Statements of Standard Accounting Practice*, together with the Companies Acts from 1980 to 1985, have significantly increased the legalistic nature of financial reports. This, in turn, has provided considerable further scope for ingenuity on the part of some businessmen, accountants and lawyers to devise schemes which, although complying with the letter of the law, result in the failure of financial statements to portray such elements of economic reality as their nature permits. Creative accounting is simply the most recent manifestation of management's determination to report financial results in the best possible light. The cycle continues.

NOTES

1. It is interesting to note that financial accounting appears to be a term coined relatively recently. There are earlier references to the financial records in contrast to cost records, but the first use of "financial accounting" to indicate the content of a book on accounting known to the writer is George O. May's *Financial Accounting. A Distillation of Experience* published in 1943.

2. International influences are explored in, for example, Hopwood (1989) who also strikes the cautionary note that "it is difficult to disentangle international and indigenous influences" (Hopwood, 1989, p.3). An illustration is the widespread view concerning US influence on the post-war development of financial reporting practices in Japan, which has recently been placed in rather different perspective by Chiba (1994). Also, no attempt is made to relate findings to international classifications of accounting practice such as are found in Nobes and Parker (1991).

3. An Italian firm of merchants, the Gallerani company of Siena, - are known to have employed double-entry bookkeeping at their London branch 1305-8 (Nobes, 1982), while the first English text on double-entry bookkeeping, by Hugh Oldcastle, was published in 1543. The widespread adoption of double-entry bookkeeping in the UK occurred much later.

4. The company's archives are located at the Derbyshire Record Office, County Offices, Matlock, Derbyshire DE4 3AG, UK.

5. The preface to Dicksee's *Auditing* makes it clear that the book was written for both students and practitioners. Edey (1989, p.63) recalls the fact that the text continued to be regarded as a basic authority in the 1930s, "though for examination use it had by then been replaced by the more concise student texts."

6. *Dynamische Bilanz* was the name used from the fourth printing which appeared in 1926. The publication was initially titled *Grundlagen dynamischer Bilanzlehre*.

7. A number of more limited adjustments made by companies in various countries to take account of changing price levels are listed in Gynther (1966, pp.220-3).

8. The main focus here is on developments in the UK and US. See Hatfield (1966) for some interesting comments on diversity in

accounting practice between the UK, the US, France and Germany during the early years of the twentieth century.

9. The CAP (which issued *Accounting Research Bulletins*) was established in the mid-1930s, replaced by the Accounting Principles Board (which issued *Opinions*) in 1959 and, in turn, succeeded by the Financial Accounting Standards Board (which issued *Financial Accounting Standards*) in 1973. The *Bulletins* and *Opinions* in common with the *Recommendations* issued in the UK between 1942 and 1969 were intended to improve standards of financial reporting, but the US pronouncements are likely to have been taken more seriously by corporate management. Whereas it was known in advance that *Bulletins* and *Opinions* would be enforced by the SEC, the *Recommendations* were no more threatening than advice from a body of experts.

10. It is worth noting that The Institute of Chartered Accountants of Scotland, with one exception (covering the Council's views on departures from the historical cost principle, issued in 1954) displayed a marked reluctance to follow the ICAEW's example and issue guidance to its members. According to Sir William Slimmings (1981, p.14) (partner in Thomson McLintock & Co. from 1946 to 1978, and the Scottish Institute's President from 1969 to 1970), the Institute's view was that "a set of accounts ought to be a custom-built document" designed to present a true and fair view of particular business circumstances, and "the Institute should not appear to interfere in the exercise of such a judgement by those whose responsibility it was to prepare accounts and to audit them."

11. The editors of *Fortune* cancelled arrangements for publication at a late stage. MacNeal attributed this change of plan to pressure brought by Price, Waterhouse & Co. (the auditors of McKesson & Robbins) and the American Institute of Accountants (Zeff, 1982, p.545). An abridged version of the article prepared for *Fortune* appeared in *The Nation* in October 1939.

12. It seems possible that Leach is referring to a situation where the auditor is faced by obdurate directors since, four lines earlier, he states that "the English Institute produced a number of useful recommendations for its members" (Leach, 1981, p.4).

13. There were, of course, other factors encouraging a move towards standardisation which there is not room to discuss here. The Accountants International Study Group was set up in 1966 to enable representatives of the profession in Canada, the US and the UK to

collect information on matters of accounting practice in various countries and attempt to identify best practice. Henry Benson, at that time President of the ICAEW and highly influential in the establishment of the Study Group, had referred to his "realisation that, if the firm was to be able to build up a national and international accounting practice, it would be quite impossible to do so without clear manuals for the guidance of partners and staff, world wide, who were engaged on professional work" (Benson, 1989, p.102). The needs of the rapidly-emerging global accountancy practices involved in auditing and advising multinational companies therefore appears to have been an important pressure on accounting change.

14. The new measure was not passed without difficulty, and in the endeavour to highlight and counter parliamentary opposition to the proposed measure on the grounds of "its interference, real or supposed, with the legitimate operations and privileges of substantial and bona fide trading associations, and especially of the railway companies", *The Times* of 4 July 1844 (p.4) considered it appropriate to emphasise its belief that "publicity is all that is necessary. Show up the roguery, and it is harmless."

15. As noted above, standardised financial statements and the audit requirement were introduced for a series of industries, commencing with the railways in 1868.

3 A RECENT HISTORY OF FINANCIAL REPORTING IN THE UK AND US

Donna L. Street
James Madison University*

*I would like to express my appreciation to Tom Lee, for providing direction for the chapter and comments on an earlier version. I am also grateful to David Tweedie and Andrew Lennard, of the Accounting Standards Board, for their assistance.

INTRODUCTION

Prior to the 1970s, accounting regulation in the UK assumed a laissez-faire system which provided minimal guidance. During this same period, regulatory guidance in the US was provided primarily by the Accounting Principles Board (APB). However, the APB was controlled primarily by public accounting firms, its *Opinions* normally failed to take a solid theoretical stand on controversial issues. In the early 1970s, a new era of regulation was introduced in both countries as public discontent and fear of government regulation led to the formation of the Accounting Standards Committee (ASC) in the UK and the Financial Accounting Standards Board (FASB) in the US. A historical review of the past twenty five years suggests that many of the standards issued during this period resulted from fire-fighting efforts to address accounting problems stemming from a constantly changing and increasingly complex environment. Accordingly, the accountancy profession, particularly in the US, must now cope with an arsenal of detailed standards. Historical analysis also indicates that, although accounting standards are the product of many interacting factors, political compromise, which is often associated with consideration of economic consequences (see Solomons, 1983 and 1986), has played an increasingly important role in the standard-setting process.

Since the 1970s, the UK and US have endorsed the view that the primary purpose of financial statements is to provide information useful in making economic decisions. Prior to this revolution in accounting thought, the focus of financial reporting was on stewardship and the measurement of income. In *A Statement on Accounting Theory and Theory Acceptance* (SATTA), an American Accounting Association (AAA, 1977) committee suggested that acceptance of the decision-usefulness model resulted from dissatisfaction with the conventional matching-attaching approach to specifying the contents of financial statements.

In the US, the user orientation received both professional recognition and widespread exposure in the Trueblood Report (AICPA, 1973, p.13).[1]

> The basic objective of financial statements is to provide information useful for making economic decisions. ... This ... requires that every accounting objective, standard, principle, procedure, and practice should serve users' needs.

This philosophy was restated in the FASB's (1978) *Statement of Financial Accounting Concept (SFAC) 1*. The user orientation gained momentum in the UK during the 1970s via issuance of *The Corporate Report* (ASSC, 1975). Growing acceptance of the user orientation in the UK is further reflected in the *Solomons Report* (Solomons, 1989a), and *Making Corporate Reports Valuable* (McMonnies, 1988). Following the example of *SFAC 1*, the International Accounting Standards Committee's (IASC) *Framework for the Preparation and Presentation of Financial Statements* (IASC, 1988), and the Accounting Standard Board's (ASB, 1991) *Statement of Principles* both indicate the primary objective of financial reports is perceived as serving the information needs of users.

Consensus of the primary professional accountancy bodies and standard-setters in the UK and US and the IASC indicates that modifications to financial reporting during the last quarter of the twentieth century should be driven by the informational needs of users. However, an historical analysis of the output of UK and US regulators indicates that, although environmental changes (which help define user needs) have dictated the agendas of standard-setters, the form of standards has been greatly influenced by political intervention - particularly from government agencies and preparers. With regulatory responsibility moving outside the accountancy profession by the formation of the ASB (formed in 1990) and the FASB, and an awareness that accounting regulations do impact behavior, visible consideration of economic consequences[2] has become vital to the success of, and perhaps even survival of, private sector regulators. In recent years, special interests have utilised claims of detrimental economic consequences to influence the work of standard-setters, thereby significantly impacting accounting standards. This chapter reviews the last twenty five years of standard-setting in the US and UK, and examines factors that have significantly impacted financial reporting.

More specifically, the chapter examines the work of UK and US standard-setters during the 1970s, 1980s, and early 1990s, focusing on factors that dictated agenda items and the impact of constituent lobbying on financial reporting. Next, the chapter briefly examines international influences on UK and US standard-setters by reviewing the impact of the European Community (EC) *Directives* on UK standards, and efforts to achieve international harmonisation of accounting standards with a focus on the role of the FASB, ASB and IASC.

EARLY 1970S: FORMATION OF REGULATORY BODIES IN UK AND US

UK: Formation of ASSC

Following a period of general complacency on the part of accountants (Napier and Noke, 1992a), financial reporting met with widespread criticism in the UK during the late 1960s. This criticism flowed from problems associated with the development of complex and innovative business practices, the growth in merger activity (Tweedie and Whittington, 1984; Whittington, 1989; and Napier and Noke, 1992b), and scandals associated with these activities (Taylor and

Turley, 1986). According to Leach (1981), an environmental event (the takeover bid) highlighted deficiencies in the UK accounting system. In particular, events such as the AEI-GEC merger and the Pergamon-Leasco affair placed the accountancy profession in the limelight (Orton, 1991; and Patient, 1992; see also Chapter Two).

With respect to the GEC takeover of AEI, it was unclear how the sudden disappearance of expected income could be tied to the adjustment of AEI's reported data, GEC's accounting methods, or to other factors (Singleton-Green, 1990). In any event, the discrepancy between forecast and actual financial results was viewed as scandalous. One year later, serious allegations surfaced concerning the accuracy of the financial statements of Pergamon Press.[3] Reaction by the press included "the system which has been exposed so lamentably this week ... simply is not good enough" (*The Economist*) and "the standing of Britain's auditing firms has never been at a lower ebb" (*The Guardian*). The chairman of the Takeover Panel, called on The Institute of Chartered Accountants of England and Wales (ICAEW) "to define more clearly what was the correct practice which had to be followed by accountants." Events such as these, and the unpleasant publicity that followed, encouraged the profession to reconsider its attitude regarding reporting practices (Tweedie, 1981).

Prior to the 1970s, there were relatively few financial reporting requirements in the UK (Singleton-Green, 1990; and Patient, 1992). Minimum disclosures were set forth in the Companies Act 1948, but the Act contained virtually no rules regarding measurement of assets, liabilities, and income. In the absence of a standard-setting body, there were no accounting standards. Official guidance was limited to an ICAEW series of *Recommendations on Accounting Principles*, which represented generally accepted "best practice." These *Recommendations* were not mandatory, and provided little assistance to the auditor in persuading a client to accept best accounting practice. They often allowed alternative approaches, none of which was "sufficiently out of line to distort a true and fair view" (Leach, 1981, p.4).

Criticism of the accountancy profession peaked with the Stamp and Leach debate (Singleton-Green, 1990) initiated in 1968 when Professor Edward Stamp, wrote to the President of the ICAEW, Sir Ronald Leach, questioning the excessive number of generally accepted accounting options available to companies. The resulting debate played out in the pages of *The Times*,[4] and led to public discontent with existing accounting principles. During the exchange, Stamp argued for accounting and auditing reforms, and more accounting research to produce "a set of rational, logical and self-consistent accounting principles." Leach defended the policies and record of the profession (Nobes and Parker 1984), arguing in favour of the status quo with one exception. He supported fuller disclosure of accounting methods (Singleton-Green, 1990). Responding to the debate, the chairman of the City Panel suggested that "it might be well if the English Institute were perhaps to define more clearly what was correct practice."

Faced with the possibility of action by a Labour government, and growing public discontent fed by a critical financial press, the accountancy profession faced a crisis (Tweedie, 1981). The Department of Trade and Industry (DTI) was reviewing the activities of the profession in case legislative action was deemed necessary. The possibility existed that self-regulation might be replaced by incorporation of accounting rules into a Companies Act. Leach was "besieged by [Institute] members demanding action ... to stem the mounting criticism of the profession in the press" (Leach, 1981, p.4).

The ICAEW's reaction appeared in its *Statement of Intent on Accounting Standards in the 1970's* (ICAEW, 1969). The publication announced ICAEW's plan to intensify efforts to narrow areas of difference and variety in accounting practice by publishing authoritative statements on best practice, recommend disclosure of accounting bases and departures from established definitive accounting standards, and recommend wider exposure for proposed standards (Leach, 1981; Nobes and Parker 1984; Singleton-Green, 1990; and Napier and Noke, 1992a). Formation of the Accounting Standards Steering Committee in 1970 (hereafter referred to as the ASC, the name assumed in 1976) represented a successful effort on the part of the accountancy profession to pre-empt governmental regulation (Napier and Noke, 1992a).

US: Demise of APB and Rise of FASB

The APB encountered many problems leading to its demise. Problems associated with accounting for the investment tax credit crippled the APB in its infancy and returned in its final years. During the early 1960s, failure to attain compliance with *Opinion 2* accompanied by a Securities Exchange Commission (SEC)[5] veto forced the APB to reverse its position (Davidson and Anderson, 1987), thereby crippling its ability to take controversial stands.

The APB also made little progress in the development of a theory to guide development of accounting standards. For example, it rejected the proposed postulates and principles set forth in *Accounting Research Studies* (ARS) *1* and *3* aimed at defining "true" income. And, APB *Statement 4*, issued in 1970, was descriptive in nature and failed to provide the theoretical guidance needed to address controversial, complex accounting issues. The final blow was the APB's failure to address significant problems in the late 1960s (e.g. accounting for inflation, and mergers and acquisitions [M&A]).[6] Critics argued that a lack of independence[7] limited the APB's objectivity when dealing with controversial issues where potential solutions could yield a material effect on income. Support mounted for a full-time, independent Board which would be better equipped to address accounting problems arising in an increasing complex economic environment.

In 1971, political pressure on Congress associated with reinstatement of the investment tax credit resulted in legislation allowing either the flow-through or deferral method of accounting (Previts and Merino, 1979). The APB was forced to withdraw an exposure draft (ED), and issued a statement criticising Congressional involvement in the establishment of accounting standards (Zeff, 1984). Congressional action alerted the accountancy profession to the possibility of intervention on other accounting issues (Previts and Merino, 1979). Evidence that corporate and government officials link political and economic consequences with accounting rules meant that the profession could no longer act without considering the concerns of constituents. In future debates, US standard-setters were forced to be more cognisant of constituents' economic concerns.

In 1971, amidst growing concerns over the future of the regulatory system, the AICPA appointed the Trueblood Committee to consider the objectives of financial reporting, and the Wheat Committee to study the process by which accounting standards should be set (Davidson and Anderson, 1987). The Trueblood Report emphasised a user-driven standard-setting process (AICPA, 1973). The Wheat Committee recommended the formation of FASB which would be comprised of full-time members with no business affiliations. The

Wheat Committee (see Davidson and Anderson, 1987, p. 122) concluded:

> The new organisational structure will facilitate participation by a number of important groups in the standards-setting task. It will thus have a broader base of support, and it will be possible to draw upon a broader range of skills both for the Standards Board itself and for its supporting organisations.

The FASB's deliberation of accounting problems would entail a due process system designed to incorporate analysis and consideration of research findings and constituent views.

The formation of the FASB marked the separation of the standard-setting process from the accountancy profession. Early indications were that the FASB was off to a promising start. In 1973, the SEC issued *Accounting Series Release 150* stating "principles, standards and practices promulgated by the FASB ... will be considered by the Commission as having substantial authoritative support." At the same time, the FASB began work on a conceptual framework project intended to provide theoretical guidance when developing accounting standards.

Objectives of Financial Reporting

During the 1970s, both the FASB and the ASC addressed the issue of the objectives of financial reporting. The views set forth in *SFAC 1* and *The Corporate Report* represented a new view on this subject. Originally, accounting was perceived as serving a stewardship function[8] which provided a means of controlling an entity's assets (Tweedie, 1981). By the 1960s, however, accounting had evolved into a system intended to serve many functions including but not limited to stewardship. In the US, the failure of *ARS 1* and *3*, which focused on measuring "true income," led researchers and practitioners to further question the objective of accounting. In response, the Trueblood Report recommended a new approach, decision-usefulness, which the FASB included in *SFAC 1*. Endorsement of this model significantly affected FASB's work from the late 1970s onward. In particular, while evaluating proposed standards, the FASB focused on a broad range of user groups.

As with the US's Committee on Accounting Procedure decades earlier, the ASC's initial pressure (primarily from the Take-Over Panel) was to produce standards quickly. Therefore, minimal effort was directed at stating objectives during the ASC's first years (Tweedie, 1981). During the early 1970s, the ASC adhered to a stewardship focus[9] directed at improving existing practice through determining "true income." But, in 1975, *The Corporate Report* indicated that financial information should seek to satisfy user needs. The impact of this change in thinking is best reflected in the work of the ASB beginning in the 1990s.

While adoption of the decision-usefulness model may be viewed as a paradigm shift from stewardship (AAA, 1977; see also Neely, 1991; and Page, 1991), it may also be interpreted as acceptance of a model which includes but is not limited to stewardship. Chen (1975) discusses two types of stewardship - financial and social. Decision-usefulness may reflect a multifaceted view of stewardship which includes Chen's dimensions as well as a responsibility to supply information for a broader group of users. Indeed, Whittington (1991) has defended the ASB's endorsement of decision-usefulness, arguing that there is no inconsistency between it and stewardship.

ACCOUNTING STANDARD-SETTING IN 1970s

During its initial decade, the FASB's agenda was dictated by environmental events (including an economic crisis and double-digit inflation), and pressing problems inherited from the APB (e.g. leasing, marketable equity securities, and oil and gas [O&G] accounting).[10] While addressing these and other problems, the Board realised that, although its independent status may minimise self-interest, it was not immune from special interests. The FASB's due process system is a highly political process. For example, in 1974, *SFAS 2* required that most research and development (R&D) costs be expensed (Zeff, 1984), thereby providing a preliminary indication that the FASB would consider the views of constituents but would not allow standards to be dictated by claims of economic consequences. The FASB continued this policy of resisting political pressure from preparers, and adhered to an anti-smoothing philosophy in 1975 with *SFAS 5* on accounting for contingencies, and *SFAS 8* on foreign exchange accounting. However, during the latter part of the 1970s, pronouncements began to reflect the effects of political intervention from government and preparer constituents. In addition, the FASB's agenda during this period was primarily determined by environmental events.

Agenda items of the ASC were also largely dictated by environmental events.[11] Issues placed on the original research agenda included changes in accounting bases, and inventory accounting, both at the heart of prior causes célèbres (Tweedie, 1981). In 1971, the ASC issued its first *Statements of Standard Accounting Practice* (SSAP) addressing issues which surfaced during the Stamp and Leach debates (Taylor and Turley, 1986). As the 1970s progressed, however, some items (e.g. investments) were dropped from the agenda, and replaced by more urgent issues (Tweedie, 1981). For example, increased merger activity prompted issuance in 1973 of an *Exposure Draft* (ED) on business combinations. This was heavily criticised, and no standard was issued on the issue at that time. Also in 1973, the collapse of Rolls Royce forced consideration of accounting for R&D.

The preceding examples suggest that not only was the ASC's agenda driven by environmental events, but its early standards were a potential target for special interests. The evolution of accounting for deferred taxes illustrates how these factors combined to shape UK standards during the 1970s. Hope and Briggs (1982) argue that *ED 11* in 1973, which recommended the deferral method, was the product of an environmental factor in the form of a need for international harmonisation. However, criticism from industry and the accountancy profession led to *SSAP 11* in 1975 which required the deferral method, but allowed companies to choose their method of calculation. A further environmental factor, high inflation, yielded large deferred tax balances, prompting preparers to question the extent to which deferred taxes should be provided. Napier and Noke (1992a) contend that widespread refusal to comply with *SSAP 11* exposed the weakness of self-enforcement by companies. In 1977, the ASC responded with *ED 19* which restricted the extent to which deferred taxes should be provided and recommended the liability method. Although *ED 19* was criticised for conceding theoretical rigor for practical expediency, *SSAP 15* was issued in 1978 with only minor adjustments.

Common Problems

Research and Development

The 1970s found the ASC and the FASB debating several similar issues and arriving at similar solutions. For example, both addressed accounting for R&D. Prompted by the Rolls Royce collapse in 1971 and actions of other standard-setters (FASB's *SFAS 2* and the IASC's *ED 9*), the ASC issued *ED 13* in 1975 (Nobes, 1991). The ED recommended immediate write-off and met with opposition from certain industries. *SSAP 13*, issued in 1977, reflects a compromise resulting from standard-setters encountering political opposition (Taylor and Turley, 1986). Although *SSAP 13* required write-off of research costs, it allowed deferral of certain development costs. Hope and Gray (1982) attribute this modification primarily to concerns of the aerospace industry which voiced concerns about the economic consequences of the original *ED*.

In the US, *SFAS 2* in 1974 required immediate write-off of R&D. But, with respect to substantially similar expenditure, environmental events and political lobbying coerced the FASB into later allowing alternative treatments for the O&G industry. In 1969, *ARS 11* had recommended elimination of "full-cost" accounting (Zeff, 1984). But the APB was unable to act in a timely manner because the O&G industry and the Big Eight accountancy firms were divided on the issue (Miller et al., 1994). Following a petition from Arthur Andersen requesting prohibition of "full-cost," the Federal Power Commission, ignoring an APB plea to delay action, issued a 1971 ruling allowing "full-cost" (Zeff, 1984). After the 1973 oil crisis, the O&G industry became a priority of Congress as efforts were directed at ensuring adequate supplies of energy (Miller et al, 1994). In 1975, Congress instructed the SEC to determine appropriate accounting for O&G reserves (Zeff, 1984). The SEC turned to the FASB, and the Board issued *SFAS 19* in 1977 requiring "successful efforts" as the basis for accounting (i.e. deferral only where future benefits are guaranteed) (Miller, et al. 1994). While the larger O&G companies and the Big Eight firms supported *SFAS 19*, the smaller companies voiced much opposition, claiming "successful efforts" would yield unfavourable economic consequences. The SEC responded by announcing that both "full-cost" and "successful efforts" were acceptable. With *SFAS 19* vetoed by the SEC, *SFAS 25* was issued by the FASB in 1979. It allowed both "full-cost" and "successful efforts" accounting.

Thus, although accounting for R&D and O&G reserves are in substance similar, SEC interference prevented the FASB from achieving comparable accounting. During the 1970s and 1980s, growth in the software development industry presented the FASB with a similar problem (Miller et al., 1994). The FASB *Interpretation 6* issued in 1975 and *SFAS 86* issued in 1984 allowed capitalisation of certain costs associated with software development, but required write-off of most R&D expenditures associated with software development. Accounting for R&D and similar expenditures therefore illustrates the impact of political lobbying and the role that consideration of economic consequences has played in standard-setting in recent times. While the ASC and the FASB originally indicated that R&D should be expensed, both eventually allowed alternative treatments. The result of compromise directed at appeasing special interests has been particularly troubling in the US, where different rules apply for different industries.

Inflation

Double-digit inflation during the 1970s greatly limited the FASB's and the ASC's efforts to address other important accounting problems. As inflation rose, historical cost (HC) statements were perceived as failing to meet user needs. In 1973, the O&G crisis aggravated inflation, and the FASB placed accounting for inflation high on its first agenda (Tweedie and Whittington, 1984). A 1974 *Discussion Memorandum* (DM) explored supplementary statements disclosing the effects of general price-level changes. Unfortunately, the proposal set forth similar recommendations to those appearing in *ARS 6* which had been opposed by the SEC Chief Accountant, who had expressed a strong preference for replacement cost (RC) accounting. In 1975, the SEC announced plans to require large companies to disclose RC data. Accordingly, the FASB modified its proposal in 1979. *SFAS 33* required supplemental disclosure of current purchasing power (CPP) and current cost accounting (CCA) information by large companies for an experimental period. Then, during the 1980s, inflation declined and interest in accounting for inflation subsided. In 1986, the experiment ended when *SFAS 89* made the disclosure of CPP and CCA information voluntary.

In the UK, the ASC issued an *ED* in 1973 advocating CPP, thus reflecting the views of the accountancy profession and industry (Taylor and Turley, 1986). But, at the same time, the UK government established the Sandilands Committee to investigate inflation accounting, thereby signaling its discontent with the ASC proposal (Tweedie and Whittington, 1984). In 1974, the ASC issued a *provisional* standard. In other words, by 1974, both the FASB and ASC had issued documents advocating CPP accounting, and encountered signs of governmental discontent (Tweedie and Whittington, 1984).

Operating in a period of unprecedented inflation, the Sandilands Committee was concerned with the issue of methods to control inflation. The Committee's deliberations were also held during a period when the retail price index was not reflective of the effect of inflation on specific goods, thereby leading to its endorsement of current value (CV) accounting. The Committee directly opposed CPP by rejecting the use of general price-level adjustments. In 1976, the ASC issued *ED 18* recommending CCA. However, implementation of the CCA proposal was blocked by members of the accountancy profession. This directed the ASC's efforts to eliminate many of the controversial and complex aspects of *ED 18*, and the *ED 24* in 1979 met with less opposition. In 1980, the ASC issued *SSAP 16* for an experimental period. This was a CCA standard deliberately modified to address industry concerns (Tweedie and Whittington, 1984). The experiment failed due to lack of compliance. As inflation rates declined in the 1980s, accounting for inflation ceased to be an urgent issue, and the ASC took no further action.

Napier and Noke (1992a) argue that the extensive debate over inflation accounting led to questions regarding whether the state could safely delegate accounting regulation to the accountancy profession. The impact of government intervention in the standard-setting process is vividly illustrated with the inflation accounting debate. Tweedie and Whittington (1984) note that the "Current Cost Revolution" was advocated by the governments of most major English-speaking nations. But its failure can be attributed to several factors. In the US, the demise of *SFAS 33* resulted from user disinterest and high preparation costs. In contrast in the UK, without the support of a governmental agency, the ASC was unable to enforce *SSAP 16*. In particular, compliance failed when a number of companies decided not to disclose the CCA information, claiming it was too costly and too subjective. The Stock Exchange failed to take action, and many audit firms were not willing to qualify the audit report on the grounds of noncompliance. However, the economic factor of a substantial decline in the rate of inflation during the 1980s was the key factor which allowed US and UK standard-setters to remove accounting for inflation from their agendas. Efforts of standard-setters to address inflation accounting thus tend to rise and fall with the rate of inflation (Mumford, 1979; and Tweedie, 1986). Given the views of special interests groups, accounting for inflation is unlikely to return as an issue unless the rate of inflation rises significantly.

Overview of 1970s

As reflected in the ASC constitution, general consensus in the UK indicated that, for a private sector professional body to achieve compliance with standards which affect many diverse parties, consideration must be given to the public interest (Taylor and Turley, 1986). Yet the public interest often conflicts with special interests. As the ASC encountered problems associated with dependence on voluntary compliance (such as with *ED 3*), it realised that the marketing of standards was one of its primary functions (Taylor and Turley, 1986). As initial efforts to increase compliance[12] proved insufficient, consultation with constituents grew to play an increasingly important role in the development of generally accepted practice, thereby providing standards which were sufficiently flexible to permit discretion in preparing financial statements (Hope and Gray, 1982). As a result, instead of promoting the public interest, standards in the 1970s often reflected compromise directed at appeasing the most vocal special interests groups. In addition, the professional accountancy bodies in the UK held great power over the ASC, since the authority to issue standards belonged to their Councils. Accordingly, standards of the ASC were frequently viewed as practical compromises with minimal theoretical underpinning (Napier and Noke, 1992a).

In the late 1970s, the US accounting profession took action to address criticisms surfacing during the Moss and Metcalf

Congressional hearings. To address this threat to self-regulation, the production of FASB standards increased significantly (Byington and Sutton, 1991). Based on a review of FASB, a 1977 report of the Financial Accounting Foundation's (FAF) Structure Committee recommended more consideration be given to the economic impact of proposed standards (Zeff, 1984). The FASB responded by commissioning research studies on the economic impact of FASB proposals. Studies of this nature continue to be a standard component of the FASB's due process system.

1980S: LOTS OF PROBLEMS AND FEW SOLUTIONS

During the early 1980s, the ASC and the FASB finalised or, in the case of inflation accounting, laid to rest several projects initiated in the 1970s. In addition, new projects resulted from environmental factors (e.g. increased merger activity and widespread abuse of off-balance sheet financing [OBSF]).[13] In the US, particularly, completion of the conceptual framework project had a significant impact on changes in financial reporting. Consideration of economic consequences continued to play a major role in the development of financial reporting.

The ASC

This decade proved to be the ASC's last. During the 1980s, the ASC issued only seven new standards (Turley, 1992). Productivity during the 1970s had been influenced by the need to codify best practice. However, problems associated with voluntary compliance, such as the withdrawal of *SSAP 16*, resulted in a lack of confidence by and in the ASC (Whittington, 1989; and Singleton-Green, 1990). This greatly hindered future progress. According to Singleton-Green (1990, p.84):

> The life of the ASC was a 20 year crisis. The committee was perpetually under fire from one direction or another: either from government or the profession or industry or the press.

Throughout the ASC's existence, questions were asked concerning the interests served by it and its authority. Accordingly, the ASC was frequently distracted by reviews of its process and activities. In response to a late 1970s review, for example, the ASC began to focus more on the marketing of its standards by means of an increasing emphasis on consultation and communication (Turley, 1992). Issues facing the ASC during the 1980s surfaced due to the interaction of several environmental factors. For example, increasingly competitive capital markets and increased M&A activity encouraged UK companies to reflect their performance in the most favorable manner possible (Whittington, 1989). During the later 1980s, the economy was booming, and companies became obsessed with ensuring that reported profits matched market expectations (Tweedie and Kellas, 1987; and Tweedie, 1993).

Management was under pressure to produce good results, either to deter hostile takeovers or to be in a position of having a strong share price to enable the company to take over other companies (Tweedie, 1993). Window dressing and OBSF provided the means for managing the debt-to-equity ratio. Immediately following the ASC's victory in achieving capitalisation of finance leases, other assets and liabilities began to disappear from the balance sheet leaving an incomplete picture of financial position. The creation of new financial instruments gained momentum and compounded the problem. Since many of these instruments were designed primarily to yield cosmetic improvements in accounting results, creative accounting flourished and became a hot topic in the press.

Throughout the 1980s, the ASC failed to act on urgent issues, and appeared anxious to avoid controversy by accommodating the needs of special interests (Whittington, 1989). For example, although environmental factors focussed ASC attention on accounting for business combinations, the ASC failed to adequately address this important issue (Turley, 1992). A due process system emphasising consultation and discussion could not react quickly to financial reporting problems surfacing due to changes in the environment. As merger activity increased, innovations in financial arrangements were linked to innovations in financial reporting, characterised as a legalistic approach to accounting. Arrangements were constructed simply to get around regulations or take advantage of available options. Involvement of accountancy firms in these schemes did not assist the ASC in producing effective standards. The large professional base of the ASC (as with the APB in the US during the 1960s) meant that it lacked sufficient authority over other groups. Without action by the ASC, accounting for these transactions yielded a focus on legal form rather than economic substance.

Singleton-Green (1990) argues that the beginning of the end came in 1984 with the issuance of a standard on accounting for goodwill (GW). *SSAP 22* allowed companies to choose between "a misleading balance sheet" or a "misleading profit and loss account," thereby providing an impression of anarchy. *SSAP 23*, on accounting for acquisitions and mergers, issued in 1985, reinforced this impression by providing companies with the opportunity to structure acquisitions in a way that allowed them to be accounted for as mergers. Following this poor performance over M&As, the ASC was faced with accounting for pensions, fixed asset accounting (left unresolved by the failure of CCA), and OBSF (Singleton-Green, 1990). Public skepticism reminiscent of the 1960s was reappearing, and characterised by the publication of a book on creative accounting by Griffiths (1986). The collapse of a number of high profile and apparently financially sound companies in 1989 and 1990 placed pressure on the accountancy profession to clean up its act or face government action (Orton, 1991). Amidst public discontent and a review by the Dearing Committee which signaled its demise, the ASC was unable to issue *SSAP*s which addressed pressing issues. However, during its last eight months, the ASC did issue *ED*s on GW, M&A, fixed assets, intangibles, fair value, and OBSF. These *ED*s and the unresolved issues were passed on to the ASC's successor for consideration during the 1990s.

The FASB

During the 1980s, the FASB finalised its conceptual framework project. Some of the views set forth, such as acknowledgment of the usefulness of cash flow data and balance sheet-oriented definitions of statement elements, greatly influenced the FASB's work. The FASB also issued a considerable number of standards, mainly addressing industry-specific topics or amending existing standards. However, the FASB did address several critical issues including pensions, cash flow, and deferred taxes.

Conceptual Framework

During its first years, the FASB devoted much effort to completion of a conceptual framework designed primarily to provide the Board with guidance when developing standards.[14] For example, *SFAC 1* declared that the primary focus of financial reporting was to provide useful information to users. *SFAC 2* provided a hierarchy of qualitative characteristics indicating that financial information should be both relevant and reliable. *SFAC 5*, which was highly criticised due to its primarily descriptive nature, set forth recognition and measurement principles. Noteworthy contributions of *SFAC 5* include acknowledgment of the importance of cash flow information and a statement of comprehensive income. *SFAC 6* (which superseded *SFAC 3*) provided definitions of financial statement elements which set the stage for cleaning-up the balance sheet.

Cash Flow

Failure of the funds statement to signal large financial failures such as Penn Central (1969) and W T Grant (1976) focused attention on the statement's limitations (O'Bryan, 1989). Heath (1978), for example, argued that the increased complexity of business transactions and refined measurement of periodic income had escalated the divergence between net income and cash flows. In addition, inflation had greatly impacted the financing needs of businesses. These and other factors combined to spur an increased demand for cash flow information. As the FASB debated cash flow reporting, the Robert Morris Associates initiated a letter-writing campaign encouraging adoption of the direct method of reporting cash flow from operations (O'Bryan, 1989). Wyatt (1988) points to this campaign as an illustration of declining professionalism in the standard-setting process. Following issuance of an *ED* requiring the direct method, preparers lobbied in support of the indirect method and won the battle.

Although *SFAS 95* encourages the direct method, the indirect method is allowed and remains the method adopted by most companies in the US.

Pensions

Like the ASC, the FASB faced numerous OBSF issues. *SFAC 5* and *6* committed the FASB to cleaning up the balance sheet via recognition of transactions satisfying new definitional and recognition requirements for a liability. Pensions and other post-retirement benefits served as an initial target. Given the complexity of the project, work on post-retirement benefits was delayed until resolution of the pensions issue. Although aimed at eliminating a source of OBSF and achieving consistency between the conceptual framework and practice, *SFAS 87* on accounting for pensions clearly reveals the impact of compromise resulting from special interest intervention. To appease preparers claiming liability recognition would result in adverse economic consequences (e.g. violation of debt covenants and reducing ability to raise additional financing), the FASB significantly modified its original proposal. Accordingly, *SFAS 87* resulted in earlier but gradual recognition of significant liabilities. The FASB (1985, para.107) stated:

> ... evolutionary change in some areas may have to be slower than in others. ... it would be conceptually appropriate and preferable to recognise a net pension liability or asset measured as the difference between the projected benefit obligation and plan assets ... However, ... these approaches would be too great a change from past practice to be adopted at the present time, in light of the difference in respondents' views and the practical considerations noted.

Other compromises (e.g. smoothing rules) further softened the impact. Explaining his dissenting vote, a FASB member Wyatt (FASB, 1985) stated:

> this statement falls short of achieving the degree of improvement in accounting for pension costs that was attainable and that users of financial statements could justifiably expect.

SFAS 87 was therefore largely driven by political concerns at the expense of theoretical criteria (i.e. liability recognition, neutrality, etc.) as contained in the FASB's conceptual framework.

Deferred Taxes

SFAC 6 noted that the deferred tax credit of APB *Opinion 11* failed to satisfy the definition of a liability, and stated that accounting for deferred taxes would likely be revisited.[15] Thus, consideration of deferred taxes appears to have been partially motivated by a desire to clean up the balance sheet. During the 1970s and 1980s, professional concern mounted as deferred tax balances increased significantly (Johnson, 1993), prompted by inflation and changing tax rates. Since these deferred items represented balance sheet "plugs," they were meaningless to analysts. Accordingly, the FASB placed deferred taxes on its agenda in 1982 and issued a *DM* in 1983. The effective date of *SFAS 96* in 1987, which required comprehensive allocation and the deferred tax method, was postponed by *SFAS 100* in 1988, *103* in 1989, and *108* in 1991. The issue was resolved with the issuance of *SFAS 109* in 1992.

Opposition to *SFAS 96* was ferocious. Companies delayed implementation for several reasons, including the costs associated with scheduling each originating and reversing difference (Johnson, 1993). In addition, opponents argued that strict limitations on the recognition of a deferred tax asset violated the going concern assumption. *SFAS 96* illustrates the impact of lobbying and the FASB's inability to act in a timely manner in the face of substantial opposition. Unfortunately, a lengthy due process period continued to characterise several issues (i.e. re post-retirement benefits, stock options, and financial instruments) addressed by the FASB during the 1980s and early 1990s. Unable to rally support for *SFAS 96*, the FASB issued *109* retaining the liability method but, in response to preparer concerns, relaxing restrictions on recognition of deferred tax assets and scheduling requirements. The FASB's revised position on deferred tax assets can also be linked to a desire to partially offset the liability arising from *SFAS 106* (1990) on accounting for post-retirement benefits.

Overview of 1980s

During the 1980s, the FASB finalised its conceptual framework, and directed significant effort to addressing inconsistencies between the framework and practice (e.g. accounting for cash flows, pensions, and deferred taxes). Unfortunately, these efforts were tainted by political compromise. When faced with constituent opposition, the FASB deviated significantly from the guidelines set forth in its framework. The FASB's failure to address important issues in a timely manner became evident with its ten-year effort to modify reporting for income taxes. This elongated due process continued to haunt the FASB during the 1990s as it tackled unresolved issues of the 1980s (e.g. OBSF). During its last ten years, the ASC faced compliance problems and issued few standards. The standards which were issued tended to codify existing practice. In its last year, the ASC issued several *ED*s addressing complex accounting problems which were inherited by the ASB. Both the ASB and FASB therefore began the 1990s with agendas packed with controversial and complex problems.

EARLY 1990s

The ASB and the FASB entered the 1990s facing accounting problems arising from an increasingly complex business environment. Environmental events including internationalisation, business failures and the resulting audit crises, and the proliferation of financial instruments presented standard-setters with an unprecedented set of complex issues. In the UK, however, the major event has been the formation of the ASB.

Formation of ASB

The Dearing Report recommended more emphasis on the quality and timeliness of accounting standards, and reduced financial reporting options (Turley, 1992). The report advised increasing the independence of standard-setters from the accountancy profession, enhancing the legal status of standards, and improving the administrative speed of the process. Formation of the ASB in 1990 introduced a new era of regulation in the UK. The ASB is independent of the profession. Standards no longer need the consent of all the professional bodies, and the ASB is better funded than the ASC (Patient, 1992; and Tweedie, 1993). Like the FASB, the ASB issues standards on its own authority (Bromwich and Hopwood, 1992b; and Turley, 1992). However, the ASB is assisted by the UK Companies Act 1989 which requires a statement indicating whether the financial statements have been prepared in accordance with accounting standards, and disclosure of any departure from standards (World Accounting Report, 1993b). The ASB has been recognised by the Secretary of State for Trade and Industry as a body that may issue standards for accounting practice. The Review Panel, which monitors compliance, has been authorised by the Secretary of State to apply to the courts for a declaration that defective financial statements do not comply with the Act, and for an order requiring revised statements (Freedman and Power, 1992; see also Ghosh, 1993; and Tweedie, 1993). The fact that the UK system continues to rely primarily on voluntary compliance places restrictions on the form of standards adopted in controversial areas. The ASB has modified or dropped some proposals. For example, the ASB dropped revenue investment disclosure proposals because of industry objections (Fisher, 1992).

Statement of Principles

In the absence of a theory,[16] the ASC was criticised for considering standards in isolation, thereby yielding conflicting standards and inconsistent treatment for similar transactions (Taylor and Turley, 1986). To address creative accounting practices and other problems facing standard-setters during the 1990s, Tweedie and Whittington (1990) recommended development of definitions of the entity, assets, liabilities, and other components of accounts based on economic substance. To bring order to accounting, the ASB immediately began work on a *Statement of Principles*. By mid-1994, seven chapters had been released in *Discussion Draft* (DD) and/or *ED* form. Chapters 1, 2, and 3 set forth objectives, qualitative characteristics, and element definitions similar to FASB's. However, Chapters 4 and 5 present innovative views. In particular, a prescriptive approach to recognition and measurement sets the stage for an evolution from HC statements.[17] Chapter 6 addresses presentation, and Chapter 7 discusses the reporting entity. The impact of the *Statement of Principles* was evident in the ASB's early *Financial Reporting Standards* (FRS) and *Financial Reporting Exposure Drafts* (FRED). For example, the adoption of an all-inclusive approach to profit and loss (P&L) is consistent with the *Statement of Principles*, and the ASB has also issued *FREDs* which explore valuation bases other than HC.

Mergers and Acquisitions and Goodwill

Accounting for M&As has long challenged UK standard-setters. The tremendous increase in M&A activity since the 1960s created increased opportunities for creative accounting by the acquirer (Napier and Noke, 1992a and 1992b). M&A's were high on the ASC's initial agenda. *ED 3* was issued in 1971. But its size test was criticised as being arbitrary, and was compared to a similar test proposed by the US APB which had been rejected (Napier and Noke, 1992b). *ED 3* was not issued as a standard, nor was it formally withdrawn. By the mid-1970s, merger accounting fell into limbo. But, the merger boom of the 1980s led to contested takeovers and again focused attention on accounting practices (McGee, 1992).

Two efforts to outlaw merger accounting were overcome during the early 1980s (Napier and Noke, 1992b). With the support of the Consultative Committee of Accountancy Bodies, the Confederation of British Industries, and the Law Society, the DTI fought to modify the draft version of the EC *Seventh Directive* so that merger accounting would be allowed. And, a 1980 court ruling *(Shearer v Bercain)* outlawed the merger method proposed by *ED 3* (Napier and Noke, 1992b; and Patient, 1992). However, the ruling was unwelcome by those involved in the take-over business and was over-turned by the

Companies Act 1981. Although the 1981 Act permitted merger accounting, vague wording left suitable criteria to be determined by the ASC (Cooke, 1985). Faced with the 1981 Act and a strong lobby from the Law Society, the ASC felt unable to restrict merger accounting. In *ED 31* in 1982, the ASC included a size test to restrict mergers.[18] The Law Society indicated that the *ED* was an unacceptable attempt to rewrite the law. Debate continued until a standard was issued in 1985. *SSAP 23* provided rules relating only to consolidated financial statements, and failed either to significantly reduce the freedom of acquirers to choose the most favourable accounting treatment, or to require an accounting of the substance of the benefits resulting from a takeover (Napier and Noke, 1992a and 1992b).

Companies immediately began to take advantage of *SSAP 23*'s loopholes. The rules were easily circumvented by vendor placings and rights (Cooke, 1985; Woolf, 1990; and Tweedie, 1993). A further abuse was the combination of merger relief in the parent statements with acquisition accounting in the group statements (Napier and Noke, 1992b). Cooke (1985, p.104) argues that *SSAP 23* was "a poor excuse for a standard particularly after 14 years and 3 months of deliberation."

The Companies Act 1985 made merger accounting conditional on its according with generally accepted accounting principles, and the Companies Act 1989 provided detailed rules on accounting for business combinations. In 1990, the ASC issued *ED 48* representing a nearly complete reversal of thinking. This left the ASB with the task of finalising the proposal and addressing the issue of compliance.

The Companies Act 1981 extended reporting requirements for goodwill (GW) (Cooke, 1985). Regarding GW, the ASC changed directions several times. In the initial *DD*, the ASC supported a single policy of amortisation, while *ED 30* proposed alternative policies (Cooke, 1985). The laissez faire content of *SSAP 22* suggested that the only way for the ASC to achieve a standard was by allowing almost any conceivable practice (Gilmore and Willmott, 1992). While *SSAP 22* stated a preference for immediate write-off to reserves, amortisation was also acceptable. *SSAP 22* reflected a pragmatic approach of codifying the majority practice of large listed companies without upsetting a minority (Cooke, 1985; and Rhodes, 1990). Hadden and Boyd (1992) argue that the ASC guidelines contributed to abuses of creative accounting by developing merger accounting rules which encouraged a bottom-line focus. Woolf (1990) lists numerous abuses associated with accounting for GW during the late 1980s.

In 1984, GW as a percentage of the net worth of acquiring companies was eleven percent. By 1987, it was forty four percent (Barwise et al, 1989). As a result, net worth of affected companies, especially in the service industries, became severely depleted, and leverage ratios gave the appearance of a crippled entity (Tweedie, 1993). Criticism came from shareholders who incorrectly believed poor investments had been made if GW was written off instantly. To counteract criticism in the late 1980s, companies introduced intangibles (including brands) (see Tweedie and Whittington, 1990) into the balance sheet to substitute for GW. Since the Companies Act 1981 does not require amortisation of acquired brands, companies were able to capitalise acquired brands while continuing to eliminate GW against reserves. This led to the potential for an intangible asset explosion in a country where considerable uncertainty existed regarding valuation for intangibles and the reliability of these valuations. To bring accounting for GW in line with international standards in 1990, the ASC issued *ED 47* proposing a ban on reserve accounting, and arguing that the resulting asset be depreciated in accordance with the law (Rhodes, 1990).[19] Reaction was hostile to the *ED* which asked managers to report lower profits and auditors to form opinions on subjective figures.

In 1990, the ASB assumed responsibility for addressing M&A's and GW. Preliminary change was introduced in 1992 in *FRS 2* on accounting for subsidiary undertakings. Although constrained by the EC *Seventh Directive*, the standard expanded the concept of dominant influence, and emphasised that non-related subsidiaries (e.g. finance companies) should be consolidated (Crichton, 1991; and World Accounting Report, 1992c). In late 1993, the ASB issued *FRED*s addressing GW and intangibles and acquisition abuses (Baker, 1994a). *FRED 6* and *7* ignited immediate controversy. *FRED 7* confirmed the ASB had refused to back down on unpopular proposals set forth in a 1993 *DD* on fair values in acquisition accounting (see Nailor, 1994). The *DD*, which differed significantly from the ASC's *ED 53*, had been welcomed by users who indicated that the changes would make the reporting of post-acquisition activities more transparent (Baker, 1994b). But, reaction from companies and accountancy firms was less favorable (Accountancy Age, 1994). The Hundred Group and the Confederation of British Industry called for a slower pace of reform

(Baker, 1993a). *FRED 7*'s proposals were viewed as the "strongest attack yet on the accounting abuses which thrived through the 1980s" (Motyl, 1993d).

FRED 7 revealed the ASB was divided on the issue of GW (Baker, 1994b; see also Motyl, 1992b; and World Accounting Report, 1992d and 1992e). Reaction from the Big Six accountancy firms indicated the ASB was taking an excessively austere line in *FRED 7* and that it was wrong to force companies to charge those expenses against profit. ASB chairman Tweedie responded noting the Board had expected "a lot of flak from industry." Currently, the ASB is considering use of a ceiling test which may make possible both a reasonable balance sheet and profit statement. The approach involves capitalising GW but only charging it to profit when its falls in value (Accountancy, 1994c). This option is favored by industry (Motyl, 1993c) and accountancy firms, but field tests indicate the proposal introduces the possibility of major write-offs in a given year (Baker, 1994b). The proposal also raises serious concerns regarding reporting reliability.

Although divided on GW, the ASB has indicated that intangible assets such as brands should be accounted for in the same manner as GW. Interbrand (brand valuation consultants) responded that this treatment was inappropriate, and the Chartered Association of Certified Accountants and the Confederation of British Industry requested the proposal be scrapped (Baker, 1994d). Ernst & Young indicated the ASB has taken a too restrictive view, and Touche Ross favoured more rather than less recognition of intangibles (World Accounting Report, 1994). In late 1992, the FRC (1993, p. 21) noted:

> The tasks of the ASB's agenda are getting progressively tougher; as the honeymoon wanes, critics are likely to feel less and less inhibited about moving onto the attack.

Despite corporate resistance (Economist editorial, 1993), the ASB issued *FRS 6* (Acquisitions and Mergers) and *FRS 7* (Fair Values in Acquisition Accounting) in 1994. These standards addressed deficiencies including inappropriate use of merger accounting to enhance earnings and, under acquisition accounting, attributing the lowest values possible to net assets acquired so that GW correspondingly increased (ASB, 1994). *FRS 6* restricts the use of merger accounting and requires disclosures ensuring a full explanation of the effect of the combination is disclosed. The ASB noted that constituents' views were considered. However, both *FRS* 6 and 7 followed the original proposals. For example, the ASB did not accept constituents' position that some inadequacies in M&A accounting could be corrected through additional disclosures. The ASB argues that deficient accounting cannot be corrected by disclosure alone. It also noted that *FRS* 6 and 7 bring UK reporting requirements closer in line with those of the US and other countries (see Tweedie, 1993).[20] Both *FRS* 6 and 7 were welcomed by the investment community. Responses to the ASB's *DD* on goodwill and intangible assets revealed a wide diversity of views (ASB, 1994). As of early 1995, the ASB was holding discussions on this issue and had yet to determine a course of action.

Business Failures and Audit Crisis

High profile business failures during the 1980s and 1990s and the resulting audit crisis had a profound effect on the accountancy profession. Press coverage spotlighted creative accounting and revealed deficiencies of the HC model, and initiated major changes in financial reporting. In the UK during the late 1980s and early 1990s, the economy was in recession and business failures occurred at a record high. A study published by the ICAEW (Pratten, 1991), attributed this trend to a lack of competitiveness and misguided government policies. Yet, the failure of high-profile companies, such as BCCI and Polly Peck, which collapsed only months after receiving unqualified audit opinions, resulted in mounting criticism of the UK accountancy profession (Rayer, 1992; and Economist editorial, 1993). Media coverage placed creative accounting[21] and the limitations of the conventional accounting model in the spotlight. The *Financial Times* reported (Mitchell, 1990):

> companies can do anything: put brands in the balance sheet; leave goodwill unamortised; depreciate buildings only as and when desired; take your pick on accounting for financial instruments and swaps; practice split-depreciation. Anything

> will do. Creative accounting rules the day ...
> practically anything goes.

The failure of Polly Peck focused considerable attention on the definition of "true and fair" reporting generally, and *SSAP 20* particularly (Hughes, 1991). Prior to its failure, about seventy percent of Polly Peck's post-tax profits were offset by foreign-currency losses. These losses were taken against reserves (after earnings) (Gwilliam and Russell, 1991a). Evidence indicates the ASC was aware of potential shortcomings of the HC model in hyper-inflationary economies. The explanatory note to *SSAP 20* referred to the need to ensure that the financials present "a true and fair view of the results of management actions." Gwilliam and Russell (1991b, p.35) argue that for the accountancy profession

> to continue along the lines of a compromise between prescriptive standards and a reliance on an overriding concept of a true and fair view is to have the worst of both worlds.

In a timely response, the ASB issued standards which dramatically reduced the scope for creative accounting (Connon, 1992), including new rules on cash flow statements, financial instruments, and profit statements (Economist editorial, 1991). Addressing the importance of a cash flow statement, Tweedie (1993) argued that the statement of source and application of funds[22] disguised weaknesses in cash flow to all but the most percipient user. The failure of Polly Peck might have been foreseen earlier had users not been misled by the final year profit and positive funds flows from operations (a result of increases in inventory and other working capital). Estimates are that negative cash flow from operations was one hundred and twenty nine million pounds. In 1992, the ASB issued *FRS 1* requiring a cash flow statement designed to expose companies that were declaring paper profits while leaking cash (Economist editorial, 1992).

Although praised for its emphasis on cash, the categorisation required, and a more clearly prescribed format, *FRS 1* was perceived to fall short of user expectations (Perks and Georgiou, 1992). Thus, in its first real test, the ASB was accused of giving way to preparer interests rather than serving user needs. *FRS 1* allowed operating cash flows to be shown on either a net or gross basis. Responses to a prior *FRED* on the subject had revealed a user preference for the direct method. But *FRS 1* allowed companies to use the indirect method -- the preference of preparers (a similar concession to that made in the US in *SFAS 95*). With small business failures soaring in the years immediately preceding issuance of *FRS 1*, the statement has been criticised for exempting small companies (*ED 54* had proposed that virtually all companies produce cash flow statements). Again, the ASB was criticised for yielding to preparer pressure. In addition, *FRS 1* contained loopholes allowing preparation of misleading statements. For example, it does not require companies to separately disclose restricted cash flows, such as those generated abroad that cannot be transferred back to the UK. Currently, the ASB is reviewing *FRS 1*, and will likely issue modifications such as a revised definition of cash equivalents.

Creative accounting practices highlighted deficiencies of the profit statement. In addition, *SSAP 6* on extraordinary items and prior period adjustments resulted in a number of significant problems, including a variety of treatments for similar items (Goodhead and Eilbeck, 1992). In 1992, extraordinary items were reported by fifty three percent of UK companies compared to nine percent in the US (Economist editorial, 1992). In 1991, the ASB issued its first *DD* directed at addressing these abuses. Despite claims that the new profit statements would "hand competitors essential information" (Neely, 1991), the ASB proceeded along its original path and, in late 1992, issued *FRED 1* signaling an initiative to clean up accounting. The proposal called for the virtual disappearance of extraordinary items, a split of activities between continuing, newly acquired, and discontinued. World Accounting Report (1992a; see also World Accounting Report, 1991 and Accountancy, 1992) argued that the layered profit statement would provide better information on which to predict future performance. *FRED 1*'s statement of total recognised gains and losses was deemed a major innovation. The statement shows property revaluations, unrealised gains and losses on trade investments and foreign currency translation differences arising from consolidation, and prior year adjustments. World Accounting Report (1992a) argued that the statement is "a clear attempt to go beyond the traditional realisation concept," and will give analysts better information. The statement has also been viewed as a vehicle to facilitate a move towards some form of current value measurement. In

FRED 1, the ASB criticised the use of earnings per share (EPS), but noted that analysts will continue to use it.[23] *FRED 1* included a definition of EPS. Despite heavy criticism aimed at the disclosure of "revenue investment" as set forth in the preceding *DD*, *FRED 1* recommended disclosure of this item. Surprising opposition to *FRED 1* came from analysts who argued that the proposals would make company earnings appear more volatile, and make interpretation more difficult (Economist, 1993). Critics also argued that *FRED 1* was too long and prescriptive, and unnecessarily complicated (Flower, 1992).

FRS 3 issued in late 1992 closely followed *FRED 1* (Goodhead and Eilbeck, 1992). Concerning the ASB's move towards an all-inclusive profit statement, Tweedie stated that one number cannot sum up a firm's performance, and investors are better off with a range of clearly-defined figures which allow them to make up their own minds (Economist, 1991). In *FRS 3*, the ASB noted that, despite comments to *FRED 1*, extraordinary items could not be totally eliminated due to the statutory heading included in the Companies Act 1985. However, legal advice indicated the ASB could severely limit use of the statutory heading. *FRED 1*'s revenue investment proposals failed to attract support, and the ASB elected to exclude them from *FRS 3*. The Board noted that these disclosures would be further considered (as they were) in the ASB's proposals for an Operating and Financial Review. Following issuance of *FRS 3*, the *Economist* (1992) argued that the definition of extraordinary items was vague and predicted continued abuse. Analysts argued *FRS 3* could provide misleading information to the uninformed (Fitzgerald, 1993a), and lead to "an earnings Babel" with accounting authorities, companies, and institutions advancing varying interpretations (Evans, 1993).

These examples reveal that, in addressing problems such as creative accounting, the ASB initially followed a philosophy of providing general guidance. Unfortunately, some companies elected not to adhere to the spirit of the standards (Accountancy, 1993a). In an Urgent Issues Task Force (UITF) statement, an early warning was sent regarding loose interpretation (Accountancy, 1993a, p.9).[24] The statement stated:

As with accounting standards, it is important when
applying UITF Abstracts to be guided by the spirit
and reasoning ... so as to achieve their underlying
purpose. Abstracts are intended to be as concise ...
and not to be detailed rule-books.....

Tweedie indicated preparer and auditor reaction would dictate the
direction of future ASB statements (Accountancy, 1993a). Actions of
constituents will answer an important question - does the accountancy
profession want "principles on which they can use their professional
judgment or are they looking for a cookbook?" (Accountancy, 1993a).

Business failures of the 1980s and early 1990s resulted in an
estimated thirty billion dollars in damages against US audit firms
(Lowe and Pany, 1993). In 1992, the US Big Six firms issued a
document expressing concerns about the impact of law suits on their
financial viability (Lee, 1992). The audit crisis prompted the
profession to reconsider its role and responsibilities, and initiated
major changes in financial reporting. For example, in 1993, the
AICPA Public Oversight Board's SEC Practice Section issued *In the
Public Interest* (CPA Journal, 1993). The report included several
recommendations directed at improving the usefulness and reliability
of financial statements. Recommendations to FASB included a
required explanation of the limitations of financial statements, and
further study of requiring market value accounting (MVA).

Market Value Accounting

Environmental changes including the audit crisis, volatility,
technological advances, an explosion of financial products, and
globalisation prompted both the FASB and ASB to address MVA
(Measelle, 1993). The ASB issued several documents, including *Fair
Values in Acquisition Accounting, The Role of Valuation in Financial
Reporting*, and *Measurement in Financial Statements* (Accountancy,
1993b).[25] This signaled an intention to address some anomalies of the
HC model. As part of its financial instruments project, FASB issued
SFAS 107 in 1991 which required fair value disclosures of most
financial instruments. *SFAS 107* represented a key event in the
evolution of financial reporting, even though it did not require

recognition. Both FASB and the ASB have faced opposition to recognition of market values. Although analysts applauded the MVA disclosures of *SFAS 107*, they opposed adoption of market values as the basis for financial statements (Association for Investment Management and Research [AIMR], 1992). In addition, the ASB's *DD*s on valuation have met with great resistance (Accountancy, 1993b; and Accountancy Age, 1994). As reflected in the development of *SFAS 115*, special interests groups impede standard-setters' efforts to require additional recognition of market values.

Following the US government's bail-out of Savings and Loan (S&L) institutions, the SEC argued that HC accounting contributed to the crisis. Breeden noted that, as early as 1978, while S&L industry balance sheets indicated a positive net worth, market values would have shown a negative net worth of nearly one hundred and twenty billion dollars (AICPA, 1992). Accordingly, the SEC strongly encouraged the accountancy profession to address the way financial institutions reported investments in equity and debt securities, and require MVA for these assets. The AICPA turned to FASB. Prior to agreeing to accelerate this portion of the financial instruments project, FASB asked the Big Six accountancy firms to sign a joint statement indicating they would support the FASB proposal. Each of the firms signed the document. This action illustrates FASB's acknowledgment of its limited ability to act on highly controversial topics in a timely manner without the support of key constituents.

A review of *SFAS 12* is necessary to fully appreciate the need for *SFAS 115*. Between 1972 and 1974, the Dow Jones Industrial Average declined by one-third. Thus, investors needed information to reflect the resulting decline in values. To appease the SEC and the insurance industry, FASB adopted the lower of cost or market portfolio theory which decreased the likelihood of write downs (Daley and Tranter, 1990). The SEC's role in the development of *SFAS 12* indicates it contributed to the use of "once-upon-a-time" accounting. Yet, the SEC chose to blame the accountancy profession for the S&L fiasco. Other FASB constituents disagreed with the SEC concerning the usefulness of market values. The Federal Reserve Board argued that forcing banks to mark-to-market could reduce industrial competitiveness. During a recession, the Board was reluctant to support action that could limit lending ability. Accountancy firms questioned the verifiability of market values, and feared the inherent subjectivity would expose them to additional litigation. Banks and

S&L's indicated that the market value of a long-term security is irrelevant when the intent is to hold the security to maturity, and MVA would introduce needless earnings volatility.

In 1992, FASB was set to vote on an *SFAS* requiring MVA with holding gains and losses flowing through income (FASB, 1991). Yet, one Board member was swayed by the banks, and changed his vote to no. *SFAS 115*, issued in 1993, reflected the compromise needed to appease FASB's constituents. Debt securities held to maturity are reported at amortised cost, and trading debt and equity securities are carried at market value with gains and losses by-passing income (violating *SFAC 6*'s comprehensive income requirement). Compromise thus yielded a standard which, although an improvement, provides loopholes for income manipulation.

Financial Instruments and Off-Balance Sheet Financing

During the 1990s, the ASB and FASB devoted much effort to addressing problems associated with financial instruments and OBSF. OBSF became a problem during the 1970s with the growth of the leasing industry. Leasing provided an opportunity to enter contracts which, in substance, were purchases. However, the legal form allowed companies to finance large equipment purchases without balance sheet recognition. In 1974, FASB attacked this abuse with *SFAS 13*.[26] In the UK, leasing increased significantly during the late 1970s and 1980s. This growth can be attributed to numerous factors including the pre-1984 tax system (Drury and Braund, 1990). But, OBSF was the factor that concerned standard setters. In 1984, the ASC issued *SSAP 21* requiring capitalisation of finance leases. Unfortunately, the prescriptive nature of both the US and UK standards allowed companies to continue to achieve OBSF (see MacDonald, 1992; and Tweedie, 1993). Thus, given the failure of prescriptive standards to control abuses, the AIMR (1992) has recommended capitalisation of all executory contracts with an initial duration of more than one year. Companies, however, responded to *SSAP 21* and *SFAS 13* by inventing other forms of OBSF.

During the 1970s, European countries moved from fixed to floating exchange rates as a means of stabilising their currencies. Exchange rates began to fluctuate significantly. These fluctuations combined with high interest rates (associated with inflation of the 1970s) motivated companies to explore the merits of currency hedging and interest rate swaps, giving birth to the financial instruments industry. During the 1980s and 1990s, the market for innovative financial instruments exploded, fueled by factors such as internationalisation, global deregulation, sophisticated analysis techniques, computer technology, and tax and regulatory changes (Stewart, 1993). These instruments provided a means of keeping one step ahead of standard-setters. Detailed prescriptive accounting rules encouraged a search for loopholes (Napier and Noke, 1992a), yielding a divergence between substance and form (Tweedie and Kellas, 1987). In the US, the Emerging Issues Task Force (EITF) devoted much time to addressing accounting for these instruments. As soon as the EITF closed one loophole, however, another instrument was designed to circumvent the rules.

In response in 1986, FASB added a major project to its agenda, specifically addressing financial instruments and OBSF. Due to the limited success of past efforts, FASB adopted a new approach. In effect, FASB plans to issue a standard defining six building blocks, and providing guidance on accounting for each. Recognition will be based on economic substance determined by dissecting any financial instrument into its building block components. If successful, the proposal could mark an important turning point in US accounting - i.e. a move from detailed prescriptive standards to emphasis on economic substance and consistent accounting for similar transactions. Given FASB's inability to advance in a timely manner, several limited scope projects were accelerated including accounting for impairment of a loan (*SFAS 114*), marketable debt and equity securities (*SFAS 115*), hedging and other risk-adjusting activities (in process), and stock options.

The stock option project has proved to be a nightmare for FASB. Following press coverage of high profile executives getting rich from options, FASB placed accounting for stock options on its agenda in 1984 at the urging of Congress and the SEC (Byrne, 1984). But the Tax Reform Act 1986 and a weak stock market softened public opinion, and stock options became part of the broader financial instruments project. Negative media coverage during the early 1990s prompted Congress to ask the SEC to address the issue of stock options (SEC, 1992). The SEC increased disclosure requirements, but turned to FASB for accounting changes. FASB reopened its eight-year old project. In 1993, FASB issued an *ED* requiring companies to record a cost in their income statements when granting stock options. The reaction was unprecedented.

During 1993, bills were introduced in the House of Representatives and Senate urging FASB not to require a charge for stock options (Matthews 1993a and 1993b). In the same year alternative legislation was introduced in the Senate which would require companies to deduct the value of options from earnings (Khalaf, 1993). In 1994, the Senate passed an unprecedented non-binding resolution (by eighty eight to nine) urging FASB to drop the project (Cheney, 1994). When accused of playing politics, FASB chairman Beresford responded that, if this were the case, FASB would have a difficult time deciding to which politician to listen (Byrne, 1993). The Business Round Table (Berton, 1993) and the Big Six accountancy firms (Accounting Today, 1994a) also went on record strongly opposing the proposed standard.

The stock option *ED* thus placed FASB in an extremely uncomfortable position. Some noted the controversy was jeopardising the role of private sector standard-setting (Berton, 1993; and Cheney, 1994). Reacting to unrelenting opposition, FASB at first delayed implementation of disclosure requirements originally intended to take affect in 1994. Then, in late 1994, FASB announced it had changed its conclusions on stock options. Under the revised approach, companies will be able to compute the expense of granting options based on either *APB 25* or new FASB guidelines. FASB's ill-fated efforts to address accounting for stock options support Bromwich and Hopwood's (1992b) assertion that it is the threat of intervention of the Congress and the SEC, following lobbying by those dissatisfied with FASB proposals, that restricts the power of the FASB.

Another form of OBSF addressed by FASB was other post-employment benefits (OPEB). When OPEBs were first offered, the cash basis provided acceptable accounting since the liability was considered immaterial, and the benefits were viewed by many as revocable (Arthur Andersen, 1991). However, due to factors such as the high rate of increase in health costs and the liberal use of OPEBs, these benefits became a very significant source of OBSF during the late 1980s and early 1990s. Conflicting views began to surface concerning the legal and social responsibilities of companies honouring these benefits. The problem was further complicated by a federal tax system which did not encourage funding of these plans

(Wright, 1990).[27] In 1990, FASB issued *SFAS 106*. Prior to issuance, many constituents argued FASB should allow continuation of pay-as-you-go accounting because accrual would require recognition of substantial liabilities.[28] Critics argued that companies would be forced to discontinue or decrease benefits. Although *SFAS 106* required accrual accounting, compromises similar to those associated with pensions are evident. In addition, FASB allowed a twenty-year transition period (which displeased financial analysts).

SFAS 106 was followed by modifications to OPEB packages (Employee Benefit Plan Review, 1993).[29] Although an argument can be made that *SFAS 106* prompted these decreased benefits and is not in the public interest, a counter-argument can be made that *SFAS 106* protects the public interest in that many companies were promising benefits they may not have been able to deliver. A 1988 study indicated that ninety percent of companies had not attempted to measure the present value of their OBS OPEB liability (Williams, et al, 1989). Since OPEBs are not protected by federal legislation, the future of US workers could have been characterised by companies terminating plans and employees having no recourse. Accordingly, retired workers could have been exposed to high health care costs and inadequate coverage. This latter argument supports the view that financial reports reflecting economic substance, as opposed to reports biased by special interests, protect the public interest. *SFAS 106* provides workers and other users with information to ascertain the likelihood that companies can fulfill their OPEB commitments. Following issuance of *SFAS 106*, the UK's UITF issued an abstract stating that the US position should become standard accounting practice in the UK (World Accounting Report, 1992f). This action by the UK may represent a trend of the twenty-first century. As standard-setters in different countries face similar issues, they may choose to borrow from the final products of others. For example, it is possible that the outcome of projects addressing common concerns such as the US/Canada joint project on segment reporting or the Australian project on leasing could be adopted by other standard-setters with minimal modification.

During the 1980s and 1990s, UK companies devised OBSF techniques in hope of influencing market ratios, facilitating loans, enhancing market image, securing competitive advantage, increasing management enumeration, and avoiding employee demands (McBarnett and Whelan, 1992a and 1992b). Financial instruments were developed in creative attempts to circumvent tax rules (Miller and Power, 1992). OBSF abuses in the UK included the sale and repurchase contact (used frequently in the distilling industry), nonrecourse finance (i.e. securitisation), and the "non-subsidiary" subsidiary (Tweedie, 1993; see also Baker, 1994c). Prior to ASB action, users were left in the dark regarding the total assets employed by a company and its overall sources of finance. One-third of UK companies were utilising some form of OBSF (Motyl, 1993b).

A common abuse in the UK throughout the 1980s was the nonconsolidation of controlled entities. The *Argyll* case in 1981, and the DTI's accompanying statement that emphasis on substance over form must not be at the expense of compliance with the law, spurred creative compliance (McBarnet and Whelan, 1992b). Abuse was further ignited by the Companies Act 1948 definition of a subsidiary which resulted in the creation of a structure which avoided consolidation i.e. the "non-subsidiary" subsidiary (McBarnet and Whelan, 1992b; see also Peasnell and Yaansah, 1988). In response to concerns over OBSF schemes, the Companies Act 1989 emphasised control rather than ownership in defining a subsidiary, thereby rendering some OBSF schemes ineffective (McGee, 1992). However, abuse continued (Pimm, 1990).

Since detailed rules led to a search for loopholes, the ICAEW proposed a need for broader standards (McBarnet and Whelan, 1992b). But, when the ASC issued *ED 42* in 1988 proposing to address OBSF through a broad conceptual approach of substance over form, the accountancy profession responded with requests for more specificity. *ED 49*, which replaced *ED 42*, also proposed a focus on substance over form. In response to *ED 49*, Arthur Andersen & Co. (1990) indicated a need for specific and detailed guidance along with specific examples. This agenda item was assumed by the ASB and resulted in *FRS 2*'s attack on the non-subsidiary subsidiary.

The ASB also issued *FRS 4* and *5* to curb OBS schemes (see Baker, 1994c for examples of OBS schemes). Pope and Puxty (1992) contend that, by forcing financial instruments to be classified as debt or equity, company law provides incentives for the financial engineering of complex instruments. Many creative accounting schemes were designed to classify debt as equity (see Wood, 1993b). Accordingly, the ASB elected to clarify the distinction (Tweedie, 1993). A 1991 *DD, Accounting for Capital Instruments*, took a firm stand on hybrids. The ASB argued that anything which is not totally equity should not be included in equity, and additional divisions should be made in equity and liabilities to accommodate new financial instruments (World Accounting Report, 1992b; and Lennard, 1993). In late 1992, *FRED 3* proposed that share capital be divided into equity and non-equity shares and debt be divided into pure debt and hybrid.[30] The *ED* also proposed that all potential costs be accrued annually to show full opportunity cost ensuring that the profit statement reflected a fair rate of interest on financial instruments. *FRED 3* proposed that preparers consider where the benefits and risks resulting from a transaction lie (Tweedie, 1993). If the benefits and risks have not been transferred, the assets and liabilities cannot go off-balance sheet. Regarding *FRED 3*, critics noted that the voluminous disclosures could confuse users (Wood, 1993a). The primary critics were investment bankers (Evans, 1993).

Issued in 1993, *FRS 4* followed closely *FRED 3*. However, *FRS 4* did reflect modifications designed to address some constituent concerns (ASB, 1993, Appendix III, para. 24-44). Notably, *FRS 4* did not require disclosure of the market value of debt and equity shares. Respondents argued that such disclosure might be misleading. The ASB concluded that, although such disclosures are not required, they are encouraged. The desirability of market value disclosures will be considered in the future.

ED 49 proposed that securitisations represent a valid sale of assets, and there is no reason for the originator to recognise the assets. In a 1991 bulletin, the ASB reversed the ASC position calling for a tough line including full balance sheet disclosure (World Accounting Report, 1992g). The ASB action faced a storm of criticism from both investment bankers and corporate treasurers (Evans, 1993). Banks argued the disclosure would make their balance sheets look risky and put an end to the very benefits of securitisation (Wood, 1993a; see also Brady, 1991). In late 1992, the ASB issued revised proposals regarding securitisation, signaling a tactical retreat. Linked presentation (i.e. netting the asset and liability) was designed to satisfy both banks and those who considered securitisation to be the "biggest evil in modern accounting" (Motyl, 1992a). Barclays Bank called the revised proposals "a considerable improvement."

The ASB stood its ground regarding other securitisations. For revolving assets, the ASB proposed that gross value appear on the balance sheet, and thereby infuriating banks. Banks argued the proposal regarding credit card securitisation came out of the blue, indicating that, not once, had the proposal surfaced during discussions with the Board. The ASB action was interpreted as an effort to ensure that credit card securitisation remain rare in the UK. Regarding clean-up options, the banks argued that there was no accounting logic to support the ASB position. The British Bankers Association cautioned the ASB to expect a good deal of comment following issuance of its forthcoming *FRED*.

In 1993, *FRED 4*, *Reporting the Substance of Transactions*, was issued. The *FRED* followed closely the preceding *DD* (World Accounting Report, 1993a). In *FRED 4*, the ASB acknowledged that counter-arguments regarding offsetting had widespread support, and specifically requested feedback on the issue (Webb, 1993). Wood (1993b) cautioned that, while *FRED 4*'s proposals removed some uncertainty, grey areas are likely. Although designed to discourage creative treatment, Wood predicted creative adoption. In 1994, the ASB issued *FRS 5* which represents a faithful reproduction of *FRED 4* (see Thompson [1994] for a description of minor modifications). *FRS 5* sets forth a principles-based approach to discourage creative accounting schemes. The ASB has warned that the UITF will come down hard on opportunists seeking to circumvent *FRS 5* (Baker, 1994c). And the ASB has cautioned that the rules will be revised as necessary to prevent OBSF (Motyl, 1993a). In late 1994, the ASB (1994) announced it had also begun work on a project addressing accounting for derivatives and other financial instruments.

Overview of Early 1990s

Throughout the early 1990's, the ASB's agenda was driven by efforts to address creative accounting and curb financial scandals. The ASB's agenda continues to include similar projects. Following the Bestwood affair, the DTI recommended the ASB tackle related party transactions as soon as possible. Financial scandals such as the Maxwell affair reinforced the significance of this agenda item prompting issuance of *FRED 8* (Accountancy, 1994b). Despite many successes, the ASB has faced much criticism. At the 1993 *Financial Times* Reporting Conference, the Board was accused of being tardy regarding production of standards, addressing key areas such as GW, being too conceptual, and placing UK businesses at a competitive disadvantage (Accountancy, 1993c; and Singleton-Green, 1993). Some accused the Board of doing too much while others argued the Board was doing too little.

In the twenty-fifth annual survey of UK financial reporting practices, the authors indicated that the ASB is at a crossroads (Accountancy, 1994a). The authors argue the ASB has adopted a disclosure-led approach which is costly to companies and has not initiated major change. Concerns have also been expressed regarding the Board's views concerning current cost accounting (Holgate, 1991). Gee (1993) argues that the ASB has ignored smaller company issues while focusing on large listed companies. A 1994 report (commissioned by the ASB) apparently failed to provide useful guidance regarding this important issue (Accountancy, 1994d and 1994e).[31] Early in its history, the ASB entered the era that all standard-setters face sooner or later. Consensus disappears and everybody disagrees with one issue or another (Singleton-Green, 1993).

The FASB's agenda items of the early 1990s were dictated by efforts to address OBSF and the financial instruments explosion. Despite efforts to address financial instruments utilising a substance-based approach, the FASB has been prompted by constituents, including the SEC and Congress, to accelerate limited scope projects. This approach has produced detailed, descriptive standards reflecting substantial compromise. The FASB's due process period has continued to be elongated, highlighting the Board's inability to act quickly in the face of constituent opposition. The disastrous stock option project prompted critics to question the FASB's continued existence.

INTERNATIONAL INFLUENCES

During the 1980s and 1990s, UK and US standard-setters have reacted to international influences. The UK has been significantly impacted by the incorporation of EC *Directives* into company law. The UK and US have also both played an active role in efforts to harmonise accounting standards.

Impact of EC Directives in UK

In 1972, the UK joined the EC, thereby binding itself to incorporate EC *Directives* into law (Patient, 1992). Incorporation of the *Fourth Directive* into the Companies Act 1981,[32] and the *Seventh Directive* into the 1989 Act resulted in law playing a much greater role in the form of corporate accounting (Bromwich and Hopwood, 1992b; McGee, 1992; Napier and Noke 1992a; and Patient, 1992), and presenting obstacles to standards-setters (Accountancy, 1991).[33] The 1981 Act marked a paradigm shift from a basic statutory framework to a more detailed statutory framework for accounting. The Continental European influence introduced a more complete codification of accounts, with fairly rigorous valuation rules and more concern with objectivity and prudence. Thus, legal restraints served as barriers to reforms promulgated by the ASC during the 1980s and the ASB during the 1990s. For example, the ASB is currently seeking legal advice as to whether capitalised GW may be held on the balance sheet and reviewed for impairment only, without automatic annual amortisation. Or, to be consistent with the Companies Act, purchased GW must be transferred to a separate GW write-off reserve.

The 1981 Act provided some indication that when legal form did not convey economic substance the "true and fair" override could be utilised by standard-setters (Tweedie, 1983; Bromwich and Hopwood, 1992b; and Patient, 1992). However, the 1981 *Argyll Foods* case prompted the DTI to state that emphasis on substance over form must not be at the expense of compliance with law (McBarnet and Whelan, 1992b). The option was further weakened by the 1989 Act which deleted the word "override" (Napier and Noke, 1992a).

During the early 1990s, the EC has pursed a strategy of minimal harmonisation and mutual recognition (Freedman and Power, 1992). The shift from a focus on standardisation to harmonisation is very important to the work of the ASB. However, there continues to be room for concern as the EC has announced intentions to address differences in the interpretation of existing *Directives* and gaps in the coverage of existing *Directives*. To protect users of financial statements based on UK generally accepted accounting principles, the ASB works closely with the EC Commission (FRC, 1993).

International Cooperation

A major environmental change, the emergence of a global economy, has introduced the need for international harmonisation of accounting standards. The rise of multinational firms, the listing of securities on foreign exchanges, the growth in cross-border financing, and the need to report and audit these organisations and activities effectively, have each provided the impetus for harmonisation. Harmonisation may help the world economy by facilitating international transactions and minimising exchange cost; standardising information to world-wide policy makers; improving financial market information; and improving government accountability (Weber, 1992).

The IASC

In 1973, the professional accountancy bodies in nine countries established the IASC to formulate and promote accounting standards to improve and harmonise accounting on a world-wide basis. Currently, representatives from accounting bodies in over one hundred countries are involved. Early work focused on identifying acceptable methods but yielded too many alternatives. During the early 1990s, the IASC focused on a major project aimed at promoting comparability. The purpose was to reduce the number of alternative methods allowed in *International Accounting Standards* (IASs) (Accountancy, 1993d). For example, *ED 45* proposed the use of the purchase method for all business combinations in which an acquirer can be identified. This illustrates the challenging task ahead of the IASC. While it is difficult to theoretically criticise limits on the use of pooling, the ASB recently received no support for a suggestion that merger accounting could be eliminated (see *FRED 6* in the UK). And US businesses strongly oppose pooling's elimination. In the US, the accounting treatment (purchase or pooling) often drives the structure of business combinations. Businesses around the world will strongly oppose *IAS*s perceived as sources of negative economic consequences such as those adversely affecting key ratios and increasing taxable income. Completion of the comparability project in 1994 brought growing recognition to the work of the IASC (Journal of Accountancy, 1994).

An important factor in determining if and when international harmonisation will be achieved will be whether the International Organisation of Securities Commission (IOSCO) or, more specifically, its members endorse IASC standards for purposes of foreign listings by multinational countries (Cairns, 1993). In 1993, IOSCO agreed with the IASC on a list of core standards and, in 1994, wrote to the IASC about the acceptability of twenty four additional standards (Accounting Today, 1994b). Fourteen of the twenty four were acceptable. Unfortunately, IOSCO then reversed its position and decided not to endorse further standards, including the fourteen previously endorsed, until the IASC completes all core standards to IOSCO's satisfaction. IASC Chairman Shiratori sharply criticised IOSCO and national securities regulators around the world for failing to work together to smooth differences in rules. In that IOSCO cannot endorse IASC standards without the unanimous agreement of its members, it is unlikely that harmonisation via *IAS*s will be achieved in the near future. As to future IASC endeavours, the working party has recommended that the IASC should work directly with other standard-setters to achieve common improvements in accounting standards as well as greater compatibility between national requirements and *IAS*s. Freedman and Power (1992) argue that recently the IASC has become prominent, and is aiming at becoming a centre of gravity for national standard-setters such as the ASB and FASB.

FASB and ASB International Endeavours

In 1988, the FASB accepted an invitation to designate a Board member as a representative to the IASC consultative group. This was FASB's first official involvement with the IASC (Beresford, 1993). The FASB's mission statement, as revised in 1991, states that one of its goals is "to promote the international comparability of accounting standards concurrent with improving the quality of financial reporting." But the FASB is adamant, and the SEC concurs, that the quality of US accounting standards will not be sacrificed to achieve harmonisation. Beresford (1993, p.13) has stated "finding ways to raise the quality of accounting principles and disclosure - not engaging in a global race to the bottom - is our objective."

The FASB's efforts to promote international harmonisation include (see Beresford, 1993) continuation of active participation in the IASC process (e.g.. FASB and the IASC are concurrently addressing EPS); participation in joint multinational standards-setting projects (e.g.. FASB and Canadian standards-setters are jointly addressing segmental reporting);[34] and expansion of the international communications programme (including foreign visits, articles for foreign publications, and conferences [e.g. recently FASB and the ASB issued a joint publication with the IASC and standard-setters from Australia and Canada entitled *Future Events: A Conceptual Study of Their Significance for Recognition and Measurement*]). Members of the FASB and the ASB meet on a regular basis to discuss common concerns. ASB participation with the IASC is not limited to the above-mentioned project. Tweedie has stated "today we (the ASB) invite IASC to join our projects and we work with it at a committee level and it makes a real contribution" (IASC Insight, 1994, p.5). Additional efforts to improve harmonisation are characterised by bilateral contacts between the ASB and other national standard-setters including those representing Australia, Canada, France, New Zealand, South Africa, Sweden, and the US (FRC, 1993). For example, the ASB has proposed to "certain standard-setters overseas that it might be helpful to combine in producing standards dealing with common problems" (FRC, 1993, p.17).

Overview on Internationalisation

In recent years, the need to harmonise accounting standards internationally has significantly impacted the work of the ASB and the FASB. EC *Directives*, as incorporated in the UK Companies Acts, hindered the work of the ASC and continue to pose obstacles to ASB reforms. On a positive note, both the ASB and FASB have worked with the IASC and other national standard-setters to promote harmonisation. But the ASB and the FASB hold that harmonisation will not come at the expense of quality. Harmonisation is an admirable goal. However, to ensure that the needs of financial statement users are adequately addressed, UK and US standard-setters are apt to continue as the primary source of accounting regulation in their respective countries in the foreseeable future. Major steps

towards harmonisation in the immediate future are most likely to
spring from cooperation between the IASC and major national
standard-setters.

CONCLUSIONS

An historical examination of accounting regulation in the UK and
US since 1970 reveals that environmental events, such as M&A
activity, inflation, business failures and the audit crisis, the
proliferation of financial instruments and OBSF, and
internationalisation, have prescribed agenda items for standard-setters.
The ability of standard-setters to effectively address important
accounting issues has been greatly inhibited by the actions of
constituents. As constituents, including governmental agencies, have
adopted the view that accounting standards impact behavior, thereby
giving rise to economic consequences, their interests in the standard-
setting process has escalated. As a result, many UK and US
accounting standards issued since 1970 fail to reflect the technically or
theoretically best practice. Instead, standards reflect compromise
designed to address the concerns of a variety of groups which are
impacted by accounting regulation. In addition, consideration of
constituent views has limited the ASC's, and continues to limit the
FASB's ability to act in a timely manner on controversial issues, and
has resulted in projects spanning more than a decade.
This historical review of standard-setting raises important
questions including whether regulators have become overly sensitive
to the concerns of preparers and auditors as opposed to taking an
independent approach; and whether a private sector body, such as
FASB or ASB, can deal with the choices involved in the assessment of
economic questions. Stamp (1980) has compared accounting
standards to legislation. Thus, perhaps an argument can be made that
accounting regulation's impacting resource allocation should be made
by officials impacted by the regulations. However, Tweedie (1986)
points out that government is certainly not immune from special
interests groups, and may be arbitrary in its rulings, particularly as the
political party changes. He further states (p.18) "the history of
government's intervention in financial reporting in the recent past does
not inspire confidence in their ability to strengthen the process of

reporting." To ensure that standard-setting remains in the private sector, the accountancy profession must work with and support the efforts of the FASB and the ASB as these bodies seek to address user needs. Look no further than the US accounting for stock options debacle of the early 1990s, or the obstacles faced by the ASB due to incorporation of EC *Directives* into company law, to determine the desirability of government intervention.

More specifically, joint efforts must be directed at addressing issues raised in the AIMR's (1992) *Financial Reporting in the 1990's and Beyond*, the AICPA's (1994) *Improving Business Reporting - A Customer Focus: Meeting the Information Needs of Investors and Creditors*, and *ICAS's* (McMonnies, 1988) *Making Corporate Reports Valuable*. The recommendations contained in these reports bear striking similarities, and include better alignment of information reported externally with the information used internally to manage the business; improve segment information; address disclosure and accounting for financial instruments;and improve quarterly (interim) reporting. The AICPA report encourages national and international standard-setters and regulators to continue joint endeavors, and increase their focus on user needs. Users are strongly encouraged by the AICPA committee to increase their degree of participation in the standard-setting process.

Activity of private sector standard-setters can be linked to crisis and change. With the accountancy profession facing public discontent and the fear of government intervention, the ASC, the ASB, and the FASB were all quite productive and able to advance financial reporting during their infancy. However, this period of cooperation between standard-setters and constituents has historically been all too short-lived. The beginning of 1995 finds the ASB in a post-honeymoon mode tackling its most controversial agenda to date. The FASB enters 1995 crippled from an unsuccessful stock option project which spanned a decade. Berton (1993) recently noted that none of the FASB's predecessors survived longer than twenty years. Given mounting criticism over issues such as mark-to-market and stock options, he cautions that FASB's days may be numbered. Berton also notes that the Financial Executive Institute is reviewing financial reporting to determine whether it reflects economic reality.

To prevent another financial reporting crisis, standard-setters must have the support of the accountancy profession. The next crisis, in either the UK or the US, could be the last for private sector accounting. Both the accountancy profession and financial statement users would be losers if accounting regulation were to move out of the private sector. To avoid such a crisis, standard-setters and their constitutents (including users) must cooperate to ensure that financial statement user needs are identified and met. Efforts must be directed at addressing the recommendations set forth by the AICPA (1994), AIMR (1992), and ICAS (McMonnies, 1988). Given the limited availability of resources, national standard-setters should work together to arrive at solutions to common problems such as financial instruments, leases and other forms of OBSF, and segment reporting.

NOTES

1.   The decision usefulness model first appeared in the accounting literature during the 1950's. See AAA (1977) for a review of this literature.

2.   Zeff (1978, p.56) defines economic consequences as "the impact of accounting reports on the decision making behavior of business, government, unions, investors and creditors."

3.   A Department of Trade and Industry inquiry later concluded that Pergamon's financial statements failed to give "a true and fair view."

4.   The debate is reproduced in Stamp and Marley (1970, pp.155-65).

5.   In 1934, the US Congress established the SEC, and assigned its legal authority to establish accounting standards. By a three to two vote, the SEC elected to delegate this authority to the accountancy profession.

6.   See Rayburn and Powers (1991).

7.   All members of the APB had to be members of the AICPA. They primarily represented small and large firms and industry.

8.   See Chen (1975) for a survey and discussion of the stewardship concept in accounting.

9.   For a review of UK accounting objectives c.1970, see Carsberg et al (1974).

10.   For a detailed chronology of 1970s FASB activity, see Zeff (1984).

11. Additional coverage of the early years of the ASC can be found in Tweedie (1981), Nobes (1984), and Singleton-Green (1990).

12. These included Explanatory Forewords to *SSAP*s (placing the duty to observe standards on members of the main professional accountancy bodies; and *Auditing Standard 102* (1989) (requiring auditors to report departures from standards).

13. Standard-setters addressed these issues through the 1980s and into the 1990s. Discussion of them appears mainly in the 1990s section of this paper.

14. The FASB's project influenced others, including the ASB's projected *Statements of Principles* and the IASC.

15. The ASB is facing a similar situation based on the asset-liability focus of its proposed *Statements of Principles* (see Bircher, 1994).

16. Two ASC documents did have theoretical underpinnings. *SSAP 2* (1971) defined fundamental accounting concepts, and *The Corporate Report* (ASC, 1975) advocated a user approach. Neither statement had significant impact on standards.

17. Following Chapter 5, concern was raised over the ASB's support of CCA (Motyl, 1993e). Such criticism emerged despite Tweedie's known opposition to CCA (Baker, 1993b). The ASB has a stated a preference for an evolutionary approach to modifying the HC model.

18. A 1984 *Statement of Intent* reduced the size test of *ED 31*. This was later increased to conform with the *Seventh Directive*.

19. The view that GW is a depreciating asset is contained in EC *Directives* and UK legislation. However, Stacy and Tweedie (1989) argue that statute is not an impenetrable barrier. They state GW could remain unamortised when there is no permanent decline in value.

20. See Rayburn and Powers (1991) for a history of accounting for business combinations. Although the FASB placed business combinations and goodwill on its agenda in 1973 (Zeff, 1984), no significant standard has been issued to replace the APB *Opinon 16*.

21. For illustrations of creative accounting, see Griffiths (1986) and Tweedie and Whittington (1990).

22. The UK standard on funds statements in 1975 appears to have been an attempt to be consistent with the US position established by the APB *Opinion 19* in 1971.

23. Quoted UK companies must disclose EPS (World Accounting Report, 1991).

24. See UITF *Ruling*, Abstract 3, regarding GW on disposal of a business.

25. See McMonnies (1988) for an institutional recommendation regarding use of net realisable values.

26. Despite an additional eleven *SFAS*s, six interpretations, and nine technical bulletins, the use of leasing to achieve OBSF continues.

27. Federal legislation regulates pension but not OPEB plans, and the tax system encourages pension funding by providing a tax deduction.

28. Unionised companies were particularly concerned about the economic consequences of accrual accounting. They had accumulated large liabilities through prior increased benefits instead of pay increases (Burns, 1992).

29. Mertz of Coopers and Lybrand believes there is flexibility within *SFAS 106* to avoid reductions in net worth (Schachner, 1993).

30. This treatment is similar to that of the US. However, the EC *Fourth Directive* requires that hybrid debt and equity be shown separately.

31. An ICAEW CCA working party recommended that small companies be exempt from most accounting standards. The ASB response to this suggestion has been negative.

32. When implementing the *Fourth Directive*, the UK government imposed minimal accounting change, and noted the accountancy profession should continue to assist in building on the statutory framework (McBarnet and Whelan, 1992b).

33. The Companies Act 1989 incorporated the *Seventh* and *Eighth Directives*, but had minimal effect on UK accounting practice. The *Seventh* was based on existing UK consolidation accounting practice. However, the Act did adopt the Continental definition of subsidiary control, thus determining the basis for excluding subsidiaries from consolidation.

34. The FASB/Canadian project differs markedly from the 1994 IASC *ED*.

4   A HISTORY OF MANAGEMENT ACCOUNTING THROUGH THE 1960S

Richard K. Fleischman*
John Carroll University

*The author acknowledges with gratitude funding support from KPMG Peat Marwick.

INTRODUCTION

To write a history of management accounting within the page constraint of this chapter is tantamount to attempting world civilisation in a single volume. Such a venture must necessarily test an author's selectivity and capsulisation talent, especially in light of the fact that this chapter attempts a broad-brush approach to display the contributions of industrial cultures apart from the Anglo-American mainstream. The reader is advised that Figure 1 (Chronology of Managerial Accounting Developments) is presented at the end of this chapter to help tie together various milestones in diverse locations around the globe. The dates provided for certain authors should not be taken to indicate their initial appearance on the historical scene; but rather, the publication dates of specific contributions to costing literature cited in the text. A significant debt is acknowledged at the outset to a small community of scholars who have devoted far greater pains than the current author in synthesising the voluminous writings that constitute managerial accounting's historical literature (e.g. Solomons, 1952; Garner, 1954; Sowell, 1973; and Chatfield, 1977).

Venerated histories of cost accounting (Littleton, 1933; Solomons, 1952; and Garner, 1954), now a half-century old, date the advent of sophisticated costing from the US scientific management movement of the 1880s and beyond. Though much has been written subsequently suggesting an earlier timetable for the origins of purposeful managerial accounting, the fact remains that the costing theorists of the "Age of Taylor" (e.g. 1903), coupled with significant developments in standard costing and budgeting, laid foundations that were more expanded and refined than scrapped through the 1960s. To some degree, the history of cost accounting to 1970 may be viewed as a backdrop for the monumental technological and methodological innovations of the past decade.

This historical survey is divided into five major sections. In the first, early and isolated instances of nascent cost accounting collectively comprising the antecedents of later sophisticated methods are examined. Second, the search for the origins of purposeful costing is narrated chronologically. Third, the take-off of the early twentieth century is analysed with particular reference to standard costing and budgeting techniques mandated by the advent of big business and big government. In the fourth section, the Johnson and Kaplan thesis that managerial accounting did not change fundamentally in the sixty years following 1925 (resulting in the US's loss of global economic hegemony) is evaluated. The conclusion features a research perspective for managerial accounting as envisioned by leading academics at the close of the 1960s.

COSTING ANTECEDENTS

The current author and his collaborators have attempted within the past five years to demonstrate that the UK Industrial Revolution was the watershed epoch during which cost accounting methodology evolved beyond the nascent and the sporadic (Fleischman and Parker, 1990; 1991; and 1992; Fleischman et al., 1991; and 1995; and Fleischman and Tyson, 1993). However, evidence of industrial accounting that is distinctly non-British predated the great departure by many centuries and some even appeared before the publication of Pacioli's *Summa*. The De Roovers have analysed the archives of the cloth manufacturing operations of the Florentine ruling family, the Medicis, and the accounts of Christopher Plantin, the Flemish printer (Edler, 1937; and De Roover, 1941). These records, mostly sixteenth century documents, reflect evidence of attention to "cost finding" and, in the case of Plantin, the movement of costs through multiple inventory accounts characteristic of modern manufacturing operations. Plantin apparently achieved a separation of direct costs from other expenses in an effort to calculate a "prix de revient," a modified French equivalent of cost of goods sold (Holzer and Rogers, 1990). Other Italian textile operations have been analysed in terms of their cost accounting with particular reference to controlling the cost factors of production - i.e. the Datinis in Prato (Brun, 1930), the Bracci in Arezzo (Melis, 1950), and Francisco del Bene & Co. (Sapori, 1932). Some of these records date to the early fourteenth century.

Other European antecedents appeared somewhat later and were not of an Italian vintage. Scheuermann (1929) described the accounting for the Fugger's mining and smelting operations in the 1548-1655 period. Though these records are more industrial bookkeeping than cost accounts, there is evidence that costs of production were reviewed (Garner, 1954). A study of the archive of the Newmill Cloth Manufactory, Haddington, Scotland has uncovered the use of costing procedures for process evaluation, product line decisions, raw material control, and "rational planning" as early as the late seventeenth century (Marshall, 1980). The Crowley iron enterprise on Tyneside, dating from the early eighteenth century, used cost accounting methods to prepare ten-week production plans, and to achieve conformity to waste standards (Young, 1923/4; Flinn 1957; and 1962; and Fleischman and Parker, 1992). James Dodson (1750), an early textbook writer, reported the system of accounts employed by Hugh Crispin, an English shoemaker, that contemporary commentators have called an early example of batch costing (Edwards, 1937b; and Solomons, 1952).

Solomons (1952) and Garner (1954) have analysed overall directions taken in the costing methodology of these early records. Generally, accounting was utilised to systematise and control transactions (such as material transfers) through various stages of a productive process, curb waste and spoilage, and bring the records of industrial enterprises into step with the double-entry bookkeeping techniques developed for mercantile ventures.

Cost accounting had an early genesis in China and Japan as well as in Europe. But here the inspiration came from government rather than the private sector. Fu (1971) and Guo (1988b) described sophisticated budgeting procedures in evidence in Zhou Dynasty

China (1122-256 BC) that featured expenditure control and accountability through periodic auditing. Subsequent Chinese rulers did not apparently perpetuate these techniques. In absence of this leadership, accounting developed slowly because of the lack of private rights, poor commercial networks, and perhaps Confucian value systems (Lin, 1992). However, heightened banking and mercantile activities in China produced a corresponding but independent development of double-entry bookkeeping similar to the Italian method at approximately the same point in time (Lin, 1992). Guo (1988b, p.8), the foremost Chinese accounting historian (see also Guo, 1982; and 1988a), has stated:

> Chinese accounting deserved to be called a bright
> pearl in the history of the development of the Eastern
> accounting. Our conclusion is thus made on the
> basis of these rich historical facts.

Kimizuka (1992) chronicled similar developments in Japan where an indigenous double-entry bookkeeping system evolved. Here also, it was government that sponsored industrial beginnings though at a much later date (c. 1700). Kobusho, a Minister of Industrialisation, was mentioned as a positive force, though Kimizuka provided no details. He concluded that progress was slow under the Tokugawas, with significant advances awaiting the Meiji Restoration.

SEARCH FOR ORIGINS

There can be no doubt that the costing antecedents described above, by virtue of their far-flung and sporadic nature, cannot constitute the origins of cost accounting in any systematic sense. Accounting historians in recent years have expanded on the judgments of a small group of economic historians with accounting expertise in an effort to identify sophisticated methodologies in the past. The richness of this literature may be attributed in part to a lack of consensus on those elements that constitute sophistication in costing. To some, the utilisation of costing data for management decision making and/or process evaluation serves a higher purpose than product costing. Are norm-based, target standards an adequate indication of sophistication or do they have to be engineered and accompanied by variance analysis? It has been suggested that a high degree of integration between costing records and financial reporting is vital for a mature accounting system (Garcke and Fells, 1887). However, the careful segregation of cost and financial accounting as a prerequisite for future progress in today's world is urged by Johnson and Kaplan (1987a; and 1987b). The fixed and variable cost dichotomy, the variety of overhead cost allocation techniques, and a focus on non-prime production costs have been variously suggested as appropriate yardsticks. And, if this variety of measuring rods is not sufficiently perplexing, modern-day researchers who attempt to use them stand accused of error by virtue of their evaluating the competencies of the past in terms of the present (Miller and Napier, 1993). It is against this background of unanswered questions about the prerequisites for purposeful costing that the search for origins has evolved.

European Industrialisation

As previously mentioned, the traditional cost accounting histories date sophisticated cost accounting from the "Age of Taylor" and the scientific management movement. Yet, in recent years, there has been a quantum leap backwards as researchers have focused on surviving business archives from the UK Industrial Revolution in a search for origins. Despite older efforts by historians to demonstrate mature accounting methods in individual firms (e.g. Roll [1930] of Boulton & Watt, McKendrick [1970] of Wedgwood, and Stone [1973] of the Charlton Mills), UK cost accounting in the late eighteenth and early nineteenth century has been largely ignored until recently. Three explanations may be advanced for this. First, the mistaken belief that profit margins were universally high, obviating the need for concern about product costing; second, the influence of Pollard (1965, p.248) who, after an extensive examination of extant business records, concluded that "the practice of using accounts as direct aids to management was not one of the achievements of the Industrial Revolution"; and third, the absence of a cost accounting literature.

The authors of the comprehensive cost accounting histories were not privy to the unpublished business documents of the Industrial

Revolution. Consequently, when the numerous accounting textbooks of the era failed to mention industrial accounting, concerned as they were only with merchant techniques, it is not difficult to understand why the period was not more closely investigated. There was some awareness of industrial topics in two leading British manuals (Hamilton, 1777; and Thompson, 1777), and in Cronhelm's (1818) reporting of a woollen manufacturer's inventory bookkeeping that later authorities regarded as superficial (Littleton, 1933; and Solomons, 1952). The earliest significant vestige of UK cost accounting literature is Babbage (1835) who advised industrialists to maintain accurate cost and time information on every manufacturing process and to institute quality control procedures.

The French contribution to cost accounting literature was in the vanguard during the Industrial Revolution period even though the factory system there trailed the UK experience by several decades. Payen (1817) related accounting systems at a carriage manufactory and a glue factory that resembled job order and process costing respectively though, of course, he did not label them as such (Garner, 1954). Payen is also credited with insights into the areas of transfer pricing, the allocation of production costs back to products, waste cost management, and the integration of cost and financial records (Garner, 1954; and Holzer and Rogers, 1990). Payen also recognised manufacturing overhead as a component of "prix de revient." De Cazaux (1825) dealt primarily with farm accounting, but he apparently had a better handle on input factors than Payen in costing individual transformation processes (Holzer and Rogers, 1990). De Cazaux was also an early theorist on budgeting (Solomons, 1952). Two years later, Godard (1827) traced the flow of costs through an industrial enterprise with particular emphasis on raw material accounting, work-in-process, deferred costs, and opportunity costs (Garner, 1954; and Holzer and Rogers, 1990). Simon (1832) conceived of the modern-sounding notion that there should be no period costs, but that items such as rent, administrative salaries, and taxes should be allocated as overhead to productive processes (Garner, 1954; and Holzer and Rogers, 1990).

Yamey (1991) has written about what he called the earliest book to be exclusively concerned with industrial accounting. Kneppel's *Oylslagers Handboek* appeared in Amsterdam circa 1789. The book dealt with an oil crushing enterprise whose accounting featured distinct cost and profit centres and a transfer pricing system. Carmona and Gutierrez (1992) related the story of the earliest cost accounting system known in Spain at the Royal Tobacco Factory where standard costs were used to control direct labour efficiency and material consumption.

Though the costing literature in the UK was sparse, it seems counter intuitive to think that the entrepreneurs of the UK Industrial Revolution would not appreciate the benefit of cost accounting given their sophistication in other areas of economic activity such as technology, capital accumulation, and marketing structure development. Fleischman and Parker (1990; and 1991) hypothesised that the business leaders did cost accounting by the seat of their pants and frequently got it right. Holzer and Rogers (1990) felt that nineteenth century French business owners similarly used self-devised accounting systems. Broadly-based studies of Industrial Revolution businesses have fueled an effort to rehabilitate the period's cost accounting (Jones, 1985; Edwards, 1989b; Edwards and Newell, 1991; and Fleischman and Parker, 1992). Fleischman and Parker (1991) examined the records of twenty five large business enterprises, mostly in the iron and textile industries, and found substantial activity in diverse areas such as cost control, responsibility management, overhead allocation, product costing, decision making, and standard costing. Additionally, case studies of individual firms have similarly yielded fruitful results (e.g. Fleischman and Parker [1990] on Carron, Walsh and Stewart [1993] on the Owen factory at New Lanark, and Fleischman et al. [1995] on Boulton & Watt revisited). Nikitin (1990) has chronicled the transition at the Saint-Gobain glass enterprise from a single-entry accounting system with no reckoning of costs prior to 1820 to a full-cost system by 1880. What was found in this archive was a fully-articulated branch accounting system wherein each branch used a common cost system to determine prices for the sale of its commodity to Paris headquarters.

US Industrialisation

Various industries and firms of the early US industrial experience have likewise been studied as potential points of discontinuity with an unsophisticated past. Johnson (1972; and 1991) examined the emergence of cost accounting at the Lyman textile mills in the 1850s. There he observed nascent examples of financial management with the utilisation of accounting to measure the efficiency of various conversion processes, and monitor the performance of individual employees. Tyson (1992) found at the Lowell textile mills comparative cost reporting in the 1830s that stimulated cost reduction and enhanced efficiency (See also, Fleischman and Tyson, 1993). Porter (1980) noted in the textile mills of the Boston Manufacturing Company a "swift transition" from mercantile to industrial accounting as early as the 1810s, a precedent for Lowell and Lyman.

Chandler (1977) credited the managers of the large American railroads during the 1850s and 1860s with devising nearly all the basic techniques of modern accounting. Cost, rather than earnings, became the criterion by which railroad managers controlled and judged their subordinates. Thus, operational rather than financial controls were introduced. Chandler, an economic historian, and Johnson, an accounting historian, have both advanced an economic rationalist approach to cost accounting origins in that they have focused attention largely upon concepts of efficiency, performance evaluation, managerial decision making, and operational control. Cost accounting developed as a rational business response to opportunities involving new technologies and markets at a point in time when market transactions no longer provided sufficient information for the efficient conduct of economic activities (Johnson, 1981; 1984; and 1986).

Recently, there has been a keen interest in and a spate of literature about the accounting innovations in evidence at the Springfield Armoury. Chandler (1977) identified the Armoury as a prototype of the modern factory and a venue where accounting controls were in evidence. The Armoury has been subsequently investigated more closely by Hoskin and Macve (1988) within a Foucauldian context. Cost accounting provided a technique of "hierarchical surveillance" that they determined rendered labour calculable and "total human accountability" achievable. The control structure in place typified what Hoskin and Macve called "grammatocentricism," a series of written rules and regulations giving rise to a distinctive discipline (Hoskin and Macve, 1986; and 1994). Tyson (1990; and 1993) has cast these accounting innovations into terms of economic rationalism, finding them a rational response to perceived economic conditions.

Early Costing Literature

As has been shown, the history of specific firms and industries manifested sophisticated costing at early points in time. However, it was not until the late nineteenth century that a costing literature appeared in significant volume. In particular, the role of the engineering profession and its journal literature in the development of standard costing is emphasised as the innovation that launched cost accounting into the modern era. Sowell (1973, p.524) wrote:

> the industrial engineer, rather than the cost accountant, recognised the need for a revolution in the industrial order and initiated ideas that grew into predetermined cost techniques.

He cited the particular contributions of the American Society of Mechanical Engineers and an influential member, Henry R. Towne (1885-86), who predated Taylor's articulation of his principles of scientific management. Smallpeice (1949) observed that professionally-trained accountants were not commonly full-time employees in UK industrial enterprises until the 1920s, and that progress was forthcoming only when engineers and accountants worked together.

Early UK theorists (Garcke and Fells, 1887; and Norton, 1889) also had significant insights on the subject. Garcke and Fells' classic *Factory Accounts, Their Principles and Practice* is often regarded as the first truly authoritative contribution to cost accounting literature. Garcke and Fells suggested the value of establishing norms of cost wherein the person best acquainted with a particular process should estimate a probable cost in terms of wages and materials. Church (1901), though critical of Taylor, did not substantively differ in his discussion of engineered standards and their utilisation in predetermining costs and comparing estimates with actual results (Sowell, 1973). Solomons (1952) credited Whitmore (1908) with detailing a standard cost system based on the ideas of Taylor and Church, though he made original contributions in his own right in handling idle time and material use variations (Parker, 1969; and Sowell, 1973). Emerson (1908-9) distinguished a new method of ascertaining costs, contemporarily coming into vogue in large plants, wherein costs were determined in advance of manufacturing rather than after. The new approach had the advantage of allowing managers to control more effectively waste and loss due to inefficiency (Sowell, 1973). Solomons (1952) pointed out, however, that these initial standard costing efforts suffered two fundamental shortcomings - first, an absence of theory regarding standard definition (e.g. ideal or practical), even though Harrison (1918-19), who probably coined the term "standard costs," addressed this issue in detail; and second, an insufficient appreciation for the informational content of different breakdown possibilities for variance analysis.

Garner's *Evolution of Cost Accounting to 1925* (1954) provides a thoughtful and exhaustive study of the period's rich literature on costing topics apart from standard costing. Thomas Battersby (1878), a Manchester accountant, ended a long mid-Victorian drought with a book in which he explored existing techniques for overhead cost allocation. Unfortunately, Battersby contented himself with fault-finding of current methodology rather than suggesting alternatives. This topic, which was to receive more attention than any other during the period, was considered more eruditely by Church (1901). Church, a UK emigrant to the US at the turn of the century, articulated an application system that may conceivably have presaged today's activity-based costing. He argued that product and period costs (shop and establishment) could be applied to products using a variety of allocation bases. He urged the establishment of production centres to facilitate these allocations (Johnson and Kaplan, 1987a). UK theorists, Garcke and Fells (1887) and Mann (1903), had opted for overhead allocation on the basis of direct labour cost or hours. On the other side of the Atlantic, the preference seemed for a machine hour basis as typified in Nicholson's work (1909). Church's system was a combination of both. Simply stated, shop charges were to be allocated based on machine hours with underapplied overhead and establishment charges distributed on a direct labour basis. Subsequently, another US writer, Whitmore (1908), refined the discussion by paying regard to considerations of idle capacity and differences among machine types in the application process.

During this period considerable attention was also paid to the systematising of source documents to control prime costs. Henry Metcalfe (1885), a US ordnance officer, developed his famous card system for providing data to enhance the accounting for direct labour and raw materials. This system was extended by other Americans,

Arnold (1899) and Diemer (1900). Meanwhile, Garcke and Fells (1887) in the UK were developing similar systems. Norton (1889), amongst his numerous contributions, is remembered for devising a model pay ticket.

More advanced topics that occupied these early theorists were transfer pricing and job order/process costing. Norton (1889) wrote about the need for transfer pricing given his ideas that each processing department should operate as a separate profit centre. The topic was refined considerably in the work of Dicksee (1911). Metcalfe (1885) did a reasonably good job in describing a job order costing system, though the differences between job order and process became obscured in Garcke and Fells (1887). The best early work on process costing appeared simultaneously in both countries (Arnold, 1899; and MacNaughton, 1899). In due course, the differences between the two costing approaches were more sharply honed (Hall, 1904; Nicholson, 1909; and Strachan, 1909).

Continental European theorists were likewise heard from during the "Age of Taylor." Holzer and Rogers (1990) cautioned us not to ignore French contributions even though they did not add to the standard costing and overhead application literature. Rather, the French were concerned with integrating double-entry bookkeeping with cost accounting. Léautey, often in collaboration with Guilbault, emphasised the accuracy of the "prix de revient" and its overhead component. Alfred and Henri Croizé (1907) made important distinctions between period and product costs (Holzer and Rogers, 1990). In Germany, meanwhile, Ballewski (1877) considered cost behaviours at different output levels, and Tolkmitt (1894) analysed the role of costing in management decision making (Coenenberg and Schoenfeld, 1990). Schmalenbach (1899), early in his illustrious career, wrote of the dichotomy between fixed and variable costs, and the appropriate exclusion of the former for cost estimation and pricing policy (Schweitzer, 1992).

Costing Developments at Turn of Century

In Japan at this time (1887), the first book on cost accounting appeared (Kimizuka, 1992). Sasaki (1992) studied railway accounting in Japan. For the earliest period, circa 1885, UK methods were closely copied. But, commencing in 1907, an indigenous accounting system for the governmental enterprise was designed ("Japanising"). In China, there were interesting literary developments in the first decade of the twentieth century. The first double-entry primers appeared between 1905 and 1907, emanating from the West and Japan, and came to coexist with native Chinese texts. A contest ensued between the "transformationists" led by Pan Xulun, who urged the wholesale acceptance of Western methods, and the "reformationists" led by Xu Yongzu, who opted for more traditional usages with selective adaptations from the imports (Gardella, 1992).

Recent historical studies on late nineteenth century industrial America have underscored the significance of the "Age of Taylor" in cost accounting history. Hopper and Armstrong (1991) attempted to demonstrate how cost accounting came of age to accomplish labour intensification through speed-ups on the production line, the extension of the work day, and seasonal layoffs. Hopper and Armstrong typify the accounting wing of a major Marxist revision known as "labour process." Braverman (1974), who underscored the centrality of labour control within the history of industrial organisations, focused on the production process as opposed to Marx's more general concern with the totality of exchange relationships between conflictual economic classes (Littler, 1986). Hopper and Armstrong chronicled the role of accounting in the deskilling process that featured variously the fragmentation of work, the cheapening of labour through task reassignment to lesser skilled workers, the empowerment of an enlarged managerial corps, and the supplanting of an older craft tradition with the Taylorite disciplinary regime.

Miller and O'Leary (1987) examined the evolution of standard costing in the early twentieth century US within a Foucauldian context. Here accounting was perceived as a knowledge input into the creation of a "modern apparatus of power" to render the worker a "calculable" individual. The Foucauldian view of labour control is somewhat less confrontational than the labour process paradigm, in that the nexus of power relationships enhances the aspirations of labour in the factory environment by providing motivation, order, and regulation to benefit the more common good (Habermas, 1987; Miller, 1987; and Knights, 1990).

RISE OF BIG BUSINESS AND BIG GOVERNMENT

The links between cost accounting as an operational control mechanism and big business are obvious. Though substantial in terms of capital investment and numbers of employees, the firms of the UK and US Industrial Revolutions were dwarfed by the vertically-integrated firms that dominated the "Age of Taylor" and beyond. Chandler (1977) described how at Carnegie Steel, the forerunner of United States Steel, the techniques of accounting control were drawn directly from the railroads. Detailed and accurate cost sheets were employed by Carnegie to aid management in evaluating processes and making product line and by-product decisions. Costs were "Carnegie's obsession." This notwithstanding, and given the state of knowledge at the time, Carnegie's inattention to non-prime costs is puzzling.

General Electric (GE), incorporated in 1892, was an early example of a centralised, functionally-departmentalised operating structure. As the first industry apart from the railroads that required heavy extramural financing, GE's management had substantial stewardship and reporting responsibilities. The cost, financial, and capital accounting systems were maintained separately, a feature Chandler (1977) considered a virtue despite the benefits of cost/financial record integration espoused by many observers. GE early on embraced Taylorism and standard costing. The accounting control systems developed at GE to link corporate headquarters with disparate operating units came to be refined at DuPont a decade later (Chandler, 1977).

Johnson and Kaplan's *Relevance Lost* (1987a) is one of the most influential books dealing with cost accounting past and present. Though their perception of efficiency gains as the primary driver of accounting change is not universally accepted by scholars, it might be conceded that the popular book has "moved accounting's history centre-stage" (Ezzamel et al., 1990, p.157). Johnson and Kaplan focused research on the DuPont Powder Company (1903) and General Motors (GM) (1912). The innovation of importance at DuPont was the development of a return-on-investment (ROI) system intended to allocate capital effectively amongst diverse internal operations rather than to evaluate managerial performance as is more often characteristic of ROI analysis. The accounting system at GM was designed to achieve centralised control with decentralised responsibility in three ways - first, by annual forecasting to achieve congruence between operating division and top management goals; second, flexible budgeting to measure promptly deviations from planned outcomes; and third, uniform performance criteria for accurate resource allocation amongst divisions. The bottom line was Johnson and Kaplan's (1987a, p.93) claim that DuPont "before World War I was using almost every management accounting procedure for planning and control known today."

In many parts of the world, cost accounting developed not in an industrial environment, but rather as a function of governmental activity. Systematic cost accounting in Japan started only at the time of the Meiji Restoration (1868) with its new commitment to western industrial methods. There had been some documented cost accounting beginnings previously, but large-scale developments awaited the first of what Someya (1989) called Japan's two accounting revolutions. Ogura reported findings at a Tokyo soy sauce plant in the 1790s and the Ohta sake brewery in the 1840s. Hirai chronicled developments in the Tanabe family's iron and steel operations in the first half of the nineteenth century (Kimizuka, 1991). The first penetration of western-style bookkeeping was in evidence at Yokosuka Steel in 1865. But the event of greater prominence was the invitation accepted by Alexander Shand, a Scot, to join the Ministry of Finance in 1872 to teach bank bookkeeping. The influence of Shand and other foreigners was reflected in the operations of the Printing Bureau, established in 1871 with two thousand five hundred employees, to supervise the issuance of paper money and governmental securities. Kimizuka (1992) thought operations here may have been the first systematic application of standard costing in the world. Cost accounting did not develop rapidly during the Meiji era though Takeda found it at Kurashiki Spinning circa 1888. Unhappily, there were very few large companies that needed sophisticated costing and almost no surviving records (Kimizuka, 1991).

World War I Era

World War I had a pronounced effect on cost accounting development in the UK where theory had apparently been running ahead of practice since the Industrial Revolution. Loft (1986; and

1990), in her study of war materiel contracting during the period, concluded that cost accounting "came into the light" as a result of the government's insistence upon a careful articulation of standards by suppliers. Parker (1986) has agreed with this timetable for the advent of sophisticated cost accounting in the UK. During World War I, moreover, the large public accountancy firms were commissioned to perform the new function of auditing the cost of goods manufactured for various governments. Arthur Young, in particular, was a leader in this movement as public accountants came to be thrust into the role of efficiency experts (Wootton and Wolk, 1992).

In the aftermath of World War I, cost accountants on both sides of the Atlantic began to form professional associations. This development was of some significance for improving the standing of industrial accountants, and upgrading the quality of research in the discipline. The Institute of Cost and Works Accountants (ICWA) was formed in 1919 despite the opposition of the Institute of Chartered Accountants in England and Wales (who urged the denial of a Royal Charter to a non-professional group operating "in the service of traders"). This fledgling organisation, directed toward people in industry working with cost accounts, was unique in Europe at the time. The ICWA was highly professional and selective in its membership. It admitted as fellows only those who held the position of chief cost accountant or equivalent, and admitted as associates only those who could satisfy the Council of their general experience in cost accountancy. The survival of the organisation has been linked to its maintenance of professionalism - e.g. the setting of examinations, the creation of a journal (*The Cost Accountant*), and the institution of local branches (Loft, 1990).

Meanwhile, the National Association of Cost Accountants (NACA) was born in the US in 1919. NACA was not as professionally-oriented as ICWA, in that it did not strive to restrict its membership through an examination structure (Loft, 1990). NACA did have a professional journal that has survived through various name changes to the modern day. It was the *NACA Bulletin* until 1957, then the *National Association of Accountants Bulletin* until 1965, and now *Management Accounting*. Likewise, the organisation has been variously called the National Association of Accountants and the Institute of Management Accountants. The professionalisation of cost accountancy also found its way to Australia at this time. The Australian Institute of Cost Accountants, based on the ICWA, was incorporated in 1921 with a stated objective to promote and advance cost accountancy beyond the requirements of the general practitioner (Gavens, 1990). Several years subsequently, the Institute of Factory and Cost Accountants was founded by Brierley (Gavens and Gibson, 1992).

The synergies between municipal government and business spawned an important cost accounting advance in the US during the late "Progressive" era. When municipal reform reached a fever pitch in the first decade of the twentieth century, the industrial sector had already embraced standard costing at least theoretically. Municipal reformers simply adapted these techniques to the urban situation. However, budgeting in the industrial sector was rarely practised. The *Proceedings of the National Municipal League* ran numerous articles on governmental budgeting commencing in 1908. Meanwhile, the *Journal of Accountancy* published a dozen articles on budgeting in its first decade (after 1905) - all on governmental budgeting and all authored by a municipal finance expert. Although there was writing on the subject of business budgeting (e.g. Lane [1897]; Hess [1903]; and Bunnell [1911]), it was not until the early 1920s that the management literature began to pick up the theme substantively. In *The Accountants' Index* for 1920, there were over one hundred articles on governmental budgets and fewer than a dozen on business while, for the 1923-27 supplement, there were forty and three hundred references, respectively (Marquette and Fleischman, 1992). At the NACA conference in 1922, Stephen Gilman conceded that "the modern business budget is an inheritance from the municipal and governmental budget" (NACA, 1922, p.263). During the 1920s, McKinsey was primarily responsible for developing a theory of business budgeting through his series of articles in *Administration* (1921) and his book *Budgetary Control* (1922).

World War II Developments

World War II produced as great an impact on cost accounting as its predecessor though in different parts of the world. The war brought the second of Someya's accounting revolutions to Japan. The rule of the military in the early 1940s resulted in the establishment of the Japanese Cost Accounting Association to unify cost accounting rules and standards for the war effort. Yet, the "deplorable shortcomings" of the system necessitated the imposition of accounting techniques by the Allied Command following surrender. Thus, there came to an end years of stagnation and non-evolution in Japanese accounting thought since the Meiji Restoration (Someya, 1989).

On November 11, 1937, the German government mandated the *Uniform Chart of Accounts* (the Goering Plan) that identified the purpose of cost accounting as pricing and unit valuation. When the Association of German Manufacturers replaced the Nazi regime after the war, the common chart of accounts became voluntary, though practically all German firms continued to adhere to it. A distinctive feature of the German approach is its orientation toward current costing as the market price of factor inputs rather than acquisition cost (Coenenberg and Schoenfeld, 1990). The German system was carried to France with the occupation. The first of the *Plans Comptables Généraux* (1942) resembled the German chart of accounts of 1937. The French, following the war, chose to continue in the direction of centralised cost reporting, though the revised 1947 plan "was well and truly launched upon French social and economic life" (Standish, 1990, p.350). Holzer and Rogers (1990) pointed out that, in France, the cost numbers are not burdened by financial reporting dictates, thereby enhancing their relevance for managerial decision making.

JOHNSON AND KAPLAN THESIS: MYTH AND REALITY

A central message of *Relevance Lost* (Johnson and Kaplan, 1987a) was to blame managerial accounting as practised in the US for the decline in the country's industrial hegemony in the global economy. The basic assumption was that managerial accounting did not adapt to the changing conditions mandated by internationalisation, and that the costing methods in use by DuPont and General Motors circa 1925 had not been substantively altered to accommodate new realities. The Johnson and Kaplan bill of particulars is lengthy and quite inclusive. A summary includes:

♦ The vast increase in indirect production costs relative to prime costs has heightened both the likelihood and the price tag of product line decision errors for international competition.

♦ The high incidence in leadership positions of financial and legal experts without hands-on production experience has led to a risk aversity wherein the existing productive environment is accepted as a given.

♦ The focus on short-term financial measures has resulted in substantial under-investment in the future as expenditures for research and development, training, and preventive maintenance are not undertaken as readily.

♦ The dominant influence of financial reporting and mandated absorption costing has perpetuated overhead application on the basis of long obsolete direct labour measures. Consequently, cost-cutting efforts are misguided and cost realities misstated.

♦ Traditional variance analysis is meaningless at best and dysfunctional at worst.

♦ Traditional management accounting techniques have failed to provide relevant process cost information as the data are not timely, are overly-aggregated, and allow for cross-subsidies as costs are shifted to more labour intensive products.

♦ Discounted cash flow, based on hurdle rates that do not account for unquantifiable factors (quality, flexibility, etc.), have created under-investment in computer-integrated manufacturing.

♦ Academe has failed to instruct new methodologies despite the potential offered by new technology (Kaplan, 1984; and Johnson and Kaplan, 1987a; and 1987b).

A Response to Johnson and Kaplan

To accept this indictment without response would in essence be tantamount to acquiescing in Johnson and Kaplan's (1987a, p.125) observation that, "by 1925, American industrial firms had developed virtually every management accounting procedure known today." One obvious area in which significant progress has been made subsequent to 1925 was direct (variable, marginal) costing. In his introduction to a collection of essays on the topic that had appeared in the *NAA Bulletin*, Marple (1965) wrote that the advent of direct costing, a technique essential for rendering cost data relevant for planning and control purposes, was the culmination of a series of developments. Steps included the use of overhead rates to eliminate fixed costs associated with idle capacity, the development of breakeven analysis, the detailed separation of fixed and variable costs for flexible budgeting, and the recognition of the impact of volume on developing cost data for decision making. In the US, the pioneers were Harris, Harrison, and Kohl, all of whom wrote the bulk of their direct costing material in the 1930s. Despite this beginning, however, most theory on the topic was developed in the UK during the 1940s, and was featured in articles on marginal costing in *The Cost Accountant* by Reese, Impey, and Smallpeice. The first textbook on the subject was Lawrence and Humphrey's *Marginal Costing* which appeared in the UK in 1947. Marple (1965) was of the opinion that theory flourished more in the UK because of the positive emphasis there on the value of marginal costing for planning and control, while in the US the articles tended to take the more negative stance of opposition to absorption costing. The decade of the 1950s saw a revival of interest in the US with the appearance of *NAA Research Series 23* on direct costing in 1953. Schweitzer (1992) described how marginal costing developments in the German-speaking world paralleled the US, and led to contribution costing, mostly as a result of Schmalenbach's influence.

In addition, since 1925, there has been a widening of the theory and practice for a variety of overhead allocation bases apart from traditional direct labour and machine hours apportionment. Hathaway was urging as early as the 1920s and 1930s an expansion of horizons to include not only production but non-production allocation bases (Seay and Schoenfeldt, 1989). Schnutenhaus (1948) identified certain fixed costs (e.g. research and development) that should not be allocated at all. Peter Drucker (1963) warned the management accounting world of the dangers inherent in using traditional, labour-based product cost data in making product line and other marketing decisions. Many of the basic concepts of activity-based costing were articulated by academics Staubus and Shillinglaw in the early 1960s and put into practice in limited fashion at GE (Johnson, 1992b).

World War II may be regarded as a watershed in that the perceived primary raison d'être of managerial accounting changed fundamentally. Scapens (1991), for example, noted a pre-war focus on cost determination that particularly emphasised product costing and the control of product costs. Subsequently, the accounting data generated came to be increasingly relevant for managerial decision making, planning, and managerial (as distinct from cost) control activities. A most important contribution to this transition was made by the classic study of Simon et al (1954). Based on field studies, Simon et al identified three functions of a controller's service - score-card, attention-directing, and problem-solving. Score-card ("how well am I doing?") and attention-direction ("what problems should I look into?") had traditionally been the focus of the controller's operation. Now problem-solving (decision making) uses of accounting information were perceived to be "a more promising direction of progress" (Simon et al, 1954, p.4).

The new direction was reflected in a variety of ways, the most significant of which was the transition to direct (variable, marginal) costing as an alternative to absorption (full) costing. Schmalenbach (1948) articulated a theory of management based on decision-oriented transfer pricing dependent upon the utilisation of linear programming (simultaneous optimisation models) developed in the US during World War II to generate marginal-utility rates (Schweitzer, 1992). Responsibility accounting matured in the late 1950s and 1960s as various mathematical techniques evolved to separate out more accurately those costs that were controllable by individual managers (Scapens, 1991). Variance analysis became more directly linked to decision making incorporating theoretical techniques espoused in Dopuch et al. (1967) and Demski (1967). Early editions of standard managerial textbooks (Horngren, Shillinglaw, and Moore and Jaedicke) embraced a greater decision making orientation by the early 1960s (Parker, 1969). Parker (1969) made the point that it was not until accounting theorists began to take serious cognisance of economic theory (e.g. Clark [1923]) that wide-spread improvements were forthcoming in discounted cash flow, cost-volume-profit analysis, and identification of costs relevant to decision making.

CONCLUSION

Dopuch and Revsine (1973) edited the proceedings of a conference that defined the state of the art in accounting research at the termination of the period under review. Speaking for management accounting, Anthony (1973), Demski (1973), and Dyckman (1973) established a research agenda for the 1970s. In identifying research directions, these leading academicians discussed managerial accounting techniques that had not yet fully made their mark either in theory or practice. Anthony (1973) specified the need for human resources accounting, improved methods for calculating the cost of capital, the determination of transfer prices under a greater variety of circumstances, the development of management control systems for service organisations that better measured output, and the embracing of new non-monetary measures of performance. Demski (1973, p.74), disagreeing with Anthony's pessimism about the possibilities of measuring the value of accounting information, pointed out that managerial accounting badly needed "a rigorous theoretical framework for assessing precisely what the role of information in the firm should be and how the policy-maker in the firm should analyze his system decisions." Dyckman's (1973) agenda included expanded behavioural research, information processing techniques, operational control systems, adjustments to cost estimations (ex ante) for changed conditions, and the adaptation of CVP analysis to uncertainty. Anthony (1973) and Dyckman (1973) additionally listed the tools they envisioned to accomplish these research goals. Included were probabilistic estimates (expected value calculations, decision tree use, Monte Carlo and sensitivity analysis), linear programming for budgeting, new mathematical techniques (e.g. matrix algebra) for variance analysis and overhead cost allocation, learning curve methodology, computer simulation, laboratory and field experimentation, and case study analysis.

The gap between managerial accounting theory and practice is a theme frequently mentioned in the literature (Anthony, 1973; and Scapens, 1991). In the early days of cost accounting's history, it was clearly evident that practice was far in advance of theory as evidenced by the absence of a costing literature prior to the 1880s. During the "Age of Taylor," theory and practice seemed to be operating nicely in tandem. By 1970, and especially into the two decades beyond, theory appears to be in the vanguard. It remains to be seen if theory is indeed ahead of practice or, more basically, if theory is irrelevant to practice.

Figure 1

Chronology of Developments in Managerial Accounting

US	UK	DATE	EUROPE	ASIA
		B.C.		Zhou Dynasty
		14th C.	Datini, Bracci, del Bene	
		1494	Pacioli's *Summa*	
		16th C.	Medici, Plantin, Fugger	
	Newmills	17th C.		Kobusho
	Dodson/ Crispin, Crowleys	18th C.		
	Hamilton, Thompson	1777		
		1789	Kneppel	
	Boulton & Watt, Wedgwood, Carron, Charlton, Owen	late 18th C.	Royal Tobacco	
		1790s		Tokyo Soy
Boston Manufacturing	Cronhelm	1817-18	Payen	
		1825	de Cazaux	
		1827	Godard	Tanabe Iron
		1832	Simon	
Lowell Mills	Babbage	1835		
Springfield Armoury		1840s	Saint-Gobain	Ohta Sake
Lyman Mills, U.S. railroads		1850s		
		1865		Yokosuka Steel
		1868		Meiji Restoration

Figure 1 (continued)

US	UK	DATE	EUROPE	ASIA
		1871		Printing Bureau
		1872		Shand
	Battersby	1877-78	Ballewski	
Carnegie Steel		1880s	Léautey	Japanese railways
Towne, Metcalfe		1885		
	Garcke & Fells	1887		Japanese costing book
	Norton	1888-89		Kurashiki Spinning
G.E.		1892		
		1894	Tolkmitt	
Lane		1897		
Arnold	MacNaughton	1899	Schmalenbach	
Diemer		1900		
Church		1901		
Taylor, Hess, DuPont	Mann	1903		
Hall		1904		
Journal of Accountancy		1905		double-entry (China)
		1907	Croizé	Japanese railways (new system)
Whitmore, Emerson		1908		
Nicholson	Strachan	1909		
Bunnell	Dicksee	1911		
G.M.		1912		
NACA, Harrison	ICWA	1919		
Accountants' Index		1920		
McKinsey, Hathaway		1921		

Figure 1 (continued)

US	UK	DATE	EUROPE	ASIA
	Clark	1923		
		1926		IFCA (Australia)
Harris, Harrison, Kohl		1930s		
Littleton		1933		
		1937	Goering Plan	
	Reese, Impey, Smallpeice	1940s		JCAA
		1942	Plans Comptables Généraux	
	Lawrence & Humphreys	1947		
		1948	Schmalenbach, Schautenhaus	
Solomons		1952		
NAA #23		1953		
Simon et al, Garner		1954		
Staubus, Shillinglaw		1960s		
Drucker		1963		
Marple, Pollard		1965		
Dopuch et al, Demski		1967		
Sowell, Dopuch & Revsine		1973		
Chatfield, Chandler		1977		
Relevance Lost		1987		

5 THE IMPACT OF ADVANCEMENTS IN MANUFACTURING AND INFORMATION TECHNOLOGY ON MANAGEMENT ACCOUNTING SYSTEMS

Thomas Tyson
St. John Fisher College

INTRODUCTION

The playing field of management accounting systems (MAS) has changed dramatically since mid-century, when accountants' responsibility for financial reporting and their control over the management information system were uncontested. But since that time, advancements in manufacturing and information technologies (AMIT) have necessitated new management techniques, and stimulated a reexamination of MAS. This paper focuses on AMIT, although many other factors such as increased foreign competition, the quality revolution, and the influence of capital market pressures could be discussed in near equal detail.

Entering the mid 1990s, AMITs are affecting every aspect of accounting activity. Accounting software packages reduce the need for specialised accounting expertise. Bar code technology, e-mail, electronic data interchange, and funds transfer, all speed data collection and communication. They also compress the time-frame for feedback, control, and decision making. On the factory floor, automated manufacturing technologies and just-in-time (JIT) organising structures have redefined inventory valuation, cost control, and product costing. Major aspects of the MAS function have been disseminated to specialists in quality control, data processing, purchasing, production, and inventory control. These specialists pursue professional status and compete with accountants for intra-organisational influence. In addition, major constituencies of MAS have disappeared as firms downsize, centralise, and eliminate hierarchies. Accounting staff will be expected to "add more value to their work, while they do so in less time and with fewer people" (Shank, 1993, p 73).

This chapter describes MAS at mid-century and uses the National Association of Cost Accountants' (NACA) 1946 description of the cost accounting field as an organising framework (NACA, 1968). It discusses how key developments in manufacturing and information technology have refashioned the purposes of MAS as presented in the 1946 document. The paper describes current controversies and speculates about the future. It contends that managing for the numbers will continue to drive business activity, but managing by the numbers may no longer predominate.

MANAGEMENT ACCOUNTING AT MID-CENTURY

The most important characteristic of MAS at mid-century was the classification and accounting of costs. The phrase "management accounting" did not appear in textbooks until the early 1950s,[1] and was not adopted by professional organisations until many years thereafter. In the US in 1919, the NACA was established. This organisation changed its name to the National Association of Accountants (NAA) in 1957, and to the Institute of Management Accountants (IMA) in 1991. Its UK counterpart, the Institute of Cost and Works Accountants, became the Institute of Cost and Management Accountants in 1972.

In 1946, the NACA editorial department prepared a document that served as "a staking out of the field of cost accounting in the territory of administration" (NACA, 1968, pp.105-6). The NACA stated that cost data should serve five key purposes - profit determination (including inventory valuation), budgetary planning, control of costs, pricing policy, and current applications of plans and policies. These five purposes will be continually referenced to show how the purposes of MAS have been impacted by AMIT.

Profit Reporting and Inventory Valuation

Listing the profit reporting purpose first illustrates the overriding influence of external financial reporting on the cost accounting field. Stating that financial accounting transactions are "the raw materials of cost accounting" (NACA, 1968, p.106) indicates that the rules of financial reporting dictated the domain of cost accounting. Past and present accounting scholars have decried the constraining influence of profit reporting requirements and capital market pressures on the domain and attributes of MAS. In 1966, The Committee to Prepare a Statement of Basic Accounting Theory (AAA, 1966, p.40) acknowledged this influence:

> The precise limits of management accounting and the extent to which its technology will expand are not readily determinable at this point in its development. There is no logical reason, however, why management accounting should be constrained by external reporting conventions of a past era.

More recent critics describe MAS as distortionary (Cooper and Kaplan, 1988), a black hole (Schemenner, 1988), and a constraint to change (Walton, 1988). In point of fact, criticisms directed exclusively at accountants are overly harsh and often unjustified. For example, accountants were instrumental in justifying a company's computer-integrated manufacturing (CIM) project by quantifying intangible benefits (Cole and Hales, 1991). Horngren (1989) noted that many companies intentionally do not modernise their cost accounting systems because of unfavorable cost-benefit criteria. Others noted that MAS modernisation projects intentionally lagged behind AMIT in other areas. The lag was not caused by accountants who resisted change but by executives who allocated resources to other areas. MAS were updated after production, product movement, and communication systems were modernised.

Johnson and Kaplan (1987a) presented one of the most influential and controversial critiques of conventional MAS. They began their award-winning monograph with these disparaging comments (1987a, p.1):

> Today's management accounting information, driven
> by the procedures and cycle of the organisation's
> financial reporting system, is too late, too
> aggregated, and too distorted to be relevant for
> managers' planning and control decisions.

Although Bromwich and Bhimani (1989, p.47) found the
argument of MAS "subservience to financial reporting objectives" less
compelling, other UK scholars generally concurred with Johnson and
Kaplan's attribution of MAS inadequacies to financial reporting. For
example, Ezzamel, Hoskin and Macve (1990, p.164) wrote:

> If one is judged by the numbers it is almost
> inevitable that one will manage by the numbers, and
> the technical criticisms of accounting's measurement
> practices and short-term focus should be directed
> equally, if not more, strongly at financial accounting,
> given the power it exercises in the UK and the US
> through the operation of the capital markets and
> regulatory bodies.

This chapter questions the inevitability of managing by the
numbers, primarily because AMITs now enable operating managers
and designated workers to obtain information about non-financial
performance indicators whose improvement has direct, bottom-line
implications.

Advancements in information technology have influenced the
scorekeeping functions of profit reporting and inventory valuation
most directly. Data processing incorporates five key steps (Wilkinson,
1986, p.10) - capturing, measuring and recording data onto source
documents, validating and classifying data, and transmitting data for
processing. Each of these steps is accomplished more accurately,
reliably, and quickly through computerisation and, more recently,
through bar coding and electronic data interchange (Tyson, 1989).

Given the quickening pace of recent AMIT, it is worth noting that
mainframe computers first became commonplace in large businesses
in the mid 1960s. Even in the early 1970s, computers still required
air-conditioned rooms and large central staff. The speed, direction,
and application of computers to accounting have been both remarkable
and unforeseen. In 1970, a prominent accounting scholar

acknowledged that computers facilitated cost allocation procedures within large firms, but he was far less astute regarding further advancements (Anthony, 1970, p.470):

> Although most companies will use computers, it is by no means clear that most companies will have their own computers. Because of the great advantage that large computers have over small computers in terms of cost per calculation, it is quite possible that all but the large companies will use time on computers owned by someone else.

Personal computers became widely available by the early 1980s, and software packages aided accounting staff in transaction processing, record keeping, and financial reporting. More recently, decision support and expert systems software have been designed for non-accounting managers and are used in budgeting, tax and cash flow projections, and strategic analysis.

Product costing and inventory valuation were also listed by the NACA under the profit reporting section. Both of these functions have been dramatically affected by AMIT and JIT purchasing and production systems. AMIT in conjunction with bar code systems enable more costs to be tracked directly to manufacturing cells and other cost objectives. Fewer costs are allocated arbitrarily and product costing becomes more accurate and rational. Detailed paper records and physical inventory counts that are required with periodic accounting systems are being replaced by cost effective perpetual systems that generate up-to-date reports on demand. According to DeLuzio (1993), traditional MAS are dysfunctional in JIT environments, and have caused the abandonment of JIT systems because of an inability to track key performance indicators.

Budgetary Planning

Costing procedures listed under the profit reporting purpose intruded into other areas and influenced how cost data would be compiled. The NACA stated that the same costing concepts, allocation procedures, and cost classifications were customarily followed in budgetary planning. In the early 1960s, MAS began to regularly incorporate responsibility accounting (RA) rather than financial accounting principles for budgeting and cost control.[2] RA principles emphasised hierarchical relationships and fairly rigid functional boundaries. Scapens (1991) viewed the penetration of the RA framework as the key factor in the progression of the cost accounting field to a managerial orientation. Graese (1964, p.388) argued that the adoption of RA principles was retarded by accountants' financial reporting orientation:

> It has only been in recent years that complete responsibility reporting systems have been adopted by a sizable number of companies... Too many accountants have been so preoccupied with conventional financial accounting presentations that they have not concentrated on developing accounting as a managerial tool.

Belkaoui (1980) felt that an RA framework was needed in hierarchy-structured organisations to provide periodic planning and control information, as well as to serve as a means of communication between functional units. Scapens (1991 p.32) summarised three 1989 Chartered Institute of Management Accounting studies commissioned to "explore the effects on management accounting practices of advances in technology." These studies concluded that budgeting was used to facilitate dialogue rather than to provide financial control.

Regardless of their specific purpose, economic rationales for RA are not without contention. Caplan (1966, p. 506) questioned the effectiveness of RA-based control reports:

> ...many management accounting techniques intended to control costs, such as budgeting and standard costing, may virtually defeat themselves because they help to create feelings of confusion, frustration, suspicion, and hostility.

More recently, Johnson (1992b) argued that RA-based cost control has been a major impairment to US competitiveness since the 1950s. More conceptually, Chua (1986) discussed two competing interpretations of accounting controls - i.e. purposeful, rational, and designed to improve organisational efficiency (as typified by Chandler and Daems [1979]); and political, non-objective, and ideological (as described by Tinker, et al [1982]). Narrowing the gap between these views appears unlikely, given the dialogue between Tinker (1991) and Solomons (1991a). Solomons' (1991b, p.311) rejoinder to Tinker's remarks reveals the breadth of this gulf:

> Tinker's reply to my paper is so full of misrepresentations of my position and of philosophical obfuscation that a full reply would have to be longer than any editor would tolerate...
> At the end of this debate, we are as far apart as ever.

Despite criticisms, RA-based MAS are still employed and recommended. McKinnon and Bruns (1992) interviewed seventy three managers in six US and six Canadian manufacturing corporations, and reported that many companies still utilise the RA framework. In regard to focused factories, Harmon (1992, p.295) concluded that "Companies using budget-based responsibility reporting of expenses will find that these systems will have continued usefulness in the future."

One of the most important advancements in budgetary planning has been the development of spreadsheet software. In the past, budgetary projections required many simplifying assumptions, but budget models are now more realistic and potentially more useful by incorporating multiple drivers, varying sales mixes, and non-linear cost relationships. Uncertainty was first incorporated into budgeting models in the late 1960s and, in conjunction with information costs, was more fully explored in the academic literature in the 1970s. Nevertheless, most accounting practitioners continue to employ simple deterministic models, perhaps because more realistic models are perceived to be overly complex.

Control of Costs

Cost control was defined by the NACA in 1946 as actions taken to "achieve a conformity of the actual results with the planned results" (NACA, 1968, p.113). Costs could be controlled either by responsible persons at the time of cost occurrence or through actions taken as a result of accounting reports. The NACA (1968, pp.107-8) noted that the accountant's role in cost control occurred principally through the latter action and in the form of standard costs:

> The control of costs involves the adoption of standards of comparison... Control is achieved through efforts to keep actual costs in line with predetermined standards and by comparison of actual costs with these standards to reveal out-of-line performance in order that steps may be taken to remove the causes.

Academic accounting organisations adopted a similarly unproblematic view regarding the usefulness of accounting data for internal control. In 1956, the American Accounting Association's (AAA) Committee on Cost Concepts and Standards (AAA, 1956, p.188) wrote that "Cost data therefore are devices by means of which management can direct individuals within the organisation to carry out plans." On the other hand, behavioural-oriented scholars have argued against the "control over" philosophy implicit in accounting-based control reports. Hopwood (1972) questioned the propriety of budget-constrained cost control versus a more flexible use of budget numbers.[3]

The effectiveness of actual-to-standard cost comparisons may have been widely accepted at mid century because accountants usually designated the content, format, and distribution of MAS reports and rarely considered behavioural factors. Caplan (1966, p.498) suggested that RA-based cost controls rested on a set of assumptions that necessitated management controls and the close monitoring of subordinates, and concluded that "decisions regarding what information is most critical, how it would be processed, and who should receive it are almost always made by accountants."

Regardless of the effectiveness of RA-based controls in prior years, their continued use is frequently challenged. "Control-with" organisational philosophies that encourage teamwork, group decision making, and worker empowerment have gained popularity, while the "control-over" approach common to top-down, RA-based and financially-driven MAS is often disdained. Johnson (1992a) argued that MAS-generated information has been detrimental because it focused employees on efficiency matters and encouraged them to manipulate processes to achieve desired accounting results. Challenges also arise from advancements in information and communication technology which facilitate intra-functional communication and abrogate the benefits that MAS provide in this area. Horngren (1989, p.31) stated that "If everybody has the same information, the role of an accounting system is less important than if the system is a major conduit."

Until the mid to late 1970s, US firms were more tolerant of process inefficiencies because of high inflation and the absence of intense Japanese competition. However by the early 1980s, many US companies were forced to adopt Japanese management philosophies and workflow strategies.[4] JIT purchasing and production, long-term relationships with vendors and employees, quality circles, zero defects, total quality management, process simplification, and continuous improvement are principles that continue to be promoted. Their emphasis on flexibility, teamwork, and cooperative behavior make RA-based, top-down, control reports increasingly problematic. Caplan (1966, p.505) recognised this predicament early on.:

> Reports of this type seem to encourage departmental activities aimed at "making a good showing" regardless of the effect on the entire organisation... Under such circumstances, it is not very likely that the cooperative efforts necessary to the efficient functioning of the organisation as a whole will be furthered by an accounting system which emphasises and, perhaps, even fosters interdepartmental conflicts.

In conjunction with "control-with" philosophies, advancements in manufacturing technologies, such as numerically controlled machines, computer-aided design and manufacturing, group manufacturing cells, flexible manufacturing systems, and robotic assembly improve the quality, consistency and reliability of manufactured products. These advancements necessitate major investments in training and development, increase overhead costs, and place further pressure on MAS to modernise.

Despite AMIT and new organisational philosophies, MAS continued to employ labour-based allocation schemes, and evaluate performance on the basis of actual-to-standard cost comparisons. The concepts underlying the NACA research staff's (NACA 1958, p.7) description of how standard costs should be used for control purposes are still presented in many cost and managerial accounting textbooks and used in practice:

> Standards should be set for each cost item of consequence. Product unit costs are built up from their components since the cost of a finished product unit is made up of materials, labour, and overhead... Effective control requires detailed standards to show how much of each material should be used, how much labour should be required for each operation, and what facilities and services will be needed.

Howell (1988) presented compelling arguments for deemphasising the use of internal standards in the new manufacturing environment. According to Howell, standard costs focus on specific goals and static conditions, while automated manufacturing environments are more flexible and dynamic. Traditional variance analysis is not as important because new manufacturing processes are more consistent and reliable. Furthermore, standard costs incorporate an expected amount of imperfection which is incompatible with the philosophy of continuous improvement.

MAS that were designed for labour-intensive, mass production environments appear increasingly irrelevant to operating managers. New organising structures like JIT and total quality control (TQC) stress the need to anticipate problems and prevent errors or shortages. These structures require real-time information to function effectively, rather than accounting reports which often lag far behind current events. In many environments, defects are detected automatically and workers are empowered to shut down production processes and correct errors regardless of the short-term accounting consequences.

Recently, in both the US and UK, activity-based costing (ABC) is being promoted as the modern approach to product costing, cost control, and cost management. AMIT facilitates ABC by making it more economically feasible to collect, compile, and cross-allocate overhead costs. Proponents of ABC argue that it eliminates cross-subsidies, generates more accurate costs, and facilitates marketing and pricing decisions. ABC leads to better cost monitoring and helps direct cost reduction efforts. Proponents also contend that traditional MAS which employ labour-based allocations and actual-to-standard cost variances are especially inappropriate in settings where labour represents only five to ten percent of total manufacturing costs.

Alternatively, ABC's critics contend that ABC systems can be costly to implement when a firm has many distinct activities and multiple cost drivers. They also point out that ABC is rarely used in Japan, where overhead costs are still allocated on the basis of direct labour (Scapens, 1991). Bromwich and Bhimani (1989) questioned the ability of ABC to improve profits because it does not address the decisions that cause large overhead costs to be incurred, nor does ABC solve the problem of allocating large blocks of common costs. Johnson (1992a, p.139) questioned the effectiveness of ABC on more substantive grounds:

> The belief that activity-based cost management tools will improve business competitiveness is a dangerous delusion. *No accounting information, not even activity-based cost management information, can help companies achieve competitive excellence...* (emphasis in original)

Pricing Policy

The NACA staff (NACA, 1968) identified in 1946 the costs that were needed for long-term pricing decisions and speculated that (NACA, 1968, p.115): "management is concerned with the long-run normal costs of the product rather than the costs which may be obtained over a shorter period." Today, the role of costs in formulating long and short-range pricing decisions is far more contentious. Drucker (1993) described cost-based pricing as the third deadly business sin. Drucker directed his comments against most US and practically all European companies for following this approach, and accredited the Japanese for using price-led costing (1993, p.A18):

The only sound way to price is to start out with what
the market is willing to pay - and thus, it must be
assumed, what the competition will charge - and
design to that price specification.

A price-based or target cost should enable a firm to capture a
predetermined market share. Target costing is most appropriate in
environments of low inflation, global competitiveness, and continual
cost reduction. Johnson (1992, p.124) indicated that "target costing is
the antithesis of traditional American cost-plus thinking." Monden
and Hamada (1991) and Hiromoto (1988) noted that target costing is
popular in Japan because many firms are market-driven rather than
cost-driven.

Current Applications of Plans and Policies

The NACA (NACA, 1968) also discussed in 1946 the cost
problems involved in selecting among alternative courses of action.
Three examples were mentioned under this subheading - make a part
by hand or machine, make or buy a part, and keep or replace
equipment. The number and complexity of decision areas have greatly
expanded and now comprise the separate field of management
accounting. Historically, the key event which stimulated this
separation was the field study led by Herbert Simon (Simon, et al
1954). Researchers conducted over four hundred interviews at seven
major US firms. They produced a framework and used terminology
that is still presented in leading cost and managerial textbooks. More
specifically, the study reported that internal accounting information
was used to answer scorecard, attention-directing, and problem-
solving questions. Researchers noted that executives viewed standard
cost and variance analysis as a valid measure of manufacturing
efficiency when they had confidence in the accounting data. However,
managers and executives relied on other sources of information and
expressed criticisms that were to reappear thirty years later. For
example, Simon et al (1954, p.26) noted that:

> Persons interviewed consistently reported that, in any instances where the production and sales executives *might* have had their attention directed to problems by accounting data, they had already learned of the problems from other sources before accounting reports appeared. (emphasis in original)

As mentioned, management accounting became a more distinct field in the late 1950s. Although no particular definition of management accounting has ever been established, the one proposed in 1958 by the AAA's Committee on Management Accounting captures many activities that fell under the "current applications" purpose identified by the NACA in their 1946 document (AAA, 1972, p.1):

> Management accounting represents the application of appropriate techniques and concepts in processing the historical and projected economic data of an entity to assist management in establishing plans for reasonable economic objectives and in the making of rational decisions with a view toward achieving these objectives. It includes the methods and concepts necessary for effective planning, for choosing among alternative business actions, and for control through the evaluation and interpretation of performance.

According to this definition, management accounting should include all of the activities that facilitate managers' planning, control, and decision making needs within the firm. Notwithstanding the views of many prominent critics, operating and executive managers have never relied exclusively on accounting information to run their businesses. The Simon study, comments by accounting practitioners, and the more recent McKinnon and Bruns (1992) monograph reveal that accounting information is an important and necessary but insufficient tool for effective business management. McKinnon and Bruns (1992) concluded that managers' reliance on accounting information is overstated by academic critics. Greer, Treasurer of The Chemstrand Corporation, expressed this view unequivocally (Greer, 1954, p.175):

From some of the current literature on the subject
one might suppose that management consists largely,
if not entirely, of taking action based on the
statements submitted by the accounting department...
This is absurd. From the vantage point of a good
many years' experience in both management and
accounting, I observe that while accounting reports
facilitate good management they are certainly not its
exclusive, or even its most important component.
They are of vital, but limited, usefulness.

Greer's comments suggest that scholars should be wary of
describing the influence of accounting on managerial decision making.
Simon et al (1954) described how managers in the 1950s relied on
direct observation, informal reports, and other verbal information
outside of the accounting system. Thus, scholars who blame MAS for
irrelevance and inadequacy may be expecting a formal information
system to meet needs it never fulfilled. At the time that Greer (1954),
Simon et al (1954) and others discussed the limitations of accounting
reports, few formal information alternatives were available.
Accountants maintained control over the content and distribution of
financial information, and technical limitations prevented operating
managers from obtaining current and reliable non-financial measures.
Mintzberg (1975) identified the weaknesses of formal MAS and
described why managers utilised informal information. Clearly,
AMIT have improved the speed, accuracy, specificity, and reliability of
formal information, and thus overcome many of the drawbacks
Mintzberg cited.

According to Johnson and Kaplan (1987), relatively few
innovations were made to MAS from the 1950s to the early 1980s.
This notwithstanding, academic accountants and their organisations
continually promoted the expansion of the cost accounting field
throughout the 1960s and early 1970s. The Committee to Prepare a
Statement of Basic Accounting Theory (AAA, 1966, p.40) explained
the need for this expansion:

Management is increasingly involved in using
quantified data in areas where qualitative judgment
prevailed a decade or two ago. When this requires
measures and techniques based on other disciplines,

the management accountant must be prepared to
fulfill these needs.

Mathematical models and various operations research techniques
including PERT systems, linear programming, and capital budgeting
were facilitated by AMIT and became popular in the 1960s. However,
applications often incorporated simplifying assumptions such as a
stable technology and an unvarying product mix.

PRESENT AND FUTURE DOMAIN OF MAS

The final sections of this paper discuss the environment of MAS
since the mid 1980s, recount criticisms of current practice, describe
recommendations to modernise MAS, and speculate about changes
that may take place. As mentioned, the 1946 NACA document limited
the cost accounting field to cost data and oriented it to the profit
reporting function. The NAA (1983) composed a definition of
management accounting that incorporated more activities but still
prioritised managers and their decision making needs.[5] While this
definition may have represented the field in the early 1980s, many
critics now argue that MAS should enlarge its constituencies to
include work teams, and expand its perspective by incorporating non-
financial measures. Others go further by asserting that MAS,
regardless of its form, should not be used to improve internal
processes. For example, Johnson (1992a, p.119) stated:

> *I see no positive contribution accounting control*
> *reports make to operations that would justify their*
> *continued production.* They provide no control
> information that is not otherwise better supplied by
> real-time charting of information from processes and
> customers. (emphasis in original)

Notwithstanding the appropriate domain of MAS, AMIT have
increased the potential to disseminate non-financial measures of
quality, innovation, and flexibility. The formalisation of
benchmarking and vendor certification also allow external measures
about suppliers, customers, and competitors to be incorporated into a

central database. According to Bromwich and Bhimani (1989, pp.48-9), the emphasis of MAS should shift from evaluating internal performance to evaluating the costs and performance of vendors.

The mix of financial and non-financial measures to formally incorporate within MAS remains challenging. McKinnon and Bruns (1992) reported that production managers tended to focus on non-financial measures, but cost measures continued to be reported for two main reasons - i.e. executive managers evaluated subordinates in financial terms, and pressures were placed on meeting financial targets. Developments in decision support and executive information systems (EIS) enable executives to spotlight critical areas and quickly explore cost and income variances of divisions, departments, and product groups. One popular product, Executive Edge information software, can be used on IBM-compatible PCs and learned within 30 minutes (Rohan, 1990).

The growing popularity of EIS software suggests that executive management will continue to manage by the numbers. In addition, information having financial consequences will be obtained and distributed to non-executive management on a more need-to-know and less formal basis, rather than through routine, periodic accounting reports. In this computerised environment, accountants will add value by educating workers and line managers about the financial consequences of quality deficiencies, warranty returns, and customer complaints. The following speculations are presented about three specific content areas of future MAS - strategy, cost reduction, and scorekeeping activities.

Strategy

Although senior managers are preoccupied with short-term operational matters,[6] several authors have suggested that MAS should focus on strategy rather than operational control. Shank (1989) discussed three ways that cost information could be analysed to facilitate strategic management - i.e. the value chain, strategic positioning, and cost drivers. Proponents of ABC contend that it is well-suited to serve these and other strategic goals. Pare (1993) discussed the strategic benefits that ABC provides in the areas of quality improvement, faster throughput, and customer relations.

Shank and Govindarajan (1989; and 1992) endorse strategic cost analysis (SCA) as the proper focus of MAS. They contend that investments in AMIT and other long-term projects are often rejected because traditional MAS fail to quantify the benefits of competitive advantage, increased customer goodwill, and greater flexibility, as well as the costs of failing to undertake leading edge projects. In support of this view, McKinnon and Bruns (1992) found that certain capital expenditures are made on an intuitive basis because of the difficulty in quantifying intangibles. Sadhwani and Tyson (1990) reported a similar finding regarding the implementation of bar code systems. Shank and Govindarajan (1989, p.xi) indicate that SCA is needed to sustain competitive advantage and "accounting exists... to facilitate the development and implementation of business strategy." Unlike in the UK and US, Japanese MAS have adopted a more strategic orientation, and use MAS to motivate and influence managers rather than to inform them with precise data about costs. Ezzamel et al (1990), Ouchi (1981), and Choi and Hiramatsu (1987) all reported that Japanese accounting measures are used primarily for decision making rather than for operational control.

Bromwich and Bhimani (1991) described the closely-related area of strategic management accounting (SMA) which recognises the importance of having information about a firm's competitors, cost structure, and strategies over a number of periods. SMA acknowledges that firms compete across various dimensions including price, time, quality, flexibility, and speed, all of which require an external focus, and implores accountants to produce non-financial measures about markets, competitors, and customers. Given the increase in global competition and further AMIT, the call for MAS to assume a more strategic orientation should intensify.

Cost Reduction

Clearly, today's manufacturing marketplace is far more competitive than the one at mid century, and the challenge firms face is to continually reduce costs. Shillinglaw (1989, p.41) viewed the shift from cost control to cost reduction as one of the three major developments that will affect MAS in the years ahead, and described it as "a radical change in focus." During the late 1940s, when the

NACA document was written, US firms were experiencing inflationary pressures and a growing demand for mass-produced durable goods. In that environment, successful performance meant meeting sales and cost targets and staying within budget. Recent critics of MAS ignore the fact that standard costs were advanced for cost control and not cost reduction. The NACA (1958, p.9) stated this point explicitly:

> While it is sometimes said that an unattainable tight standard provides an incentive to reduce costs, it seems that this use of the standard confuses the objectives of cost reduction and cost control. Cost reduction proceeds by finding ways to achieve a given result through improved design, better methods, new layouts, incentive plans, etc. Hence cost reduction results in the establishment of new standards. On the other hand, cost control is a process of maintaining performance at as near existing standards as possible.

Cost control-oriented MAS sufficed into the 1960s and 1970s, in part because producers had relatively greater market power than customers. Large manufacturers provided a limited number of standard products and serviced customers who were far more tolerant of long lead times and quality deficiencies. But, since the mid 1970s, AMIT and global competition have intensified and major customers demand personal attention and greater value. In many industries, profit margins fell as producers reduced prices to maintain existing customers and attract new ones. Intense competition, in conjunction with AMIT, combined to exert pressure on MAS to modernise. Not unexpectedly, MAS which continued to employ labour-based allocation schemes and standard cost analysis were criticised as ineffectual and inappropriate.

In more automated manufacturing environments where continual cost reduction is expected, running actual costing has growing conceptual merit and technical feasibility. As the costs of data collection, storage, and communication fall, updating running actuals becomes increasingly cost effective. Performance reports that show year-to-date prior and current period actual cost performance reinforce the notion of continuous improvement, and serve as an irrefutable benchmark of what can be accomplished. In conjunction with longer-range target costs which are critical for competitive success, running actuals can provide a realistic benchmark of performance to date and the improvements still needed.

In general, AMIT create the need and the means to reduce costs. Competitors are enticed to build highly automated and flexible manufacturing plants in various global locations. Given continual AMIT, companies must reduce costs just to stay abreast with competitors who face the same market pressures. The means to reduce costs comes from AMIT which enable cost and non-financial data to be captured and processed more efficiently. Data capture and communication technology, in conjunction with cost allocation software, permit a firm to accurately trace and assign costs to cost objectives and better evaluate product-line profitability and competitiveness.

Scorekeeping Activities

At mid century, accountants were heavily involved in the transaction processing activities of purchasing, payroll, job and process costing, and inventory control. As a result of AMIT, these and other scorekeeping functions are performed automatically and monitored by individuals who lack accounting skills, let alone expertise. For example, bar code technology facilitates inventory control and the management of fixed assets. However, bar code applications are rarely championed by accountants.[7] According to Belkaoui (1989, p.39), the accountancy profession is losing its monopoly as the provider of accounting services. Given the impact of AMIT on these scorekeeping functions, management accountants may need to pay greater attention to the behavioural impact of scorecard measures if they wish to maintain their influence in these areas. They will need to better understand the range of reactions to negative performance reports, shrinking budgets, and sweeping cost reduction programs. Belkaoui (1980, p.10) called for a more eclectic MAS that placed greater focus on decision making:

In brief, management accounting should go beyond
cost accounting and integrate various material from
organisation   theory,   behavioural   sciences,
information theory, etc., in a multidisciplinary
approach aimed at facilitating the production of
information for internal decision making.

Recently, a number of scholars, especially those of UK origin,
have adopted a behavioural orientation and "a definite ethical-
normative bias" (Mattessich 1992, p.184).   Responding to their
recommendations will require management accountants to increase
their awareness of the social, political, and ideological uses and impact
of accounting information.   Mattessich (1992, p.185) noted that the
UK normative school was pursuing two related directions - i.e. a more
moderate, interpretive approach, and a more radical, critical
perspective.   In both schools, researchers generally contend that
"accounting cannot be neutral and must be held responsible for the
social consequences it `helps' to engender." Bromwich and Bhimani
(1989) reviewed twelve UK case studies conducted in the mid 1980s
regarding the interface between management accounting and
information technology and also called for greater behavioural
considerations.

CONCLUSIONS

This chapter has shown how developments in AMIT pertain to the
purposes of the cost accounting field as identified in the NACA's 1946
document.   It described a number of changes that have affected the
content and purpose of MAS over the past fifty years. These changes
are loosely summarised in Figure 1 below.
    In the chapter are presented certain changes that might be
forthcoming to MAS in the mid 1990s and beyond. In general, these
changes indicate that future MAS will have a broader scope, serve
strategic management objectives, and be forced to adopt a value-added
approach. It has been shown that MAS were not fully relevant at mid
century nor are they totally irrelevant today, as many critics contend.
More reasonably, and in a voice now rarely heard, Greer (1954, p.176)

called for a balanced perspective regarding the importance of MAS, and for the accountant to "approach his task with humility."

Figure 1

Mid Century vs. Mid 1990s MAS

Mid Century MAS	Mid 1990s MAS
Manual Data Collection	Automated Data Collection
Focus on Cost Control	Focus on Cost Reduction
Labour-Based Allocation	ABC-Based Allocation
Standard Cost	Target Cost
Cost-Based Pricing	Price-Based Costing
Financial Reporting Orientation	Decision Making Orientation
Profit and Product Focus	Customer and Quality Focus
Financial Measures Predominate	Non-Financial Measures Incorporated

Regardless of accounting's relevance for decision making purposes, many scholars maintain that MAS will continue to serve as an important accountability mechanism. Baiman (1990, p.368) argued that the agency model provided "a coherent framework with which to analyse managerial accounting issues." Agency's critics question the usefulness of theoretical models to solve actual business problems. For example, Anthony (1989) felt that agency relationships could not be stated realistically in mathematical models, while Kaplan (1984) questioned their usefulness to solve practical problems. Scapens (1991) acknowledged that agency theory offered insights into the nature of management accounting, but he expressed concerns about its practicality. These and other prominent scholars contend that MAS will only remain viable by adding value in non-traditional, decision making applications. Bromwich and Bhimani (1989, p.56) described how MAS must adapt:

Within the new manufacturing environment, monitors of quality, delivery time, inventory reduction and machine performance are seen as replacing measures of labour productivity, machine and capacity utilisation and standard cost variances. Accordingly, information systems need to shift their focus from traditional quantitative financial data to operating quality and other measures.

Clearly, pressures are being placed on MAS to become more relevant for operational decision making and to focus more on strategic concerns. Other critics contend that MAS should not be geared exclusively to top management nor designed for cost control or performance evaluation purposes. Johnson (1992a, p.201) expressed the latter point unequivocally:

The dynamic of global competitiveness makes it necessary for companies to replace top-down control systems with bottom-up empowerment. Companies that refuse to make the change will fail to be competitive in the long-run.

Regardless of the exact orientation of future MAS, the functions and domain of current MAS are fundamentally different from those that existed at mid century. Today's global marketplace demands much greater access to accurate, current, and strategic information in order to compete effectively. Without question, AMIT have revolutionised management techniques, manufacturing processes, and management accounting systems.

NOTES

1. Anthony (1989) described the transition from cost to management accounting and identified Vatter (1950), Robnett, Hill, and Beckett (1951) and Anthony (1955) as accounting textbooks first using the term "managerial" or "management" in their title. Even by 1957, a popular US cost accounting textbook failed to index the phrase "management accounting" (Matz, Curry and Frank, 1957).

2. According to Anthony (1989), the term "responsibility center" was first used in an article by John Higgins in 1952.

3. See Parker et al (1989) for a detailed discussion of literature in this area.

4. Johnson and Kaplan (1987a) accredited the Japanese for stimulating AMIT in Westerm firms.

5. The NAA (1983) defined management accounting as: "[T]he process of identification, measurement, accumulation, analysis, preparation, interpretation, and communication of financial information used by management to plan, evaluate and control within an organisation and to assure appropriate use and accountability for its resources."

6. McKinnon and Bruns (1992, p.19) reported that the senior-level managers they interviewed "seldom raised issues of strategy or strategic direction."

7. See Sadhwani and Tyson (1990) for a detailed description of the accounting applications and implications of bar code systems.

6 A HISTORY OF THE PROFESSIONALISATION OF ACCOUNTANCY IN THE UK AND THE US

Thomas A. Lee
University of Alabama*

*I am grateful for comments and suggestions from a number of colleagues including Dick Fleischman, Moyra Kedslie, Lee Parker, Bob Parker, and Steve Walker

INTRODUCTION

It is hard to believe there may have been a golden age in the history of accountancy, when professional accountants lived in a world free of public criticism from regulators, academics, and journalists. An organised accountancy profession emerged in the mid to late 1800s. Written accounting and auditing standards originated in the late 1910s, and were mandated in the mid-1960s. Informed criticism by non-accountants of accounting and auditing practices appeared occasionally from the mid-1800s onward, grew persistent particularly in the early 1930s through the 1960s, and became a permanent feature of accountancy in the 1980s. From time to time, significant criticism from individual accountants provided an internalised dimension to the critical debate.

The history of internal and external criticism of accountancy has been punctuated by occasional cases dealing with professional negligence (e.g. court cases such as *Kingston Cotton Mill* [1896] and *Royal Mail* [1931] in the UK, and the regulatory investigation of *McKesson & Robbins* [1941] in the US). However, prior to the 1980s, it is not apparent that these cases had a significant impact on members of the general public other than damaged investors and creditors. Legal arguments were made typically with expert testimony from leading practitioners. In effect, accountants determined, practiced and interpreted accounting and auditing standards, and worked occasionally with regulators to do so. Except for the availability of court proceedings in litigious circumstances, and despite infrequent external criticism, there were few ways of enforcing the professional covenant in accountancy. Individual accountants may have been scrutinised in court or exposed in newspapers. But the institutional process of accountancy was a relatively private matter for much of its history.

Today, this situation has changed. The accountancy profession is a regular target for informed journalists, academics, and politicians anxious to demonstrate causal connections between accountancy practices and business failures (e.g. Polly Peck and Bank of Commerce and Credit International in the UK, and the Savings and Loan crisis in the US). Sustained attacks have placed professional accountants in a very public arena. The primary effect has been to create a significant crisis of confidence about the reliability of accountancy services and the credibility of accountants and their institutional processes.

Although all professions are from time to time subject to public scrutiny and criticism, the current situation in accountancy is unique because of its persistence and strength. It is worth reviewing to explain how and why the accountancy profession has reached this position. In particular, tracing the history of the professionalisation of accountants provides one means of understanding the current situation in an appropriate context. The main purpose of this chapter, therefore, is to present a broad historical review of the creation of the accountancy profession. Using historical studies of the earliest times to the present day, an attempt is made to explain how accountants organised into professional groupings. In particular, the focus is on the conflicting phenomena of economic self-interest and public interest.

The chapter is divided into several sections - the nature and history of professionalisation; accountants before professionalisation; the birth of the accountancy profession; establishing and defending the professionalisation of accountancy; challenges and responses in professional accountancy; and a retrospect and prospective for professional accountants. The methodology of the chapter is a traditional one used in historical studies, and based on explained narrative using secondary sources. The text also contains a critical approach, in which the explained narrative is subjected to interpretation. Interested readers are recommended to consult Previts et al (1990) for an account of these methodological matters.

NATURE AND HISTORY OF
PROFESSIONALISATION

Before proceeding to a history of the accountancy profession, it is appropriate to outline briefly the nature and history of professions and, in particular, distinguish professional activities from other occupations. The review has been compiled from a variety of authoritative sources (e.g. Carr-Saunders and Wilson, 1933; Krause, 1971; Johnson, 1972; Bledstein, 1976; Larson, 1977; and Freidson, 1986).

The term "professional" is typically used in ways that give it an ambiguous flavour. For example, a football player, a plumber and an accountant each can be described as a professional because they are paid to do a job subject to observable minimum quality standards. In this chapter, however, a narrower focus is adopted. It concentrates on occupations organised in institutional form, whose practitioners are committed explicitly to serve the public interest, and who offer client services related directly to an intellectually-based body of knowledge.

Professions emerged as institutionalised occupations in a Victorian Britain coping with significant economic and social changes (i.e. large increases in population, population shifts from country to town, industrialisation of commerce and trade, a decline of the church, and state intervention in matters of poverty, health, and education) (e.g. Smout, 1986). Organised professions became important means by which the Victorian middle class exercised cultural control, and they assisted in the removal of the social status quo created by church and guild (e.g. Bledstein, 1976). The professional was perceived as an independent and knowledgeable practitioner in total control of his occupation. He rapidly became an unchallenged leader in his community, with an explicit moral obligation to act in the public interest.

The traditional literature on the subject suggests professional tasks have a consistent history and reputation as privileged work with altruistic objectives (e.g. Carr-Saunders and Wilson, 1933). However, there is an alternative historical view of the role of professionals. This suggests they organised to gain market control of an occupational service by means of monopolistic exclusion of individuals deemed unworthy or unqualified to provide it (e.g. Larson, 1977). Professionals created explicit mechanisms to operationalise this strategy, including entry prerequisites, institutionalised programmes of academic education, and work-related training and experience. Unless an individual had satisfied these criteria, professional membership was impossible, and certain service opportunities were denied. In other words, a profession could be interpreted as a created and maintained work monopoly. Such a monopoly was institutionalised when the state granted exclusive rights of service only to certified professionals (e.g. as with the audit function in the UK in 1948).

Relevant entry, education, training, experience and membership characteristics are mechanisms which contain the possibility of introducing rationality to client problems. In particular, they are perceived as bringing competence to the resolution of such problems. The professional strategy is to create client dependence on the provision of the professionalised service, subtly inducing a sense of crisis or a structure of uncertainty for the client, yet promising to bring stability to the situation.

Hooks (1992) presents an argument that the professionalisation of accountancy should be explained in terms of work function and social class. Relevant functionalist characteristics are well-known, and form the traditional way of describing professionals (e.g. membership of an institutional association, an examined body of knowledge, institutional control over student intake, training and experience requirements, licensing arrangements, and self-regulation). Such characteristics are also interpretable as explicit signals to distinguish professionals from other classified social groups. They assist a profession to maximise its economic and social status by revealing the existence of mechanisms to provide and control service quality.

A professionalised occupation retains its economic and social status by maintaining the mystery of its body of knowledge. Opening up such knowledge to others outside the profession increases competition to provide its client services, and therefore dilutes its power, status and rewards. Protecting knowledge makes good economic sense for the professional, and has been a recurrent theme in the history of accountancy.

BEFORE PROFESSIONALISATION

Accountancy existed for several thousand years either as an activity formed as a subset of a larger occupation (e.g. estate management or tax collection), or as a separate occupation practiced by individuals without organisational structures in place. It is difficult to classify early accountancy as a profession in the sense of the term defined in the previous section. However, lack of such a classification does not mean early accountants were unprofessional in the conduct of their work.

If accounting is defined broadly as a function to produce abstract representations forming memories of past economic events within specific relationships, it has existed as an occupation for many thousands of years. There is evidence of accounting predating both counting and writing, and of these systems being introduced to facilitate accounting for complex economic situations (e.g. Stone, 1969; Mattessich, 1987; Costouros and Stull, 1989; and Parker, 1989). The earliest accounting appears to have been physical in nature to accommodate available materials and user skills (e.g. clay envelopes, tablets, and bone tallies). However, it gradually evolved from pictograms to ideograms to phonograms as a result of developments in writing and counting.

Numerous writers describe systems of accounting in early civilisations (e.g. Boyd, 1905a and 1905b; de Ste Croix, 1956; Keister 1963, 1970 and 1986; Hain, 1966; Stone, 1969; Costouros, 1979; Garbutt, 1984; Stevelink, 1985; and Baxter, 1989). Accountants (or scribes) were employed to record receipts and payments relating to business, banking, governmental, and personal transactions. The main purpose of accounting appears to have been the provision of transactional memories to operationalise accountability in managed systems, and to ensure adequate control in economic relationships. The scribes dealt with a variety of communication, legal and commercial tasks in addition to accounting, were trained typically in organised schools, and often occupied high societal positions.

Auditing also has a long history, but has not been researched as extensively as accounting. Its existence in early civilisations is noted briefly in several of the above citations, with more detailed histories provided by Boyd (1905c) and Lee (1971). The idea of audit appears to have been practiced in several civilisations, mainly as a form of internal monitoring within overall systems of organisational control. Audits took place originally in the context of tax collection or estate management, and became familiar features of municipal financing in the Middle Ages. Audits were often heard in private or public, and auditors were frequently non-accountants (e.g. estate owners or town citizens).

Despite the brevity of this review of the history of early accountancy, one conclusion is reasonably clear, and that is the occupation of accountant or auditor existed in many civilisations spanning several thousand years. However, despite evidence of a high social position for scribes in several of these civilisations, as well as the existence of education and training facilities to train them, accountancy appears to have been unorganised in the contemporary sense of the existence of institutionalised professional bodies.

It is reasonable to speculate a reason for this lack of professional organisation over several thousand years. The most obvious explanation is that it was economically unnecessary for accountancy to be professionalised. Market control over accountancy services existed without institutionalised organisation because the required knowledge and skills were restricted to a relatively few individuals with the literacy required to be accountants. There was no need either to protect the body of knowledge of accountancy or to regulate the activities of its practitioners. Protection and regulation were virtually guaranteed because of educational barriers preventing access to the secrets of accountancy practices. Alternatively, the required accounting or auditing depended on technologies which could be managed by untrained or illiterate individuals, thus making accountancy an occupation open to the public (e.g. Stone, 1975; Jacobsen, 1983; and Baxter, 1989).

Barriers of entry to accountancy were reduced during the European Renaissance (e.g. Fogo, 1905; Geijsbeeck, 1914; and de Roover, 1956). First, literacy in the general population slowly increased, creating access to formal knowledge systems for a larger but still relatively small group of individuals. Second, an efficient dissemination of formal knowledge in book form became possible as a result of printing innovations and cheaper writing materials. Third, commercial schools were formed to educate bankers and merchants in subjects including bookkeeping. And, fourth, the population of bankers and merchants increased in association with expansion in trade. Thus, the ability to account in a complex format such as double-entry bookkeeping came within the reach of a growing proportion of the total population.

From the fourteenth century onwards, the occupation of accountant typically was co-mingled with that of manager or businessman (De Roover, 1956; Lane, 1977; Noke, 1981; and Nobes, 1982). It was also combined increasingly with that of teacher and writer (Fogo, 1905; de Roover, 1938; Nobes, 1979; Yamey, 1980; Martinelli, 1983; McMickle and Vangermeersch, 1987; and Mepham, 1988). In particular, from the fifteenth century onwards, following the publication of Pacioli's text, there was a deprivatisation of accountancy knowledge. It was academically legitimised with the presence of bookkeeping as part of a general educational curriculum in the eighteenth and nineteenth centuries (Mepham and Stone, 1977; De Groote, 1978; and Mepham, 1988).

But other changes were taking place. The first change relates to the organisation of economic activity (i.e. the trading evolution from ad hoc transactions to finite trading ventures, and then to continuing business entities). Trading and manufacturing innovations over several centuries created economic opportunities and managerial incentives to institute relevant accounting information systems (e.g. Johnson, 1981; and Fleischman and Parker, 1990 and 1992). There is also evidence of early cost accounting innovations by industrial engineers (Wells, 1977). Several historians have researched this period (e.g. Solomons, 1952; and Garner, 1954). Of significance is evidence of an increased use of accounting beyond the well-established role of economic memory and into managerial decision making, and the growing complexity of the accounting body of knowledge because of the technologies of data allocation and matching.

Accountancy was coming of age. Its influence in economic affairs became important to the management of business organisations. It should therefore be of little surprise that signs appeared of accountants organising formally, if not into professional groupings, then at least into something similar to guilds. For example, at the end of the seventeenth century in Italy, associations of accountants were founded (Boyd, 1905d).

By the end of the eighteenth century in Scotland, business directories of major cities regularly listed individuals as accountants despite their lack of organisation (Brown, 1905a; Stewart, 1986; and Mepham, 1988). The eighteenth century accountants identified by Brown (1905a) were the forerunners of accountants who formed the first professional society of accountants in Scotland in 1853. As Brown discusses, there were a number of well-known accountants working in public practice in Scotland before professionalisation. Examples of innovative accountants in non-public practice in the UK before and during the Industrial Revolution have also been researched, as has the specific use of accounting and accountants to control the operations of continuing businesses from the sixteenth century onwards (e.g. Solomons, 1952; Burley, 1958; McKendrick, 1970; Robertson, 1970 and 1984; Stone, 1973; Forrester, 1980; Baladouni, 1986; Edwards and Newell, 1991; and Walsh and Stewart, 1993). The stage was set in the UK for formal professionalisation to take place in the mid 1800s.

BIRTH OF PROFESSIONALISATION

The above review of the pre-professionalisation history of accountancy raises an interesting question. Given the long history of accountancy and accountants, why did a very small group of mid nineteenth century Scottish accountants in public practice feel compelled to organise in institutional form? The typical response is professionalisation was a natural consequence of the economic and organisational changes of the Industrial Revolution. That is, with industrialisation, demand for accountancy services grew, and accountants organised to take advantage of considerable economic opportunities (e.g. Garrett, 1961; Howitt, 1966; Stewart, 1986, Kedslie, 1990; and Miranti, 1991).

More detailed analyses and arguments, however, suggest a more complex rationale. For example, in addition to the industrialisation argument, Stewart (1986) suggests Scottish professionalisation was a response to competitive pressures and a need to provide a unified view on accountancy matters. Brown (1905b) states Edinburgh accountants had made several unsuccessful attempts to provide this unification prior to 1853. However, in 1853, they were successful and formed The

Society of Accountants in Edinburgh, with a royal charter following in 1854.

Brown makes no suggestions regarding the reasons for professionalisation in Edinburgh. But Macdonald (1985), Parker (1986), Walker (1988), and Kedslie (1990) each argue a major catalyst was a proposed change in bankruptcy law which would have allowed lawyers to undertake work then dominated by Scottish accountants. Thus, at least one major reason for professionalisation was economic in nature, and consistent with the suggestion of Stewart that accountants were reacting to competitive pressures. The possibility also exists of nationalistic rivalry underlying professionalisation events.

A number of writers reveal the close relationship between accountants and lawyers in bankruptcies and sequestrations during the nineteenth century (Brown, 1905a; Macdonald, 1985; Parker, 1986; Walker, 1988; and Kedslie, 1990). Accountants in public practice typically dealt with the accounting aspects of such matters. Walker (1988; and 1993) also provides evidence that voluntary insolvencies and judicial factories were an important part of public accountancy practice at that time. However, accountants covered a variety of other functions (e.g. merchants accounts, accounting for canal, rail, and banking companies, estate management, insurance and stockbroking, and legal work) (Brown, 1905b; and Kedslie, 1990). Few accountants appear to have been employed in industrial accounting or commercial auditing.

The conventional evidence of accounting history therefore suggests the existence of a small but growing public accountancy community in Scotland by the mid 1800s. Members of this community are portrayed as facing a potential economic threat because of proposed bankruptcy law changes. Unsurprisingly, they are perceived as reacting to protect their economic self-interest. They are described as organising to form institutions which justified the term "profession", thus mimicking previously-established bodies in other areas such as law, medicine and architecture (Walker, 1988; and Kedslie, 1990).

In particular, as Brown (1905b) documents, sixty one Edinburgh accountants petitioned Queen Victoria in 1853 to form The Society of Accountants in Edinburgh. The petition pointed out the public interest focus of the proposed organisation. Accountants needed to unite into one body to ensure their legal and actuarial work was completed by appropriately qualified accountants for the benefit of the public. A Glasgow body was chartered in 1855 on petition by forty nine accountants who also adopted an actuarial and legal basis to their argument to protect the public interest (Brown, 1905b). Once formed, the two Scottish bodies proceeded to resist the proposed bankruptcy laws and ensure the continuing employment of accountants in such work (Brown, 1905b; and Walker, 1995).

The conventional evidence of the origins of accountancy professionalisation in Scotland is reassessed by Walker (1995). In a study of economic, political, and social factors at work in mid nineteenth century Scotland, an alternative explanation is provided which, nevertheless, is consistent with previous histories. As in other studies (e.g. Kedslie, 1990), the impetus for professional organisation by Scottish accountants in public practice is identified as a significant threat to their economic self-interest (i.e. a London proposal to base Scottish insolvency practice on English legal provisions which required lawyers rather than accountants to act as administrators). The practical reason for the proposal was an English concern about the effectiveness of Scottish bankruptcy law, and its economically-damaging effects on English businesses trading in Scotland. The intellectual argument for reform was related to the case for improving free trade.

Scottish accountants in public practice organised in Edinburgh to defeat the threat. They not only organised, but presented their case in the context of a prevailing Scottish nationalism. They engineered a successful debate to obtain public support, convincing senior members of the Scottish legal profession and Scottish Members of Parliament that the English proposal to reform should be resisted. This was accomplished between 1854 and 1856.

ESTABLISHING AND DEFENDING THE PROFESSION

What the above analysis reveals is evidence of an organised profession deliberately created to provide market control of accountancy services. It is consistent with the professionalisation model outlined by sociologists such as Johnson (1972), Larson (1977), and Freidson (1986). In particular, the Scottish accountancy bodies sought legitimacy for their member activities in Royal Charters. The primary significance of this was the creation of institutions with royal permission to self-regulate professional accountants and accountancy, and to describe their members as chartered accountants. Brown (1905b) points out the immediate use of this designation following formation. It was a deliberate act publicly to separate chartered accountants from other individuals labelled as accountants, provide a basis for public confidence in the work of chartered accountants, and thereby stimulate demand for their accountancy services.

Both Walker (1988) and Kedslie (1990) provide evidence of the strengthening of the Scottish professionalisation process by means of hurdles relating to entry, education, examination, and training. These hurdles had the dual effect of revealing professional accountancy explicitly as a learned occupation with high standards, and also restricting the number of institutionalised members. The nature of these requirements has been researched by Walker (1988) who reveals early accountancy professionalisation in Scotland to be an almost exclusive middle class activity, and particularly associated through family, friendship, and client relations to lawyers and landed gentry.

A similar sequence of professionalisation occurred in England, with the formation of local societies of accountants in the 1870s, followed by merger in 1880 into The Institute of Chartered Accountants in England and Wales (Brown, 1905c; and Howitt, 1966). Unlike the Scottish formation, however, the English movement appears to have been little more than a series of "copy-cat" activities as local accountants sought the public credibility and authority attained by Scottish chartered accountants. It has to be presumed that such credibility was recognised as having positive economic benefits. In addition, English professionalisation was initially characterised by competitive disputes between the London-based bodies and those in other regions. These disputes were concerned with elitism and the concentration of power and influence in accountancy matters by accountants working in London firms. To portray public unity on accountancy matters, however, talks quickly took place to amalgamate five of the English bodies into The Institute of Chartered Accountants in England and Wales. According to Howitt (1966), the Institute proceeded quickly to impose standards of entry, examination and training, and was also involved in influencing changes in law relating to accountancy work (e.g. re bankruptcy and municipal auditing).

Internal Rivalries

However, all was not well in UK accountancy. Garrett (1961) describes the founding of The Society of Incorporated Accountants in England in 1885. It was licenced by the Board of Trade as a competitive response to the conditions of entry imposed by The Institute of Chartered Accountants in England and Wales. Of particular concern were the Institute's requirement of an apprenticeship system, and the restricting of the work activities of its members to those of a public accountancy nature. Society membership was UK-wide with regional organisations and members in both the public and private sectors of the economy. An examination system was initiated, and specific professional designations agreed. There also appears to have been a concern with influencing legislation affecting accountancy work (Garrett, 1961).

The early history of the UK accountancy profession is characterised by a form of unity among the royal chartered bodies, despite pre- and post-foundation English concerns regarding a centralisation of power in London. Arguably, this unity may have been a consequence of an institutional feeling of superiority over non-chartered accountants. Chartered accountants were regarded as the elite of the profession (Brown, 1905e), and their organisations cooperated in various ways. For example, the Scottish bodies adopted similar entry and training requirements, formed a joint national examination system in 1893, consulted over responses to proposed bankruptcy and corporate legislation, issued a national directory of chartered accountants in 1896, arranged joint lecture courses; had similar student societies and written *Transactions* of proceedings, and eventually merged in 1951 (Brown, 1905b; and Kedslie, 1990).

However, creating and maintaining a profession did not prove to be an easy task for UK accountants. Several writers comment on attempts by Scottish and English accountancy bodies to obtain statutory registration of the title of professional accountant (e.g. Garrett, 1961; Howitt, 1966; Macdonald, 1985; and Kedslie, 1990). A variety of reasons combined to create rivalry and competition in accountancy over a period of more than fifty years (e.g. a proliferation of bodies serving different membership needs and occupying traditionally competitive geographical locations, the specific use of the title chartered accountant by members of the chartered bodies to create exclusiveness and economic benefit, and the organisational aggressiveness of latecomers to the professional accountancy market).

Statutory registration of suitably qualified individuals to practice accountancy was seen by the leaders of the competing bodies as the most sensible way of protecting the public interest against substandard accountants. Many registration attempts in the form of parliamentary bills were made by the chartered and incorporated bodies. All failed for various reasons, not least of which was an underlying rivalry between the Scottish and English chartered bodies concerning their respective geographical jurisdictions (Macdonald, 1985). In addition, the Scottish chartered bodies had used the court system successfully to defend their right to the exclusive use of the invented and abbreviated title CA when that was challenged by two non-chartered bodies in the period 1854 to 1914 (Walker, 1991). The chartered bodies argued their professional monopoly provided a higher value of public service because of the competence of their members, and that competition devalued the chartered accountant designation. Scottish chartered accountants such as Marwick, Touche, and Niven, together with a number of English colleagues such as Guthrie, used this argument when they emigrated to the US and helped to found its accountancy profession (Brown, 1905d, Carey, 1969b, Wise, 1982, and Kedslie, 1990).

US Experience

The most obvious feature of early UK professionalisation is the pursuit by accountants and their institutions of economic self-interest in the name of a public interest. Use of entry, exam and training requirements, lobbying over legislative matters, defending the exclusive use of professional designations, and attempting statutory registration, each illustrate this point. A similar pattern emerged in the US in the late 1880s, although the specific rationale for professionalisation was different from that of the Scots chartered accountants.

Several writers have researched the US history of professional accountancy (e.g. Brown, 1905d; Carey, 1969b and 1970; Merino, 1975; Previts and Merino, 1979; and Miranti, 1990). Their work requires to be read in the context of considerable change in US economic and social conditions between 1870 and 1900, including industrialisation and urbanisation. Economic opportunities for investment by UK companies and individuals opened the way for a significant influx of experienced Scottish and English chartered accountants. They quickly organised as firms of accountants, and sought the professional credibility to which they were accustomed in the UK. They found no institutionalised bodies in the US devoted to public accountancy, and began to form institutions similar to those of the Scottish and English chartered accountants.

The first body of US professional accountants was the Institute of Accounts, founded in 1882. Membership was open to any accountant passing its admission test. The Institute's main function was the education of accountants. Several other bodies were founded from 1882 onwards. One such body was the American Association of Public Accountants (1887) which was concerned solely with a public accountancy membership. Its structure and constitution was patterned on the UK chartered accountancy model, and its membership initially comprised thirty one individuals based in the north-east of the US.

These professionals were mainly UK chartered accountants concerned with stewarding UK investments in US agricultural, manufacturing, and railroad industries. They appear to have founded the Association to obtain professional status and economic rewards perceived to be unavailable from membership of the Institute of Accounts. The Institute was open to all professional accountants. The Association restricted its membership to individuals in public practice. An initial problem for the Association's members was changing a public perception of accountants as bookkeepers rather than professionals (Carey, 1969b). That they did so is evidenced by the use of early members of the Association by US bankers financing various industries.

In 1895 and 1896, the Association and the Institute individually and then collectively sought to create legislation in the State of New York to licence professional accountants who met prescribed educational and residential requirements, emphasising a public interest focus in US accountancy, and mirroring similar UK events. Unlike the UK situation, however, the US outcome was state-accredited professional accountancy in which, following prescribed examination and training, a licence was granted by the state in which the individual accountant worked. Only licensed accountants could use the title certified public accountant. Following New York, this system was adopted in several other states. Each state founded a society of accountants to regulate and administer its certified public accountants separate from federal bodies such as the Association.

Early US accountants were concerned to demonstrate publicly their high professionalism in terms of education, training and ethics (Carey, 1969b). Much of this concern was due to external criticism of accounting and auditing standards, and internal concern about the variety of entry standards of state societies. A need for overall control was perceived and, in 1902, the Federation of Societies of Public Accountants was formed. It merged with the Association in 1905, was retitled as the Institute of Certified Public Accountants in the United States of America in 1916, and further changed to the American Institute of Accountants in 1917. The new Institute attempted to provide uniformity in professional standards to enhance the title certified public accountant, seek new areas of service for its members (particularly in the governmental sector), and work with regulators to standardise accounting and auditing practices at an acceptable quality level.

The above analysis describes briefly a system of professionalisation in the US different from that created in the UK. The US system was founded on accreditation by the state, and provided an economic monopoly for certified public accountants effectively in the name of the public. Such a monopoly could not be provided by the UK system of control of professional accountants by institutionalised bodies, even though the title chartered accountant was protected by the courts. In addition, the US system created an explicit duality of potential responsibility by the accountant to the state and his professional body.

What was similar in the UK and US, however, was the phenomenon of economic self-interest driving the professionalisation process in the name of a public interest. Also similar was the existence of nationalistic rivalry (Scots and English in the UK, and British and Americans in the US), and the seeking of economic opportunity by influencing legislators and regulators. In the US, however, the pursuit of uniform accounting and auditing standards (e.g. the Federal Reserve Bulletin *Uniform Accounting* in 1917) in conjunction with the state was different from the UK where standardisation was not a professional issue until the 1940s.

Historians such as Carey (1969b and 1970), Previts and Merino (1979), and Miranti (1990) provide considerable detail about other aspects of the early history of the US accountancy profession. They evidence the early development of university and college-based accountancy education, a concern of practitioners with the need for and quality of financial accounting and auditing standards, the reciprocation between states regarding the professional designation of certified public accountant, and a move toward a uniform examination. Merino (1975) also observes the concern of early US professional accountants with a culture of professionalism including integrity, character, and personal responsibility and judgment. She demonstrates an early professional concern with ethics and individual accountability.

Image Building

By the beginning of the twentieth century, the US accountancy profession had laid its institutional foundations and established a bridgehead in terms of relations with the state. The title of certified public accountant was protected and explicit standards of professional conduct were being discussed. However, despite a federal body of professional accountants and numerous state societies, not everything was under institutional control. The various bodies of accountants lacked the prestige and status associated with the UK chartered bodies. Each state regulated the practice of accountancy by means of legislation and state societies. US institutions were structured as trade associations, and major variations existed between states in the quality of accountants and accountancy services. In effect, the US profession entered the twentieth century with a need to initiate actions designed to create an image consistent with public perceptions of professionalised activities (Carey, 1969b).

Of particular concern was the need to make explicit the virtues and benefits of professional accountancy. Thus, as previously indicated, most state societies attempted to site accountancy education in reputable universities (Carey, 1969b; Previts and Merino, 1979; and Langenderfer, 1987). This had two effects reflecting a co-habiting of economic self-interest and public interest. The first effect deflected the economic burden of accountancy education away from professional firms and bodies. The second effect assisted in legitimising the educational basis of professional accountancy. These developments were accompanied by a slow but persistent interest by academics and practitioners in accounting research concerned with accounting theory and the development of a body of acceptable accounting principles (Previts and Merino, 1979; Langenderfer, 1987; and Lee, 1993). This interest was the foundation for a critical debate on accounting principles in the 1930s onwards (Carey, 1969b and 1970; Storey, 1977; and Zeff, 1982a).

Internal US Schism

Establishing the professionalism of US accountants proved to be a difficult task because of internal disputation (Carey, 1969b, Previts and Merino, 1979, and Miranti, 1990). Leaders of the American Institute of Accountants modelled it on the Scottish and English chartered accountancy bodies, with an apparent aim of making it appear to be a self-regulating federal body of American chartered accountants. A road block to this goal was the variable system of state-based licensing of certified public accountants. The Institute's leadership sought control of a self-regulating, independent profession of individual accountants rather than have a system in which government controlled the right to do business in accountancy. However, the large majority of Institute members were state-licensed and had allegiances to their individual states. A schism was created in the Institute which lasted from 1916 to 1936.

The Institute initially set high entry standards of examination and experience which contrasted markedly with those of most of the licensing states. Its membership was open to all qualified accountants and not restricted to certified public accountants. State-licensed accountants objected to the entry conditions. The conflict appears to have been between accountants in large, east coast firms and those in small, provincial firms. In 1920, the leadership of the Institute removed all professional designations from its membership records (including that of certified public accountant).

Dissatisfaction reached a point at which a rival organisation, the American Society of Certified Public Accountants, was founded in 1921. Its founder described accountancy not as a profession but as a business of the very highest type, thus emphasising the economic nature of the professionalisation process. The Society's initial objective was protection of the title certified public accountant, and admission was based solely on possession of this certification.

Eventually, a dialogue commenced to restore professional unity, with emphasis on admitting certified public accountants to the Institute, forming state chapters of the Institute, and creating greater uniformity in examinations. The Institute and the Society merged in 1936 into the American Institute of (later, Certified Public) Accountants, with a membership of only certified public accountants and a uniform examination which was adopted by all states in 1952.

What Carey describes as the "great schism" reflects the internal rivalry generated by a combination of economics, professional status, national differences, and geographical allegiances.   Such rivalry appeared in the UK earlier than in the US.   In both countries, however, the battle was an economic one to determine who was entitled to practice as an accountant.   Of no lesser significance was the associated struggle to establish the right to regulate accountants.   In the UK, the professional bodies established and maintained that right. In the US, the main professional body has never attained such an autonomous position because of state licensing.

Education and Journals

These US developments were different from their UK counterparts because UK accountants had created an institutionalised environment separate from the state, and were left to self-regulate.   There was less concern over the siting of accountancy education in learned universities.   Only in Scotland was that a major consideration, with provisions for compulsary university classes in law, the creation of part-time chairs of accountancy at Scottish universities (filled by leading practitioners), and the institution of accountancy classes managed by the Scottish bodies of chartered accountants (Brown, 1905b).   These developments were not followed in the larger English community, and it is perhaps not surprising to find less interaction between practice and academe in the early history of the English bodies (Garrett, 1961; and Howitt, 1966).

The use of the journal (e.g., the *Journal of Accountancy* from 1905, and *The Accounting Review* from 1926) was a further important means in the US of publicly signalling the knowledge base of accountancy, and the intellectual leadership of the profession (Carey, 1969b; and Previts and Merino, 1979). It was a strategy already in use in the UK with the *The Accountant* (founded in 1874) and *The Accountants' Magazine* (founded in 1897) (Brown, 1905b; Garrett, 1961; and Howitt, 1966). These journals identified accounting, auditing, tax, legal, and business issues affecting professional accountants. They provided a means of publicising and criticising the accountancy body of knowledge, and the elite accountants developing and teaching it (Kitchen and Parker, 1980).

Other means of presenting the professionalism of accountants and their associations took a very explicit physical form. For example, early efforts were made in the UK to found libraries as depositories of accountancy knowledge (Brown, 1905b; Garrett, 1961; and Howitt, 1966). Similar developments occurred during a later period in the US (Carey, 1969b). In addition, consistent with more generalised evidence of impression management by nineteenth and twentieth century organisations (Ewen, 1988; Harvey, 1989; and Featherstone, 1991), the main UK accountancy bodies acquired or erected magnificent buildings on key city sites (Brown, 1905b; Garrett, 1961; Howitt, 1966; and Macdonald, 1989). These events can be characterised as part of the UK accountancy profession's drive to respectability and social standing. The histories of Carey (1969b) and Previts and Merino (1979) suggest this was not a priority of the early US professionals.

Expanding Services

The early accountancy profession extended its menu of services when economic opportunities arose. Kedslie (1990) describes how early Scottish chartered accountants developed a range of services beyond those existing at the time of foundation, including accounting and auditing work for corporate entities and municipalities. Hein (1963; and 1978) documents accountants' involvement in periodic parliamentary reviews of UK corporate legislation. Carey (1969b) and Miranti (1990) describe the US experience with audit, tax and advisory services.

The UK history of expanding professional accountancy services is characterised by a long-standing, complex economic and social dependency which existed between accountants and lawyers, and a strained relationship between accountants and the state (Bromwich and Hopwood, 1992a; and Freedman and Power, 1992). The equivalent US situation has permitted more harmonious and productive relations between the state and the institutions of accountancy. The issues at stake in both the UK and the US, however, have been identical (i.e. a desire by professional accountants to secure the right to provide specific accountancy services, and their need to control the debate on which standards to apply to such work).

Napier and Noke (1992a) provide a history of this process in the UK. The first part ranges from the late nineteenth century to the mid twentieth century, and suggests restrained involvement by accountants. In particular, they appear to have gradually extended their political influence in corporate accounting and auditing without explicitly lobbying legislators, and without writing practice standards in these areas. This development seems to have been a natural extension of their established work in bankruptcies and liquidations (i.e. they did not have to lobby for new work, and operated in a relatively liberal and flexible environment without explicit standards). This conclusion is consistent with the findings of other historical researchers (Hein, 1963 and 1978; Aranya, 1974; Edwards, 1976; and Kitchen, 1982).

The second phase identified by Napier and Noke suggests a more pro-active role by accountants from the 1940s onwards. It followed legal cases dealing with accounting and auditing failures and subsequent criticism, and reflects a growing awareness by UK accountants that their economic self-interest was not well served by ignoring their public responsibilities. As Nobes and Parker (1984) demonstrate, the major professional bodies began writing accounting and auditing standards, first as non-mandatory *Recommendations on Accounting Principles*, then as required *Statements of Standard Accounting Practice*. UK accountants also influenced corporate legislation (e.g. by evidence to company law reform committees) and, in the Companies Act 1948, obtained a legal monopoly of corporate audit services.

The more recent history of UK professional accountancy standards contains a persistent cycle of criticism of perceived accounting and auditing failures, public expectations of accounting and auditing performance, extended prescriptions in standard-setting, reduced public concerns, followed by further sustained criticism as a result of new business failures (Lee, 1979; and Mumford, 1979). The most significant change over time has been the increased writing of accounting and auditing standards by accountants (e.g. chronologically, by the Taxation and Research Committee of the English Institute, then the Accounting Standards Steering Committee and, most recently, the Accounting Standards Board). Thus, even though appropriate accounting and auditing practice is ultimately a matter to be decided by lawyers in the UK, the precise practices used by accountants and auditors have been historically determined within the accountancy profession.

The histories of American researchers such as Carey (1969b and 1970), Storey (1977), Previts and Merino (1979), Zeff (1982a), Boockholdt (1983), Davidson and Anderson (1987), and Miranti (1990) suggest a similar overall pattern in the US, but with one specific difference. The US change from laissez faire to prescription of standards took place earlier than in the UK as a result of the Great Depression. Following a period of relative flexibility in and persistent criticism of accountancy practice, leaders of the US profession realised it needed to control the debate over what is termed generally accepted accounting principles. The evolution from recommendation to mandate is clear (i.e. from non-mandatory *Accounting Research Bulletins* and *Accounting Principles Board Opinions* of the American Institute of Certified Public Accountants to *Statements of Financial Accounting Standards* of the Financial Accounting Standards Board). Also relatively clear is the move from part-time professional committees (e.g. the Committee on Accounting Procedure) to full-time, quasi-independent boards (e.g. the Financial Accounting Standards Board).

In this respect, the state (largely represented by the Securities Exchange Commission from the early 1930s onwards) has tended to permit the accountancy profession to manage the standards process. This may have been a legacy of the early relationships built between the various institutions of US professional accountancy and legislators and regulators, in which accountants demonstrated their willingness and competence to institute quality standards. However, the US profession has not had complete control over standards, and regulators have occasionally criticised and intervened to assist in improving accounting and auditing practices (Miller and Redding, 1994). Indeed, relationships between the Securities Exchange Commission and the American Institute of Certified Public Accountants have been far from harmonious in relatively recent times (Ohlson, 1982).

What the histories of UK and US standard-setting suggest is a delicate process managed by the professional accountancy bodies of balancing self-interest against public interest. Professional accountants have persistently attempted to retain control over standards and standard-setting. They have done so by maintaining a dialogue with the agents of the state sufficient to give comfort to the latter that standards can be prescribed by accountants in the public interest. In recent times, such comfort has been given by separating the institutions of standard-setting from the professional bodies (e.g. the Accounting Standards Board in the UK, and the Financial Accounting Standards Board in the US). The issue at stake is an economic one. Loss of control over standards suggests loss of control over the body of knowledge, and loss of the body of knowledge brings into question the appropriateness of the professional monopoly of service.

Contemporary accounting researchers have specifically focused how the institutions of professional accountancy have faced up to this issue over recent decades. For example, Richardson (1988) reports evidence that audit practitioners maximise their rewards by responding to politically-sensitive issues, and standardising their practices in these areas. This suggests professional accountants have responded to issues only when they perceive an economic incentive to do so. Byington and Sutton (1991) provide evidence consistent with this observation. Identifying four events between 1938 and 1985 which significantly threatened the autonomy of professional accountants, they found significant increases in published accounting and auditing standards in the four years following each event.

In the area of auditing, Humphrey et al (1993) outline a history of accountants' responses to the fraud detection expectation in which, while appearing to accept more responsibility, they have in fact reduced their role. Sikka et al (1992) conclude there was a late nineteenth century tendency by accountants and lawyers to diminish the importance of fraud detection in auditing for economic reasons, and a late twentieth century pressure by government to reverse that position as a result of increased economic crime in the corporate sector.

Fogarty et al (1991) describe the above institutionalised responses as a complex strategy of doing "nothing" (i.e. decoupling pronouncements of ideal accountings and audits from corrective actions by responding to concerns and maintaining the status quo so long as this is economically viable). Such a strategy is a familiar feature of the history of the accountancy profession. For example, in relation to the expectations gap debate, Humphrey et al (1992) identify the accountancy profession's ability to control and manage the debate in order to maintain the status quo regarding the role of the auditor. Controlling the debate has reaffirmed accountants' professionalism, but deflected attention away from the audit and auditors toward the limitations of the proposed reforms and reformers.

Fogarty et al (1991) confirm this strategy in a wider historical context of the accountancy profession under continuous siege. They examine several responses to such pressure including the lack of clarification of fraud detection duties, increased competition for audit services, even for risky clients, diversification to non-attest services, demands for legal reform to reduce liability costs, cost containment measures to reduce audit time, expectations gap projects with ambiguous statements of audit roles, and failures to develop better accounting and auditing practices, discipline deviant accountants, issue qualified audit opinions, and improve quality control procedures. They argue these responses to persistent criticism make good economic sense so long as it is viable to absorb legal liability losses without changing the nature of the audit. The strategy of doing "nothing" can also be argued to have political as well as economic benefits for the accountancy profession. Power (1993a; and 1993b) states standard-setters have for some time adopted a political approach to issues which is cosmetic in substance and rich in form. In particular, he perceives the profession defining issues, setting up institutional structures to respond, and issuing standards or guidance to practitioners which maintain a "zone of discretion" for the practitioner.

Doing "nothing" has been revealed in other ways. For example, Fogarty et al (1993) evidence the history of a professional body's failure to respond to reported accounting errors by its members because there were no economic incentives for the body to publicly expose its members. Parker (1993) analyses published disciplinary cases in the Australian accountancy profession over three decades and, with evidence of few exclusions from membership, concludes the economic self-interest of accountants dominated their duty to the public interest. Sikka et al (1989) recount a documented situation in which a major UK professional accountancy body prevented individual external scrutiny of its standard-setting process, yet allowed such access to one of the largest professional firms.

Each of the above research studies provides some evidence of the recent behaviour of professional accountants when under pressure to respond to issues. They reveal the inherent difficulty of being a professional with an explicit covenant to serve the public interest in situations where there are considerable economic incentives to adhere to self-interest. The interesting feature of this analysis is the conflict is positioned at the institutional level. The above studies concern pressures on and responses from the institutions of the accountancy profession. This is counter to the strategy of these institutions which, historically, appears to invest in the status quo by focusing on the failures of individual accountants, thus diverting attention from the institutional effect (Willmott, 1990).

The professionalisation of accountancy has provided institutional structures to permit accountants to maximise their self-interest in a publicly interested way. Davis and Stawser (1993) give a researched example of this conflicting situation. They observe the profession's historical involvement in the debate over accounting for inventory, and the eventual domination of individual client interests over the public state interest. The broader studies by Briloff (1990) and Mitchell and Sikka (1993) of recent histories of accounting and auditing failures come to a similar conclusion (i.e. client interests have superseded the public interest, thus leading to concerns that the accountancy profession has failed to make the powerful accountable, and has remained unaccountable itself).

Body of Knowledge

Evident in the US over several decades since the 1960s and, more recently in the UK, is the accountancy profession's desire to find an intellectual basis for its practices, thus making explicit the possibility the latter are based on a rational body of knowledge. Although most writers on the subject touch briefly on its history (e.g. Peasnell, 1982; Hines, 1989; and Archer, 1992), there is no definitive historical analysis.

Using Zeff's (1984) chronology as a data base, it is reasonably clear that the US institutionalised search for an intellectual basis for accounting practice started with the 1938 study of Sanders, Hatfield and Moore, and the 1940 study of Paton and Littleton. Both studies rationalised conventional practice. The 1961 and 1962 studies of Moonitz and Sprouse, however, challenged the status quo, evoked considerable opposition, and were quickly shelved (Zeff, 1982b). The issue was not revisited until a 1970 study on concepts and principles, and the 1973 Trueblood Report. The former pronounced on conventional practice. The latter provided a conceptual framework for accounting change. It was later developed by the Financial Accounting Standards Board into a series of conceptual statements.

A similar and later sequence of events occurred in the UK (Peasnell, 1982; and Archer, 1992). A conceptual framework study was published in 1975, shelved for more than fifteen years, and reappeared in the conceptual proposals of the Accounting Standards Board in 1991. Despite this continuous effort in the UK and US to expose a theoretical body of knowledge, there is a consistent view from researchers that it has not changed the nature of accounting practice (Peasnell, 1982; Hines, 1989; and Archer, 1992). The historian is then left with the distinct impression that, if practice has not changed, the conceptual framework project's purpose is something other than for improving practice. Perhaps its presence is no more than a ploy to demonstrate the existence of a body of knowledge sufficient to maintain accountants' professional status and economic monopoly (Hines, 1989).

Further Developments

Langenderfer (1987) discusses the on-going attempts of US accountants to legitimise accountancy education. Initially, this process concerned the institution of university degree-based studies (Carey, 1969b; and Previts and Merino, 1979), and contrasts with the traditional UK method of part-time non-university study within an apprenticeship system. Only recently has the US system been introduced to the UK. In both countries, however, university courses are now subject to accreditation procedures by peer review. In addition, expected qualifications for academic and student accountants have become more rigorous. The nature of the academic accountancy community has also changed (i.e. from practice-based teaching by part-time practitioner-educators to a profession of full-time educators teaching theory and practice, and researching a range of topics). These changes arguably have enhanced the professional status of accountancy. But they have also created schisms in the accountancy community concerning the relevance of both teaching and research, and raised questions regarding the status of accountancy as a profession (Lee, 1989 and 1995; Zeff, 1989; Bricker and Previts, 1990; and Strait and Bull, 1992). Not only is the public interest potentially at risk with a divided accountancy profession, but so too is the latter's economic well-being when the credibility of its body of knowledge and educators are doubted.

Change has also been a feature of the institutional and organisational framework of the accountancy profession. Renshall (1984) provides a UK analysis, while Wootton and Wolk (1992) give a US perspective (see also Carey, 1969b and 1970; Previts and Merino, 1979; and Ohlson, 1982). These analyses demonstrate considerable change in the profession's structure. Over many decades, there has been a significant increase in the number of professional accountants and students, coupled with a continuous consolidation of practice firms and institutional bodies. Accountancy has become a multinational activity and an important part of private enterprise economies. The range of professional services has extended beyond the traditional areas of accounting, auditing, and taxation. The profession's relationship with government has been continuous and increasingly significant.

But growth and change have brought attendant problems. In combination, they raise the question of whether contemporary accountants are professionals or business executives (Dyckman, 1974; and Zeff, 1987). Dyckman's concerns include the self-interest of professional accountants dominating their public interest commitment, lack of effective response to criticisms of practice by professional bodies, inability to find an acceptable theoretical foundation to accountancy practices, and failure to punish accountants who have breached ethical standards. Zeff's comments are similar, concentrating on the issues of accountants responding to competitive pressures by treating management rather than ownership as the client, offering a wide range of non-accounting business services, and lacking intellectual leadership on accounting and auditing problems.

According to its critics, what has happened to the accountancy profession is a loss of its sense of public mission, making it indistinguishable from any other form of profit-based business. Indeed, approximately one hundred years following its foundation, the American Institute of Certified Public Accountants was prompted in the 1980s to amend its statement of mission to make explicit its commitment to the public interest.

In the US, savings and loan banking failures are linked with perceived failures in accounting and auditing services (Briloff, 1990). A similar phenomenon exists in the UK with respect to corporate disasters such as Polly Peck, British Bank of Commerce and Credit International, and Maxwell Communications (Mitchell et al, 1991). Law suits, public scrutiny and press comment, and large court awards or out-of-court settlements have become familiar features of accountancy life. The economic size of the problem is seen in a statement issued by the largest US audit firms (Cook et al, 1992). Although this is argued to be part of a bigger problem facing all professions, its impact on accountancy in recent times has been to create a crisis of survival for the profession.

RETROSPECT AND PROSPECT

The history of professional accountancy is relatively recent in the context of the existence of accountants and auditors. It is essentially an economic text with a cover entitled the public interest. In terms of the above historical analysis, the fundamental influence driving professionalisation is economic in nature. Professional accountants came together to provide an institutional structure to protect an economic monopoly of work then under threat. The process has been repeated over several decades, with the institutional structure elaborated to maintain and expand service monopolies. Professional rivals were defeated or eventually absorbed by merger, and attempts were made to obtain a state monopoly by registration. A strategy of using explicit signals of professionalism was practiced, and the range of services increased. The size of the profession grew, accompanied by a concentration of practice units and institutional organisations through merger.

The accountancy profession developed over a relatively few decades into a powerful and authoritative sector of a modern economy. But this progression has not been free of major problems. The most significant is the growing and persistent public criticism of accountants and their services. Of concern is the association of accountancy with business failure, and the apparent inability of accountants and auditors to assist in the accountability process. This criticism originated before professionalisation as a public concern about the ability of public accountants to effectively discharge legally-based responsibilities, and evolved over many decades into a concern about the flexibility of accounting practices, and the inadequacy of audit verification procedures. Today, criticism involves doubts about the ability of accountants and auditors to resist managerial pressures to misreport.

These criticisms have gradually been externalised through the financial press, forcing the institutions of accountancy to respond more publicly. They have done so in a way which has had two effects. The first is a gradual exposure of the accountancy body of knowledge through conceptual statements, standards, and guidance recommendations. These explicit signals of the knowledge underlying accountancy practice have removed some of the mystique of accountancy, and made it easier for non-accountants to criticise practice. The second effect has been the institutional adoption of a strategy of doing "nothing," in which issues are responded to without altering the status quo of accountancy practice.

The combination of these effects ensures the accountancy profession will continue to face the historically long-lived issue of whether its accountants wish to be professionals or members of trade associations. The explicit covenant to protect the public interest has to be taken seriously, perhaps for the first time in the history of the accountancy profession. It can no longer be taken as a legitimised ticket to provide a range of services without public accountability but with significant economic and social rewards. Instead, it has to be regarded as a vocation, in which service for a designated client also involves duties to a wider public, and where failure to satisfy these duties results in public accountability and punishment. These are issues which require public debate. They are issues which have a long history of being ignored.

7 INFORMATION TECHNOLOGY
AND
THE ACCOUNTANCY PROFESSION

Fenton F. Robb
Formerly, University of Edinburgh *

*I am indebted to my colleagues, particularly to Tom Lee, Rolland Munro and Simon Lilley, for their inspiration and help; the discussants at the Pacioli Seminar at Edinburgh in 1994; and the anonymous reviewers for their constructive suggestions. However, no reader should hold any other than the author responsible for any errors, omissions and offences committed here.

INTRODUCTION

The purpose of this chapter is to review some aspects of the interaction between information technology (IT) and the accountancy profession. This first section details the organisation of the chapter. A history of information technology is sketched in the second section. The many ways in which IT actively affects people and shapes their attitudes and behaviour are discussed in the third section. A reflection on how organisations are changing under the influence of new technologies, and how the accountancy profession may be deeply involved with these changes are revealed in the fourth section. The final section presents concluding remarks with respect to IT and the accountancy profession.

A HISTORY OF INFORMATION TECHNOLOGY

There are many streams of thought as to the causes of present information technologies. The stream of thought presented in this chapter has been selected with partiality to suit the writer's argument. No special privilege for the particular viewpoint is claimed.

Early efforts to categorise events and objects, and to graph and mechanise logical and causal relations, are first discussed. The history of adaptive machines is traced. An examination is then undertaken of how these machines support mass data processing for operational purposes, such as bookkeeping and the generation of information for forecasting and decision making. An attempt is made to relate this to what is afoot in the accountancy profession.

Logical Technologies

Analysis and Synthesis

For generations, people have attempted to produce conceptual, graphical, mechanical and, recently, electrical and electronic devices for solving logical and mathematical problems by analysis. However, before any logical or mathematical operations can be performed, there has to be divisions and categories of things and events. To find the origins of these would entail looking for the origins of language as a means of dividing the world and assigning different values (moral, cultural, spiritual, economic, and so on) to its parts.

As long as four thousand years ago, in the Golden Crescent between the Tigris and Euphrates Rivers, many types of written records were kept on tablets of all kinds of shapes and sizes (Keister, 1963; and 1970). Not only did these record possessions and commodity movements, they also listed the formation and dissolution of commercial relations such as partnerships, and recorded transactions between people and groups of people. These records, like the tallies and tokens which have survived to the present time, described conversations creating obligations. When the obligations were discharged, the records were cancelled by being returned and broken. Already IT, and what it portrayed, were implicated one with the other, and with people and their institutions. Here we see early evidence to support McLuhan's (1964) assertion that the form of the message may be more important than its content, even that the medium is the message.

Until the present century, much of what passed as "science" was devoted simply to classification in the belief that sorting things into groups with similar characteristics would provide new knowledge (e.g. about origins). There are, for example, nineteen category labels in modern botany, although only six or seven "taxa" are generally used. With respect to the history of the sciences, the interest in taxonomy and classification has, in general, dwindled. For a time, there was interest in finding causal explanations. Now the emphasis seems to be on making accurate reports of observations and the drawing from these statistical arguments about correlation, rather than the attribution of causation.

Many centuries ago, Aristotle used tree-like graphs to divide and classify the primary and secondary "substances," and distinguish "species" from "genus." Branching tree-graphs can represent the "dumb" machines that contributed so much to the early development of modern IT. Document sorting boxes were perhaps the earliest office machines. The automatic Hollerith sorter/tabulator in the 1890s performed the same work using punched cards. Electric telegraphs, such as Reuter's ticker-tape, used punched tape. Both punched cards and punched tapes became favoured ways of entering programs and data into early mainframe computers.

Another stream of activity was devoted to synthesising knowledge by combining different fragments of data to form information. In the thirteenth century, Friar Ramon Lull invented a set of tables for arranging all possible combinations of *a priori* principles or categories in every branch of knowledge. He claimed this would enable one to know everything. Despite Swift's (1726) parody, this device was certainly not trivial. By re-arranging letters, words and ideas into unfamiliar patterns, Lull must have produced some surprises, if not heresies, and stimulated creative conversations just as in a brain-storming session today. How similar it is to the famous Think Tank. Is it not the same, in principle, as decision-making using a random number generator? One of the most important benefits of political, professional, and academic conferences, browsing in an open library, and foreign travel is the inspiration of new ideas gained from chance remarks and random encounters with other people and things.

Of course, none of the ways of generating random associations of letters, words, ideas, and opinions, guarantee that the relationships between them, though they might make sense or even be true, are logically consistent and valid. Consistency and logical validity have been very highly prized for so long, particularly among accountants, that it is almost heretical to question their value.

Logical and Causal Relations

If the premises of a valid logical argument are true, then its conclusion is true. Ever since Aristotle presented rules for valid logical argument, there have been problems testing real life arguments against his pure form. In the seventeenth century, Leibniz and others dealt with this problem using circles to depict class propositions and syllogisms. Later, Euler and Venn developed similar diagrams, and now these form the foundation for the "new" mathematics introduced widely in the 1960s. These diagrams can depict only a strictly limited number of variables, so that many people tried to add further dimensions to them. Charles Pierce, for example, believed that his system of graphs and a "sheet of assertion" (made of rubber which he stretched and shaped to connect the signs on his graphs) would reveal new truths. His symbolism bears a resemblance to the topological graphs used by Lewin (1952) in his group dynamics work between the World Wars, and to some of the diagrams used by today's "soft" systems methodologies. These include those used by Checkland (1981), programs like COPE (as reported by Eden et al, 1983), and STELLA that uses computers to aid cognitive mapping.

Gardner (1983), who provides many insights into the history of such machines, awards Charles Stanhope the title of inventor of the first engine for solving both logical and arithmetical problems rigorously. Stanhope's *Demonstrator*, anticipating William Hamilton's quantification of the predicate, made the distinction between "some" and "all" of the predicate, and thus increased the number of basic propositions from which we can construct syllogisms. Lewis Carroll's Game of Logic Machine (c.1886) demonstrated that valid syllogisms could contain both negative and positive terms. Jevons, too, was among the many inventors of progressively more successful engines for conducting operations in formal logic and, thus, mechanising the syllogism.

George Boole was the originator of the modern truth-value based propositional calculus, and the symbolic study of class relations. In fact, Boolean algebra is a special case of the more general mathematical structure known as a lattice. Lattice is at the heart of the so-called neural network mentioned below. This eventually led to understanding and symbolising switching networks, and the modern approach to computation that employs at least binary (i.e. true or false, yes or no, on or off, 1 or 0) logic. There were great debates about the comparative usefulness of analogue machines (using continuously variable voltages and currents to depict many valued logical operations) and digital, two-state, computers. The digital solutions won the day.

Lately, there has been greater interest in representing degrees of truth or the likelihood of something belonging to a particular class of things, using many valued logics, such as Zadeth's probabilistic fuzzy logic or Reichenbach's three-valued quantum logic (i.e. true, false, and indeterminate) (see Geach, 1981). As Hacking (1990) reports, probabilistic reasoning takes advantage of the nineteenth century invention of chance as a rational explanatory device. Some think these modifications of logic emulate human thought processes more convincingly than strictly formal two-state logic can ever do. Despite all this, others (e.g. Johnson-Laird, 1983) hold that human thought is really more about model building and relating ideas than it is about the operations of logic - digital, fuzzy, or otherwise. They claim credible models of people's perceptions and thought processes could be built without having to depict reasoning at all.

Very similar to logical diagrams are those graphs and graphical engines that reflect causal relations. Some depict actual operational connections between events in time. Vessels and burettes of coloured water connected by pipes and valves have depicted accounting and stock control systems. Such a device is an analogue computer. Today, the more common examples of devices simulating causal relations are planning charts, signed digraphs, and flow charts. Charts can also symbolise normative causal relations describing what should be the causal relations between things such as in a machine drawing, a wiring diagram, a diagram of accounts, a critical path chart, or a chart of a command structure. Max Weber called this "the iron cage of bureaucratic life" (Runciman, 1978). The Program Evaluation and Review Technique (PERT) combines representations of prescribed relations with actual relations.

Stavros Foundos, a London accountant, developed a logical engine around 1977 which might have been used anywhere where binary or ternary decision trees could find application. But for the arrival of the cheap digital computer, this logical machine might well have found applications as a ready reckoner in law, taxation, business decision-making, cost allocation, financial accounting, medical diagnosis, operations research, and game theory (George, 1980). Computer programs now embody all these charts of logical and causal relations, and support accountants and managers in their daily work.

Adaptive Technologies

Cybernetic Feedback and Accounting

A quite different stream of thought developed in the world of the engineer. Water wheels and steam engines powered factories during the Industrial Revolution. The power source often drove a single shaft and this, in turn, powered many machine tools. Although individual tools started and stopped as the work required, the speed at which the main shaft turned, and the energy it could deliver, had to remain constant. James Watt was probably the first to theorise and apply the cybernetic principle of negative feedback. Watt designed and built mechanical "governors" to replace the human engine driver who throttled the supply of steam or water to the engine or the mill wheel.

Successes associated with cybernetic principles include code-breaking (Hodges, 1983), "predictors" that directed anti-aircraft fire (Wiener, 1948), and a number of machines such as the Homeostat of Ashby (1952). During and after World War II, there was great enthusiasm for building machines that reflected aspects of human intelligence. For example, Grey Walter's *Docilis* was one of many mechanical "turtles" that developed Pavlovian conditioned reflexes by bumping into things, thereby discovering how to get around obstacles. Other machines sought light, sound, and heat within certain thresholds and under certain stipulated conditions. Under other circumstances, these same stimuli had no effect or repelled them. These machines learned to make themselves comfortable under varying conditions. Claud Shannon's electric mouse learned how to run mazes. Other mechanical animals could find electric sockets for recharging their batteries. All of these, and many others of their generation, employed the same cybernetic principle, and laid the ground for the emerging theory of communication (Shannon and Weaver, 1963). Pask (1964) reported some three hundred and fifty such machines or simulations of machines in the early 1960s.

The same principle has been familiar to accountants for many years as variance analysis and budgetary control. These remain the main devices for "steering" most functions in companies. Hofstede (1978) argues that the application of cybernetic control such as management-by-objectives to non-routine and non-industrial processes will certainly fail. Others contend that it inhibits learning by the system, or "deutero-learning" (after Argyris and Schon [1978]), because it provides strong incentives to cover up mistakes and to throttle initiative. Recent work by Tse (1993) has shown how the behaviour of organisations controlled in this manner can be significantly destabilised by the amount of slack built into control parameters such as cost standards.

Gaming Machines and Experts

The theory of games (Spencer-Brown, 1969) is also realised in machines, and has found an important place in strategic planning and control despite "some very sinister possibilities" noted by Wiener (1954). The first uses, apart from experiments with chess playing machines, were mainly military. The theory played a variety of roles from strategic planning and control, parodied in Kubrick's film *Dr. Strangelove*, to the tactical training of submarine commanders.

Computer-supported business games train managers and accountants and model real life business situations. They act as test beds for different strategies and provide answers to "what if?" questions. Some of these machines learn from experience or trial and error, and others are successful because they can recall from memory similar situations and acceptable solutions. Some machines modelled human personality traits (Loehlin, 1968; and McCulloch, 1970), suffered neuroses, and simulated human reactions to stress (Raphael, 1976). Such models had potential use in demonstrating the behaviour of patients suffering the effects of trauma, customers in sales situations (Robb, 1984), or managers under pressure. Today, such models have the potential to depict the landscape of the mind, and permit noninvasive exploration of that unfamiliar territory in a kind of virtual reality.

Expert systems, the latest in this family of research, come in many varieties. Loaded with a "tree of knowledge" derived from the interrogation of experts by skilled knowledge engineers, these systems can diagnose a situation by interrogating someone in a systematic way. Or, they may advise how to reach a particular solution by stipulating what are its sufficient conditions. Expert systems can also explain how they come to their conclusions. These systems have attracted considerable attention from accountants, and there are many in use commercially, often embedded in conventional decision-support programs.

This section has shown that today's technologies have emerged from the fortuitous interactions of many different streams of thought. Three aspects of this are reflected upon further. First, with hindsight, the causal trains of thought of the past always seem to converge on the present. This is an illusion that is experienced when standing anywhere in a network, and viewing what is around. The viewpoint preferentially selects the history that looks as if it led to the present, and firmly excludes everything else.

There is a second experience which may occur in seeking reasons for the present situation. This is the perception that progress is a continuously flowing process. However, if the changes are looked at in detail, it is found that, far from being continuous, what is seen as progress proceeds in fits and starts; discontinuity is the order of the day; continuity is more a fabrication of perceptions than a reflection of any objective reality. Jaques (1982) holds the view that there is always present a duality in the perception of time. Time can be perceived as both continuous and discrete, but never at the same moment.[1]

Finally, successes are seen but only rarely is notice taken of the multitude of side-tracks, dead ends, and total failures. This concentration on successes may obscure the possibility that failures are much more important ways of learning than successes. Similar problems exist with the physical things that make up technology. Everything in view is thought of as part of a continuous causal chain, everything not noticed matters not, and a few successful developments provide more important lessons than a multitude of failures.

Bulk Processing Information

The printed word has become the main medium of communication in society. It is responsible for much of the uniformity of social organisation, and for the monotonous adoption to the contemporaneously fashionable "one right way." The written word can be seen as a means of standardising definitions and meanings and of promulgating procedures. Its adoption marked important changes in the ways in which society was organised.

Typewriters and Their Successors

The printing press was domesticated with the arrival of the typewriter in the nineteenth century. Once the keyboard had become standardised and the mechanism arranged so that the typist could see the work, this mechanical wonder became very popular. Copying devices complemented the typewriter and extended the sphere of influence of the typewritten word. By the turn of the century, automatic cash registers incorporating the features of list-adding machines with a secure cash box were in extensive use. In the early 1950s, bookkeeping machines (large list-adders) simultaneously typed many-copied orders and invoices on continuous stationary, posted entries to ledger cards, and kept running totals of the value and numbers of transactions entered.

Big Engines

The first general purpose electronic computer was ENIAC, built in the US and used mainly for military purposes. ENIAC could perform about three hundred multiplications per second using eighteen thousand thermionic valves. Each valve emitted as much heat as a small electric light bulb. The computer required a substantial cooling plant and a clinically-clean environment. Today, speeds are measured in hundreds of millions of instructions per second, only very large machines are cooled, and all are compatible with the normal office environment.

The main stream of computer-supported IT started when the first business machines, UNIVAC-1 and the IBM 650, were introduced in the marketplace about 1954. Larger companies used these great machines for simple, repetitive, and labour intensive tasks such as payroll, billing, and the processing of accounts. In the early days the production of information other than for accounting purposes was often just a by-product of bookkeeping. Gradually this changed. Management consulting, purportedly based on scientific principles, addressed rate-setting, time and motion study, material usage control, and waste control/recovery. Computer processing of the masses of data needed to operate incentive bonus schemes was a welcome reality. The new profession of cost and management accountants emerged and needed computer support of their practices.

The set-up costs for each different kind of transaction processing were very high. Every time the kind of operation changed, the machine had to be set up again, almost from scratch. Setting up entailed setting switches, plugged connections, and running program cards or tapes which put the machine into the mode for carrying out the next kind of operation. Previously most office work was regular and continuous. Now the work schedules revolved around this somewhat unreliable machine. This new constraint had quite a significant effect on the flow of work everywhere in the company, such as in planning the production line, stores, purchasing, sales, and cash receiving offices. It became increasingly necessary to program work in the office as if for a production line. And the skills required of the different kinds of office worker became very differentiated. For example, a typical general office might have the following: shorthand or steno-typists, copy typists, audio typists, filing clerks and progress chasers, operators of comptometers, list adders, bookkeeping machines, card/tape punch/verifiers, sorting machines, mailing machines, telephone exchange, and so on. Due to the skills and knowledge required, there were not many people who could do more than a few of these jobs. There is little in the literature noting this very important change.

Monsters No Longer

In the late 1960s and early 1970s, transistors replaced the big hot valves. Transistors, in turn, were replaced by microchips and integrated circuits. Power increased while size and cost dropped. These computers generated less heat and became much more reliable. Programmers prepared their work off-line and prototype-tested it before mounting on the machines. As set-up time reduced, more real-time processing was possible. And, as reliability increased, the work became more regular. Dumb terminals, intelligent terminals, and then multi-purpose workstations slowly replaced the card and tape readers. At first, these provided new means of input and, later, helped end-users to call up programs and control computer operations.

Originally dubbed scientific, the minicomputer edged its way into the market for special purposes, including modelling and processing on-off calculations. Compared with the mainframe, the minicomputer was much easier for non-professionals to program. Many companies installed minicomputers as a type of self-service support for the new and considerably more numerate generation of managers, engineers, and research workers which had matured after World War II. In a period of very full employment of these people, the provision of computing facilities strongly attracted the brighter candidates. This new generation of professionals had the benefit of computing power available without interfering with routine accounting work.

Contemporary Information Technologies

Microcomputers

Perhaps the most surprisingly useful development was the personal microcomputer. Apple introduced a microcomputer in the early 1980s which was significantly smaller, cheaper, much simpler to program, and easily networked. This computer soon became integrated with all kinds of other equipment such as colour printers, laser-read compact discs, display projectors, local and wide area communication systems, and the mainframe itself. The costs of data storage and retrieval also dropped dramatically.

The typical microcomputer now has a high-definition colour screen, word processor with spelling checker, thesaurus, grammar checker, and convenient editing facilities. The microcomputer also has a spreadsheet which is able to perform a wide variety of mathematical, statistical, and graphic operations. All work can be done in a "windows" environment, and is driven by a "mouse" (and perhaps an extended keyboard). Versions of the microcomputer, such as laptops, are very portable, and can have printers attached. Modems and acoustic couplers connect machines over normal telephone lines or satellite radio links. Microcomputers are now delivering far more power than the early mainframes (some of which are still in use) at prices comparable with those of electric typewriters.

Higher level programming languages, culminating in intelligent enquiring languages (among the fourth generation languages or 4GLs), help quite unskilled users to run specialised applications and make complex searches of data bases. Along with packages for word processing and spreadsheets, the software readily available now includes desk-top publishing, drawing and painting, 3-D designing, image processing and graphics animation, critical path analysis, planning by PERT, diary facilities, telephone answering and dialing, fax and e-mail, database management, interactive maps, and the means of compressing and extracting files to save storage space. The personal computer is user-friendly, and puts the end-user in the driving seat.

Distributed Computing

In the early days, the big engines were centrally located close to the work which made output readily available to management. Often big new headquarters grew up around the computer centre. With the availability of cheaper and more reliable communications, the location of computers and their sizes became much less important. There is now a very marked tendency to decentralise administration. In some installations, a network of microcomputers can perform operations just as well as a single large mainframe. This is distributed processing, and it is particularly attractive to new companies because they do not need to make large investments in specialised expertise and elaborate computing departments.

Distributed processing has reached impressive sophistication. For example, in supermarket chains, the bar code readers at the checkout, connected to computers, can update the stock record for every item in the store and re-order stock, check that each item carries the correct price and print out a detailed receipt, charge the total to the customer's bank account using a debit card as authorisation, make the appropriate bookkeeping entries, and provide sales returns for the buyers at headquarters. The computer can do these functions at the time of transaction or be downloaded overnight when the network is less occupied.

Strategic Management of Information Technology

Big problems emerged in the early days of large-scale computing. Some companies made strategic commitments to source from only one supplier in order to maintain compatibility of hardware and software, and sustain some continuity of knowledge and skills. Under pressure from competition, there were many failures among hardware suppliers and great difficulty in sustaining continuity. In at least one case, a supplier announced that it would no longer support earlier installations, and tried to force customers into making drastic and costly system changes. Customers responded by forming a pressure group. They succeeded in making the supplier provide bridging programs to ensure that the new machines could emulate those which they replaced to enable older software to continue in use. Some companies now find themselves in a difficult situation. They allowed the technology to invade the company in a piecemeal way, and are now heavily reliant on out-dated equipment, incompatible systems, cumbersome programs, expensive-to-maintain machinery, and an aging and irreplaceable staff nearing retirement. Networking may provide some solutions to the dilemma.

Decisions involving IT are complex and exasperating. Different technologies progress at different rates, and they do so intermittently. This creates difficulties in maintaining compatibility between components of the system, and leads to exasperation because the past is absolutely no guide to the future. The progress of the technology is not well behaved and linear. It moves in fits and starts. New breakthroughs are hailed and forgotten in months. Suppliers of hardware and software play complex games with copyrights, patents, and technical expertise. Uncertainty rules everywhere.

There are continuing pleas for company boards to become more IT-literate, and for more clearly-defined IT strategies (Fitzgerald, 1993). Development of long-term strategies have often been unrealistic because of uncertainty and the speed of change. Attempts to meet the strategies have been time-consuming and distracting from other important aspects of corporate affairs. There is a need to adopt less rigid ways of managing the development of IT as Robb (1986) has indicated. It is no surprise that some companies, instead of putting more IT specialists on the board, put the whole IT function out to contractors. The situation may be stabilising, however, and the function of planning the strategic management of IT may have become more mature and realistic. There may be opportunities for the accountancy profession to move into IT. First, of course, the profession has to demonstrate its superior expertise in the field.

And From Here?

Even mature operating systems, such as MS-DOS, can behave in strange ways or suddenly collapse, as every regular PC user will testify. There are new operating systems on the way, but whether they will be compatible with what has come before remains an open question. There are still many outstanding problems such as compatibility, the connection of computers with each other, and the wide variety of digital communications now in regular use. Of course, everything that already exists will get better, but there will also be some very novel products and services widely available to enhance or replace some products. For example, the increase in the use of home computers connected to cable or telephone networks will make home banking and shopping easier. The existing IT in wholesale and retail distribution could make the supermarket, with its vast car parks, a thing of the past. Home banking is already becoming popular. Home shopping seems an even more likely opportunity. Computers will continue to get smaller and faster and deliver better value for money. High temperature superconducting circuits are in use already. Even smaller and more complex integrated circuits are possible using new substrates in place of silicon. But the advantages will have to be very substantial to justify such a dramatic change in the basic material. New materials are already being considered for incorporation in cellular or molecular computers.

Even the keyboard is under threat. A plain sheet of paper, quite unconnected to the computer, with the diagram of a keyboard drawn on it and a miniature video camera fixed to the computer screen watching the user's fingers, may combine to produce a "virtual" keyboard. This could shrink portable machines even further. It could also provide physically more secure access to machines working in hostile environments such as operating theatres, heavy industry, and cash dispensers. More intelligent document readers will be less vulnerable to failure through difficulties in reading poor typescript. Where the spoken word is appropriate, voice synthesisers will be used. Handwriting readers are still at a primitive stage, and generally require either highly stylised writing or quite long periods of training.

The use of paper as a communication medium will decline as inter-terminal communications become faster, cheaper, and capable of carrying visual and animated material as easily as tables and texts are sent today. Investment in wide-band optical cabling may restrict progress in the domestic market, but commercial and industrial premises are already becoming well served. A personal computer with a videophone is already in production, and video-conferencing between the users of up to eight computers will soon be possible.

In the field of IT, there is always a hope that someone will invent an entirely new form of computing to replace the conventional linear processor. If truly concurrent processing could be achieved, there would be a massive increase in reliability and performance. An entirely novel architecture, a genuine departure from the von Neumann tradition, called the artificial neural network, is now available. A neural network typically consists of three layers of computing elements. All the elements in the middle layer connect to all those in the layers above and below by adjustable connections. The strength of the signal transmitted through a connection depends on the "weight" given to it and to all its neighbours by previous training sequences of trial and error and feedback, or "back-propagation" of error. This network has demonstrated the ability to generate its own program without using algorithmic logic, just by training, or learning from experience. The network is particularly effective at detecting and recalling patterns of inputs. Already important applications include providing secure visual identification of the faces, fingerprints, or voices of people when using cash dispensers or seeking to enter secure premises. An artificial neural network can also provide an alternative way of seeking out correlations from large masses of data, and eliminating extraneous noise from communication systems.

The accountancy profession employs educated and experienced human intelligence of a high order. Educated and experienced human intelligence is a scarce, very costly, and often transient commodity.

This makes the quest for artificial intelligence a great economic opportunity as well as a very interesting intellectual project. Neural networks might further the quest for artificial intelligence, but there still seems to be three serious impediments remaining. First, the most obvious, is that there is no agreed upon notion of what constitutes intelligence. With each step forward, once the surprise has worn off, it is said that the step (whatever the step was) was not a sufficient reflection of human-like activity to be "really" intelligent. Second, whereas most computing systems in the past have been hierarchical, or at least dependent on a central controller, nervous systems seem to work concurrently, and there is still much to be learned about how to run "democratic" computers. For example, can a machine be enabled to write a program to accelerate its own learning processes? Does a machine really need a program at all? Or, could a machine teach itself how to learn more quickly?

The third problem is that of scale. The world's most powerful computer, Thinking Machine's CM5 at Los Alamos, consists of just over a thousand parallel processors. But, when a cat makes a learned movement with its paw, about one hundred million different neurones fire almost simultaneously. Despite all this, the accountancy profession should remain alert to developments to neural networks and expert systems. Generally, much of accountancy could be both learned and taught by such machines. Neural networks might become the Pacioli of the future, and make the secrets of the profession available to a much wider public. They might even eliminate the need for using people for accounting altogether!

PEOPLE AND INFORMATION TECHNOLOGY

This section discusses how accountants and specialists have fared during the IT revolution.

Clerks, Accountants and Computing Experts

As previously mentioned, the first extensive mechanisation of clerical work started in the accounts departments of quite large companies. Although the mainframes and their associated systems were under the general control of the accounting function, those who ran the computers were specialists in such areas as programming, operations, system analysis and design, and archiving.

Technology at Arm's Length

Most accountants and auditors preferred not to get involved in what was patently electro-mechanical engineering. These professionals tended to treat the whole computing function, from data preparation to printing, as just a huge black box. The computer was simply speedier, possibly cheaper, and sometimes a bit more reliable than a roomful of clerks. In arriving at this judgment, many professional accountants, like very many others, quite underestimated the impact of IT on organisational form. Machines were audited by running dummy transactions and comparing the output with standard answers. There were few attempts to audit the machine codes and programs being employed. The systems were comparatively simple and free-standing and not, as so often is the case now, connected to networks of remote processors. In short, many of the accountants responsible for IT took an arm's length view of the whole situation, and some serious consequences followed.

New Rare Breed of Specialist

The computer introduced an entirely novel group of highly trained or experienced specialists, often in a class quite apart from general office workers. The typical computing department under a data processing manager consisted of a systems manager in charge of groups of systems analysts; a programming manager with teams of programmers; an operations manager to control the data preparation supervisor; the operations supervisor whose operators ran the machines; and the control supervisor whose staff planned the operating schedules, and the issue of instructions and programs to the operators. In addition, there was often a computer department services manager responsible for the data processing audit, maintenance of standards, recruitment, selection and training of staff, and data administration. The keeping of records of all programs and of all changes made often entailed having an archivist as well. The network manager, responsible for maintaining compatibility and security of all machines and applications across local or wide area networks, became increasingly important. Many of the activities of these people are now supported by computing facilities.

Most of these specialists lived in a world of their own, apart from the rest of the company and somewhat alienated. They were physically divorced from their colleagues, often living in relatively modern, air-conditioned, and clean conditions which were rarely typical of office work in the seventies. Because the big temperamental machines demanded shift and weekend work, the working hours of these very highly-paid specialists were quite different from those of executives, office workers, and were often more akin to those on a factory floor.

Most companies found there was a constant queue for new programming and for new systems analysis and design. Systems and computer specialists were in very short supply, and commanded very high rewards. Most attention was directed to meeting the demands for new systems. In the early days, the maintenance of computing systems suffered. Often these specialists had educational backgrounds different from their superiors and had quite different interests. Their first, and usually enthusiastic, commitment was to a technology that required their constant attention and much nurturing. Some were quite uninformed about their company's business or even the strategic role that data processing played in company affairs.

Specialists Confounded

As the technology changed, the specialists often found themselves marooned with very narrow skills and able to cope only with the particular systems on which they had served their apprenticeships. They, with the help of the hardware suppliers, often defended these systems long after they had become outdated and unsustainable. Few in the company outside their ranks had sufficient knowledge to challenge their judgment on technical matters. Initially the driving force for innovation, some of these experts became very resistant to suggestions for change. Instead, they viewed change as threatening years of hard work. Few of these specialists took kindly to user-driven computing, both when minicomputers became widely available and when the much more serious challenge to their positions arose with the microcomputer. These highly specialised and narrowly adapted people were not only the gatekeepers to the use of the technology, they were also the gatekeepers to its evolution. Sometimes, these individuals stood against any innovation such as the introduction of user-driven micro computing. Later, when most companies had almost filled their portfolios of new IT, maintenance of old systems became the main task of specialists. As this became routine, job satisfaction of the specialists diminished. Their creative urge was frustrated, and many of the brightest drifted away to other more intellectually demanding activities.

The microcomputer drove IT even further away from the direct control of the accountants, but it did serve to overcome the problem of queues for system design and programming. Even where companies had no policy at all for adopting microcomputers, computer buffs brought their hobby to work and inspired others with it. Soon many of the small "nice to have" programs were up and running, often in spite of the computer department. The new alternative technology presented itself as a strange mixture of hardware and operating systems of varying sophistication. Initially, mastery of BASIC or a similar language was essential. But soon word processors and spreadsheets made such skills redundant. The need for support of a new kind grew because the expertise that the big engines needed was inappropriate. There were very few outside experts to help. Suppliers of hardware and software were over-stretched. Many products came to market inadequately tested, and machine and program failures abounded.

The management of computing suddenly became very complex and beyond the competence of many IT specialists. Small data bases sprang up here and there, and incompatible hardware proliferated in wild variety. Management made almost desperate attempts to ensure that the ownership of information held on all data bases belonged to the company as a whole. Despite this, as people came and went over time, user departments lost important data. Programs and data were inadequately documented and poorly protected. Data bases became corrupted. Home-grown systems were allowed to crash irrecoverably, and users constantly produced incompatible systems. The users became a powerful class in real competition with the specialists. If the computer specialists did not meet their demands, they would meet them themselves, and in their own idiosyncratic ways. Computing ceased to be a technological problem and became, and remains, mainly a "people" problem.

One solution was to try to network all the systems so they could share common data bases. Because of the variety of operating systems introduced by the enthusiasts, networking in large companies became a nightmare. The management of IT was too important to be left with the technologists. Managerialism invaded the field, and new specialisms are appearing now to act as gatekeepers. Network managers tried both to create compatibility between systems developed by end-users, and develop seamless communications between all the systems in use. Information resource managers include in their duties ensuring that information is properly a corporate property; functions do not keep information to themselves; there are proper security standards; and users design, document, secure and archive programs properly. These new specialisms may soon become very highly developed in their own right. They may well become professionalised and succeed in closing ranks against such outsiders as accountants. The accountancy profession may lose all the great advantages the profession had at the outset of the IT revolution.

Money Numbers and Information

Accountants have contested with other professions for the control of the company's information (e.g. with engineers measuring the weight of coal needed to produce a pound of steam). The assumption was that more information would provide the means of exercising more effective control. Since money numbers were often the only systematic records available over long periods, they were adopted as the foundation of most organisational control systems. So-called management accounting was a money-number response to meet an apparent need for control information. But the accountancy profession only recognised this lately. Management accounting, already an expensive practice, is perhaps becoming even more expensive by the adoption of zero-based or activity-based accounting (the fashions change frequently). This reflects only a small and very narrow aspect of a very complex interacting and interactive system. For example, what is the point of knowing to the nearest decimal place the direct production cost of a product when price and volume of sales are arbitrarily determined by a fickle market, indirect costs determined by an arbitrary allocation of overheads, or interest rates determined by the views of government? Yet management accounting is taken with such seriousness that line managers may have to be counselled by accountants when they look at cost indicators. These indicators can do no more than reveal to line managers what they should have already determined from their management information system.

Money numbers are quite inadequate measures of economy, efficiency, and effectiveness, the watchwords of the managerial culture. Few managers manage money. Instead, they manage the disposition and control of very physical resources. Managers measure such things as machine performance, standard minutes required to perform specific work, and the disposal of stock before its sell-by date. The money-evaluation of information still presents an intractable problem despite the patent fact that IT is now probably the first among the regular big spenders.

The largest accountancy firms have diversified so widely, into so many different activities, that it is legitimate to question whether some are accountants at all. So great is the variety of services offered, it seems unlikely that the accountancy profession as a whole will adapt very easily to the new technology. However, there will be a few pockets of substantial expertise such as in computer-audit that opens up the black box. The designers and owners of all the information systems in the company might have once been accountants. My belief is that a crucial moment has passed, and accountants will not be able to regain that most important power base. The repositioning of the accountancy profession is due as much to the professionalising of managers and to the emergence of the managerial discourse, as it is to the new IT. So, how did management come to aspire to the lofty category of a profession? How do managers seem to challenge the accountancy profession for the head of the boardroom table?

Professionalising Managers

It may seem odd to point to printing as the efficient cause for the emergence of what has come to be called management today. Printing is, perhaps, the most significant of all IT in history. The ancient Chinese are said to have invented printing, but it was Gutenberg's press that enabled the printed word to reach out to educate, inform, and discipline people far and wide. With Pacioli and his contemporaries, printing became the vehicle for the professionalisation of the businessman. Contrary to the conventional wisdom of his time, the publication of Pacioli's handbook on bookkeeping de-mystified an arcane practice and revealed to all the dark secrets of bookkeeping. Of course, the numbers of people who had access to these secrets must have been few. Pacioli (1494) indicated that anyone with cash, an accounting, mathematical ability, and an orderly set of properly kept books could be a successful businessman. Perhaps Pacioli was really promoting the professionalisation of the businessman when he preached the gospel of double-entry?

By the late eighteenth century in the West, the printing press and increasing literacy were seemingly leading people away from mindless tradition, ignorance, and fear of the unknown towards a "daring to know." This is associated with the Age of Reason, the genesis of modern scientific inquiry, and the development of many useful technologies (Eisenstein, 1979). After Adam Smith's (1776) *tour de force*, a management view emerged that (despite all efforts to decry, castigate, or ignore it) remains to this day the dominant view of all those in business. Efficiency, economy, and effectiveness, the commodification of the firm, and the respect of market forces as determinants of the value of things and people alike, have largely eclipsed notions of trust, accountability, prudence, personal responsibility, and custodianship. The values of the manager are measurable and readily embraced by IT. Paradoxically, those of the accountancy profession are not.

Traditions of dismissing ivory tower academics, and of admiring practical men (the more unlettered the better), flourished and still persist. Of course, this has served the accountancy profession well by allowing it to maintain a veil over its secrets, and ensuring the continuation of arcane rites and practices by a comparatively small band of initiates. Neither literacy nor numeracy, beyond the level of the three R's (reading, (w)riting and (a)rithmetic), was essential for membership in the managerial community. It has taken a long time for Pacioli's penny to drop. Only in the last few decades has the need to educate managers and businessmen in matters of accountancy been widely acknowledged. But what has been provided by the educational system are techniques and methodologies rather than a liberal education. The practical use of the tools of the manager has been drilled into many, but few have any deep understanding of the assumptions, evidence, and principles which underlie the craft.

Technology and Managerial Detachment

Managers once walked about and conversed with their work force on the job. The managerial revolution started in the early twentieth century (Burnham, 1941), and successfully established managers as a new class in society quite distinct from those of the older professions, the owners and their agents, accountants, technicians, salaried staff, and wage earners. Managers had little choice but to converse eye-ball to eye-ball with their workforce. Although the workforce was indeed literate, there were no practical means of communicating other than by word of mouth until the typewriter made its mark. With the advent of the typewriter, managers retreated into the less challenging tranquillity of their offices, and issued instructions in writing. The transcription of notebook jottings into formal typewritten reports aided communications in the other direction from the workplace to the now remote managers.

Access to the typing pool became a coveted asset, but pool typists often became gatekeepers, giving priority to the work of some and delaying that of others. Access to a secretary or typist became a status symbol. The personal secretaries, secretarial assistants, and administrative assistants often exerted amazing power in the way they controlled access to the "boss." The management literature has little to say about the role of the typewriter (machine or person) in the power game of business organisations. Typists remained in this position until the personal computer eventually liberated managers, and forced managers to control their own work flow simply by forcing managers to do it themselves. Now the comparable status symbol is possession of a personal computer.

Documents, Devices and Drilled People

IT in the form of "documents, devices, and drilled people" allows management by remote control, just as its precursors, the chart, compass, and astrolabe and the skills of sailors, navigators, and astronomers, enabled management at a distance in the days of the merchant venturers (Law, 1986).   The typewriter also supported, maybe even created, a tremendous growth of bureaucratic hierarchies. From the interactions between businessmen, accountants, managers, typists, typewriters, and typescripts, a new way is seen of viewing and manipulating the world. The typewritten words and statistical reports initiated by managers came to carry nearly as much authority as the table of money numbers from the accountant. The same halo of truth beyond question now surrounds computer-produced information.

The technology of the typewriter and its successors performed a role similar to that performed by Pacioli's technology. This is the case when technology is defined as those things necessary to the successful businessman, and excluded absolutely everything that he could not put on the right and the left side of a book. Through the form of its technology alone (by its method of communicating rather than by the content of its communications), the typewriter, interacting with the people around it, defined what was to be managed, what it was to be a manager, and what were the things being managed. The manager could now see the world only as abstracted, simplified, refined, and constrained to contain only those aspects that typewriting could communicate. In short, it was simple enough to be describable in short words and in short reports. All else was, and maybe still is, irrelevant.

This is a reminder of an aspect of IT that serves to undermine the incompetent.   The statistics of past work performance, reports of appraisal interviews, of what managers did, said, and reported they thought, moved from the personal and private to the public domain. Records, especially those of failures, might remain forever, to be seen by virtually anyone. Did this not serve to make managers more conservative and cautious? Does this persistence of records not encourage managers to move from job to job to escape the pursuing records of their failures? Will not the ease of information gathering and recording using today's IT increase vastly what is held in evidence? Could it not be that record-keeping has killed off the spirit of enterprise except amongst the most foolhardy?

In the early days of the IT revolution, there was an explosive increase in the volume of information produced. Managers ignored much of it. Now computer-supported exception reporting is more widely employed, and shared data bases and inquiring systems allow accountants and managers to determine for themselves what is important and what is not.   The flood of information seems containable. The hazard lurking here is that management may well relax and leave the computers to look after the work. But, if the thresholds for making the exception reports have been wrongly set, then what?

How Information Is Used

This section examines what typical managers do with information received.

Information for Managerial Control

Managers are often content to find satisficing short-term solutions to their problems, rather than optimising long-term ones. They, like everyone else, have only limited perceptual and information-processing capabilities. Simon (1957) called this bounded rationality, so there are strict limits to the complexity with which managers can cope. Managers have to address many incompatible goals (Flood and Carson, 1988). They are often much more concerned with interchanging opinion and gossip with others than with formulating and understanding computational models of problem situations (Mintzberg, 1973). Often managers just try to muddle through (Lindblom, 1959; and Tversky and Kahneman, 1980).

When managers do address data and try to make sense out of the information set, there is strong evidence that they ignore base-rate data (the prior probabilities resident in a given situation) if these do not seem to fit into their own causal scheme of things. Managers do not intuitively multiply the probabilities of the components of a compound event when estimating the probability of that event (Cohen and Hansel, 1958). Because managers ignore or discount disconfirming evidence, they are subject to illusory correlations that persist in the face of disconfirming evidence (Chapman and Chapman, 1967; and Einhorn and Hogarth, 1978). Even when it is more efficient to seek disconfirming evidence, they do not seek it (Wason, 1960). Managers tend to overestimate the probability of conjunctive events and underestimate that of disjunctive events (Cohen et al, 1972). They have overconfidence in predictions based on scant evidence, and quite redundant information enhances their level of confidence. Managers tend to ignore sample sizes and focus instead on other sample and population variables (Peterson et al, 1965). They overestimate the appearance of randomness in small runs (i.e. managers commit the gambler's fallacy - the ill-founded belief that a system such as a roulette wheel has a memory, and that after a run of one result the probability of another result increases). And they take extreme observations as representative of underlying processes (Kahneman et al, 1982).

Information in Novel Situations

The directions in which managers' attention moves when confronted by problem situations are also of interest. When things start to go wrong, they direct attention to imposing more control like the existing control mechanisms, rather than to reviewing the nature of those controls and considering how to change them. Managers tend to ignore or suppress actions that do not conform to this view (Pfeffer, 1977). Management usually views itself as the sole causal agent in the organisation, and this minimises the influence of non-managerial agents (Hofstede, 1978). Middle management groups and the relationships between them can change only infrequently, but senior management tends to change strategies much more frequently (Aitken et al, 1980). Senior management presumes, usually erroneously, that the existing systems with just a little adaptation are capable of implementing quite substantial changes (Clegg 1975; and Kantar, 1984).

Information and Accountancy Profession

This writer knows of no research to discover whether members of the accountancy profession, with their presumed-to-be-superior educational qualifications, are as prone to misunderstand numeric and statistical information as were managers.

Education and the End of Conversation

The writer's preception is that many students of accountancy are only reluctantly numerate, and have limited fascination with statistics, management science, operational research, systems dynamics or information systems analysis and design. Computing science is not their most popular subject, and few seem interested in either logic or mathematics. The writer's evidence is small, but his belief is strong that either earlier schooling, or later pecuniary ambitions, have largely swamped accounting students' interests in anything other than gaining an entry qualification to a respectable and rewarding occupation. In establishing what the educational requirements for the accountancy profession might best be in the future, perhaps a research effort should be undertaken. This effort would examine whether accountancy is still a profession with a real interest in furthering an understanding of its own domain and the domains around it, not just a craft to be practised in a routine way. The other question which is seemingly rarely addressed is why managers pay such scant attention to the implications of the information they get. Managers pay so much for information and still demand more. As accountants are among those confronted by such demands, they may well believe that information is management's "comfort toy," but it is not really in their own interest to let the world into that secret!

IT will play an ever-increasing role in teaching accountancy, if for no other reason than classes and tutorials everywhere are becoming so large that teaching is becoming de-personalised. The world into which students today are entering is dominated by IT. But, arguably, this technology has an immense and almost insuperable shortcoming in both everyday use and in use as a teaching medium. This idea is not one that has concerned many discussing the subject in the literature. IT is excellent at communicating. Communications are the means of ensuring regulation and compliance with norms. Although IT provides powerful means of communicating between people who share the same views of the world and who do not need to debate the meanings of words and ideas, it really does inhibit conversations (Robb, 1987; 1993a; and 1993b).

Conversations are the media for the critical review of presently-held truths. They entail dialectical interaction between people who do not share exactly the same view of the world. Conversations enable people to appreciate some situations as novel, allow the setting up of new posts from which the world can be viewed in a different light and with a new perspective, and require new and shared distinctions to be drawn.   They are the way that organised society redefines the boundaries around its core values, and adapts them to the constantly changing situation in the world of personal discourse.   Conversations are also the means by which the "world beyond" can be explored, the undefined, undistinguished world still unexplained in the terms of present conversations.   Conversations are the engine of creativity and the means of changing those norms.   Total disagreement and total agreement both eliminate conversations.   Vitality stops if conversation stops.

IT provides facilities for human interaction that are so primitive, compared with everyday life, that real conversations are impossible. Individuals can say nothing spontaneously, convey no nuances or colours, and have to put everything on the record.   Because people have to use the written word, there must be long delays between the moves in any conversational game as whole sentences of grammatically correct form are constructed and transmitted.   All non-verbal indicators are filtered out.

Programmed-learning texts and machine-supported teaching were in use long before the appearance of electronic computers (Pask, 1960; and Cram, 1961).   Now multi-media computer-based learning stations connected to many sources of information are becoming available. The main constraint is the availability of suitable course material. However, document readers could download conventional course material on to electronic media.   Over the longer term, multimedia interactive teaching, learning, and testing programs will be created much more easily and cheaply.   This will become the norm for most instruction, just as the printed textbook eventually did after there had been much debate about whether the printed word was as true as the hand-inscribed word.   The suppliers of packaged application programs have already improved their help facilities so that off-the-screen instruction in personal computing is becoming much less necessary. To take full advantage of this, end-users, managers, directors, and accountants alike will, if they have not done so already, have to acquire considerable keyboard skills, real understandings of the capabilities of their applications programs, and a responsible approach to security and filing.   The distinctions between IT specialists and users will become increasingly blurred.   In time, even the board of directors will be computer-literate, if only because the illiterate will have retired!

This is all very well, but the key to successful teaching and learning lies in just that conversation which modern teaching and IT so patently lack (Robb, 1993b). There is hope yet, perhaps. As long ago as 1972, Gordon Pask and the writer constructed and successfully demonstrated a device CHARLIE-GAS at the National Ideal Homes Exhibition at Olympia (Robb, 1979). This was an automatic salesman which discovered the cognitive style of its potential customer, and adapted its presentation accordingly, at the same time as offering the product best suited to the customer's need.[2] To the writer's knowledge, little has been done since then to develop adaptive conversational computing on a commercial scale. Yet, the need is obvious, and the knowledge and technology are available. Perhaps we have to wait until IT delivers virtual reality, and includes people with different cognitive maps in the scene. In the meantime, IT must drag individuals, probably unwittingly, into a pit of conversational silence. A long time has passed since poetry and rhetoric had a place in the business discourse. Now, conversation will probably decay, and gradually people will come to believe that computer mediated signalling is all that is needed. With no very clear idea where technology is going, with ever larger classes, and with such naive computer assistance, education (as distinct from teaching a skill) is going to become very difficult indeed.

ORGANISATIONS, PRESENT AND FUTURE

IT has mediated organisational changes in various ways. These all affect the accountancy profession and include the tendency towards what appears to be participative and shared management, the ever more detailed nature of surveillance, the development of internal markets, and changing boundaries of organisations.

Participative and Shared Management

There are many ways in which managers try to persuade staff to share more of the responsibility of management. These have various guises such as commitment to customer service, just-in-time, right first time, towards total quality, re-engineering the organisation, and so on. Charters or mission statements and similar protestations of commitment express the rhetoric of these efforts to change. Pertinent to this discussion, there are elaborate information systems set up to monitor performance and to hold people personally accountable for specific aspects of the work, despite the rhetoric which often stresses team-work and cooperative effort. In the frantic search for performance indicators, practically everything that is measurable about people has to be measured (Hacking, 1990). The classification of attributes of people in order to make measurements has the effects of forming them to fit what the measurers, usually (anonymous) institutions, deem to be good (Hanson, 1993).

Appearances are deceptive. The ability provided by information systems to measure outputs in all their aspects, not just costs, is enabling the development of output-oriented control. Output control focuses on the end-products of work and, in theory at least, pays much less attention to the method of production. No one discusses what happens when games are played with numbers to ensure success.[3] Research, such as that performed by Lilley (1993), is urgently needed to reflect upon the interaction between IT and the new managerial agenda.

Universal Surveillance

Newer forms of organisation may appear to allow greater autonomy to the periphery, to the group, or to the individual. But IT enables ever more stringent and detailed control from the centre as the need should arise. The early technologies of surveillance and control were limited in their scope and resolution. Statistically-defined samples were used as surrogates for the populations of interest, and controls were exercised on the assumption that individuals would conform to the behaviour presented by stereotypes. The new IT makes intensive and intimate surveillance possible. Its nature is such that those being surveyed become ever more exactly defined and individuated, while those who conduct the surveillance become ever more remote and anonymous (as Foucault [1980] has observed). Indeed, effective control of individual behaviour can be exercised by an information system which has just the potential to observe. Real observers may not be needed at all. For example, the roadside box which might, or might not, contain a speed camera has been found to provide an effective deterrent to speeding.

Development of Internal Markets

IT makes the formation of internal markets within companies possible, and with this comes entirely new ways of organising work. Contractual relations between parts of the company dissolve the hierarchical arrangement of authority and responsibility, and they move higher management even further away from the action. Each autonomous unit is responsible for organising its own work, forming its own contracts with other parts of the company or with other suppliers, and (if things go wrong) for negotiating the allocation of responsibility and excess costs. IT has created great opportunities for the accountancy profession to move into situations such as these. IT can assist in forming contracts, evaluating competitive tenders, and making the adjustments for variations and errors. If money-accountants are needed in business, they would seem more likely to be able to flourish as financial advisors, arbitrators or, as recently proposed, as assessors of financial reports (McInnes, 1993). All these activities could become as pertinent to each of the sub-units as they are to the whole.

Changing Boundaries of Organisations

The boundaries of the accounting entity have often had to change because of mergers and divestments, as the commodification of companies goes on. Accountancy has had to wrestle with merging incompatible systems when companies merge, and redesigning information systems when companies divide. The rate of change of ownership and of types of custodianship, already high, will increase as ever more ingenuity bears on these issues. The boundaries of organisations are also likely to continue to change over time in quite another way, as ideas such as "companies should take social responsibility" and "the polluter pays" gain ground. In the future, as technology becomes more mature, and when technical developments enable databases in both the public and private domains to become more accessible, changes of accounting boundaries to encompass this kind of redefinition will become much easier. It will become progressively more feasible to meet the growing demands for accountability of a pluralistic society.

As Mepham (1987) demonstrated some time ago, accounting (and information processing generally) can be performed by recording transactions in a database and extracting accounts in whatever forms are required by running different pre-designed programs (tailored to some generally agreed accounting standard) to meet the needs of each stakeholder. The profession has in this notion another opportunity of extending its expertise to embrace not only money numbers but all the data, numeric and written, available in the company.

CONCLUSIONS

IT has done much to support accountancy in the practical business of preparing financial statements and operating money control systems. It will do much more in the future to teach (if not to educate) accountants. However, the profession has not profoundly influenced the development of IT. The profession did have an opportunity of capturing the power over the production of information when IT was first applied by accountants to bulk data processing. But it did not take full advantage of its position.

Most accountants allowed computer experts to develop and control the corporate use of IT. In time, newer technologies displaced successive generations of experts and, at every major change, there was an opportunity for the accountancy profession to reassert itself and assume a dominant position. The changes are continuing, and the profession has the opportunity now to address the issues of planning the development of IT. The profession could have a hand in moves towards standardisation, and accountancy could play a part in promoting new systems with flexibility and compatibility with existing systems. The profession could also assume an important, maybe a dominant, role in solving the problems of network management and of standardising inter-company digital communications. The profession needs information systems that can easily present information in a wide variety of formats. The pluralistic company needs information tailored properly for all its stakeholders. Systems should be seamless in use. Yet, when the needs arise, they should be divisible into viable parts or capable of forming viable wholes. This aspect of information systems has received scant attention. The accountancy profession deals with mergers and demergers and internal as well as external markets, so it has some interest in this.

The accountancy profession could vastly widen its scope by relinquishing narrow definitions of accountancy that refer to money numbers, and adopt a more practical and catholic position. Accountancy uses all kinds of information to chronicle, explain, forecast, plan, execute, and control activities. Some might argue that information and its supporting technology are quite separate and distinct, and the technology should be able to deliver the needed information. Certainly, IT will if there is a large market and if product development receives sufficient resources. However, the user-clients have already absorbed much technology and have got into quite a situation in the process. IT has already delivered big labour savings, and the profession has yet to come up with a rational way of justifying IT investment on any other grounds.

The writer's belief is that the profession is very alert to the opportunities for auditing computer-supported accounting systems. But should accountancy not extend its interest into the technical auditing of managerial information and control systems too? Their reliability and security from interference are becoming ever more important as they provide the bases for compliance with elaborate contractual arrangements and complex systems of reward (and punishment) associated with both internal and external markets.

The question is proposed about whether the profession will succumb to the growing managerial discourse. Accountancy, whatever its shortcoming, portrays itself as being about accountability and responsibility, prudence, custodianship, and preventing the abuse of power. The new discourse is all about effectiveness, economy, and efficiency within very narrow fields, sub-units of companies, and short time frames. The managerial discourse has armed with the full panoply of IT and is a formidable force. Will the profession become as well accoutred? And, can it prevail, or will it in turn succumb and be sidelined? The gravest shortcoming of IT is its pathetic incapacity to adapt interactively with its users in a conversational mode. It is not the sole responsibility of the accountancy profession to remedy this. It is the responsibility of everyone and anyone concerned with saving education, the professions, and the whole of society from mindless mechanisation by well-meaning but ill-equipped technologists.

This chapter has shown that managers have a tremendous respect for information. Yet they pay little regard to what information can tell them. It has been suggested that it might be worth the effort to determine just how much accountants understand such matters. Discussion is needed concerning whether the notions of reason and calculation on which both the profession and IT founded themselves are strictly sufficient. Forecasting and planning were thought to be as essential in business as in government. They have failed spectacularly in politics. Business keeps its secrets better (but planning in that domain has fared no better). Correlations have been repeatedly confused with causal relations, and much of what has passed for knowledge in business and administration is mere superstition. In their pursuit of efficiency, economy and effectiveness, accountants and their academic supporters have assiduously ignored the effects of their narrow perspectives on the environment, the structure and ethics of society, and the morale of individuals. The Comptroller and Auditor General has now added a fourth E, the environment to this list (Bourn, 1993). Maybe the accountancy profession will eventually follow this lead.

Now the world is far more uncertain. The future no longer seems predictable. Market forces (chance by another name), not business cycles, seem to rule. Every institution in society is being challenged and every expert is on trial. Experience is discounted; the past is no guide to the future. The new formula seems to be "do the best you can with as little as possible." No one tries to account for the costs of accounting and management information, and our ever more elaborate information and accounting systems are probably absorbing far more scarce resources than they are worth. The use of information may be just a ritual needed to rationalise and sanctify recommendations and decisions that have already been made and taken for other reasons, as advanced by Weick (1979). There is a real and terrifying possibility that all this investment in technology, all this anxiety, and effort have no further purpose.

NOTES

1.   This may well lie at the heart of the accountancy dilemma, the problem of depicting both the flow of resources and their value at any particular moment.

2.   Many customers preferred dealing with the machine because it was not biased. In fact, it proved to be much more adaptive than its human counterparts!   It was built from bits of an old telephone exchange and a multi-track tape recorder.   It owed nothing to digital computing.   It was, however, a first tentative step towards a psychologically-adaptive machine able to engage in something which passed for conversation because it spoke its customer's language in some sense.

3.   For example, the railway's Customers' Charter promised compensation to passengers if the trains ran late.   At first, the company defined that late was to be measured at the ultimate destination.   This provoked a public outcry, and, reluctantly, the company agreed that late should be measured at each destination on the route.   In the event, many trains ran late by this revised definition and it cost the company very dear.   The solution was to add minutes to running times published in the time tables right across the network. Now all the trains are running later than they were all of the time, but very few fail to match the published timetable, so very much less compensation has to be paid out.   Success!

BIBLIOGRAPHY

AAA Committee on Cost Concepts and Standards (1956), "Tentative Statement of Cost Concepts Underlying Reports for Management Purposes," *The Accounting Review*, April, pp.182-93.

AAA Committee to Prepare a Statement of Basic Accounting Theory (1966), *A Statement of Basic Accounting Theory*, American Accounting Association, Sarasota: FL.

AAA Committee on Courses in Managerial Accounting (1972), "Report of the Committee on Courses in Managerial Accounting," *Supplement to The Accounting Review*, Vol.47, pp.1-13.

AAA Committee on Concepts and Standards for External Financial Reports (1977), *Statement on Accounting Theory and Theory Acceptance*, American Accounting Association, Sarasota: FL.

Accountancy (1991), "EC Obstacle to Harmonisation," *Accountancy*, May, p.12.

Accountancy (1992), "The Great Accounts Shake-Up Begins," *Accountancy*, May, p.9.

Accountancy (1993a), "Profession Faces a Regulation Cookbook," *Accountancy*, January, p.9.

Accountancy (1993b), "ASB Discussion Paper Gets Short Shrift," *Accountancy*, August, p.11.

Accountancy (1993c), "ASB Under Fire," *Accountancy*, November, p.16.

Accountancy (1993d), "IASs Must Be Used, Pledges New Chief," *Accountancy*, February, p.16.

Accountancy (1994a), "ASB at `Crossroads,'" *Accountancy*, April, p.17.

Accountancy (1994b), "FRED 8 Could Have Stopped Maxwell," *Accountancy*, April, p.17.

Accountancy (1994c), "Testing the Ceiling," *Accountancy*, February, p.1.

Accountancy (1994d), "Standard Relief for Small Companies," *Accountancy*, December, p.11.

Accountancy (1994e), "Big GAAP/Little GAAP: The True and Fair Override," *Accountancy*, December, p.23.

Accountancy Age (1994), "UK: E&Y Slam Provisions Proposals," *Accountancy Age*, 28 April, p.3.

Accounting Standards Steering Committee (ASSC) (1971), "Disclosure of Accounting Policies," *Statement of Standard Accounting Practice 2*, Accounting Standards Steering Committee, London.

Accounting Standards Steering Committee (ASSC) (1975), "The Corporate Report," *Discussion Paper*, Accounting Standards Steering Committee, London.

Accounting Today (1994a), Comment, *Accounting Today*, 7 February, p.4.

Accounting Today (1994b), "IASC's Shiratori Slams IOSCO for Reporting Differences," *Accounting Today*, 12 December, pp.12 and 60.

Aho, J. A. (1985), "Rhetoric and the Invention of Double-Entry Bookkeeping," *Rhetorica*, Winter, pp.21-43.

AICPA (1973), *Objectives of Financial Statements*, American Institute of Certified Public Accountants, New York: NY.

AICPA (1992), "Mark to Market Accounting: Theory, Politics, and Economic Consequences," *Case No. 92-05*, American Institute of Certified Public Accountants, New York: NY.

AICPA (1994), "Improving Business Reporting - A Customer Focus: Meeting the Information Needs of Investors and Creditors," *Report of the AICPA Special Committee on Financial Reporting*, American Institute of Certified Public Accountants, New York: NY.

AIMR Financial Policy Committee (1992), *Financial Reporting in the 1990s and Beyond*, Association for Investment Management and Research: New York: NY.

Aitken, M., Bacharach, S. and French, L. (1980), "Organisation Structure, Work Process and Proposal Making in Administrative Bureaucracies," *Academy of Management Journal*, pp.631-52.

Anthony, R. N. (1955), *Management Accounting*, Irwin, Homewood, IL.

Anthony, R. N. (1970), *Management Accounting Principles*, Revised Edition, Irwin, Homewood, IL.

Anthony, R. N. (1973), "Some Fruitful Directions for Research in Management Accounting," in Dopuch, N. and Revsine, L. (eds.), *Accounting Research 1960-1970: A Critical Evaluation*, University of Illinois Press, Urbana: IL, pp.37-68.

Anthony, R. N. (1989), "Reminiscences About Management Accounting," *Journal of Management Accounting Research*, Fall, pp.1-20.

Antinori, C. (1959), Transcription of Luca Pacioli, *Summa de Arithmetica... Distinctio IX - Tractatus XI*, in *Rivista Bancaria - Minerva Bancaria*, Milan.

Aranya, N. (1974), "The Influence of Pressure Groups on Financial Statements in Britain," *Abacus*, June, pp.3-12.

Archer, S. (1992), "On the Methodology of a Conceptual Framework for Financial Accounting Part I: An Historical and Jurisprudential Analysis," *Accounting, Business and Financial History*, September, pp.199-227.

Argyris, C. and Schon, D. A. (1978), *Organisational Learning: A Theory of Action Perspective*, Addison-Wesley, Reading: MA.

Arnold, H. L. (1899), *The Complete Cost-Keeper*, The Engineering Magazine Press, New York: NY.

Arthur Andersen & Co. (1990), *Letter to ASC*, 28 September, Institute of Chartered Accountants in England and Wales Library.

Arthur Andersen & Co. (1991), *Post-Retirement Benefits Other Than Pensions: An Explanation of FASB Statement 106 and a Discussion of Implementation and Business Issues*, Arthur Andersen & Co., Chicago: IL.

ASB (1991), "The Objective of Financial Statements and the Qualitative Characteristics of Financial Information," *Exposure Draft Statement of Principles*, Accounting Standards Board, London.

ASB (1993), "Accounting for Capital Instruments," *Financial Reporting Standard 4*, Accounting Standards Board, London.

ASB (1994), *Inside Track*, No.1, October.

Ashby, W. R. (1952), *Design for a Brain*, Chapman and Hall, London.

Babbage, C. (1835), *On the Economy of Machinery and Manufactures*, Augustus Kelley Publishers, New York: NY (1963 reprint).

Baiman, S. (1990), "Agency Research in Management Accounting: A Second Look," *Accounting, Organisations and Society*, Vol.15 (4), pp.341-71.

Baker, N. (1993a), "ASB Predicts Bloody Reforms Battle," *Accountancy Age*, 28 October, p.1.

Baker, N. (1993b), "E&Y Attack on ASB Backfires," *Accountancy Age*, 23 September, p.10.

Baker, N. (1994a), "Goodwill, Acquisitions Rows to Begin," *Accountancy Age*, 6 January, p.1.

Baker, N. (1994b), "Goodwill and FRED 7 Will Test ASB's Strength," *Accountancy Age*, 6 January, p.11.

Baker N. (1994c), "Substance Wins Out for Off Balance Sheet Ruling," *Accountancy Age*, 13 April, p.13.

Baker N. (1994d), "Treatment of Goodwill Keeps ASB Pinned Down," *Accountancy Age*, 5 May, p.11.

Baladouni, V. (1986), "Financial Reporting in the Early Years of the East India Company," *The Accounting Historians Journal*, Spring, pp.19-30.

Ballewski, D. (1877), *Die Calculation von Maschinenfabriken*, Magdeburg.

Barwise, P., Higson, C., Likierman, A. and March, P. (1989), *Accounting for Brands*, Institute of Chartered Accountants in England and Wales, London.

Baskin, J. B. (1988), "The Development of Corporate Financial Markets in Britain and the United States 1600-1914: Overcome Asymmetric Information," *Business History Review*, Summer, pp.199-237.

Battersby, T. (1878), *The Perfect Double-Entry Bookkeeper*, J. Heywood, Manchester.

Baxter, W. T. (1981), "Accounting History as a Worthwhile Study," *The Accounting Historians Notebook*, Spring, pp.5-8.

Baxter, W. T. (1989), "Early Accounting: The Tally and Checkerboard," *The Accounting Historians Journal*, December, pp.43-83.

Belkaoui, A. (1980), *Conceptual Foundations of Management Accounting*, Addison-Wesley, Reading: MA.

Belkaoui, A. (1989), *The Coming Crisis in Accounting*, Quorum Books, New York: NY.

Benson, H. (1989), *Accounting for Life*, Kogan Page, London.

Beresford, D. R. (1993), "International Harmonisation of Accounting Standards and Cooperation between the United States and Japan," *FASB Viewpoints*, 7 July, pp.10-15.

Berton, L. (1993), "Accounting Rules Board Is Under Fire As It Nears Decision on Two Key Issues," *Wall Street Journal*, 6 April, p.A2.

Bircher, P. (1988), "Company Law Reform and the Board of Trade, 1929-1943," *Accounting and Business Research*, Spring, pp.107-19.

Bircher, P. (1994), "A Taxing Decision Ahead for the ASB," *Accountancy*, September, p.100.

Bledstein, B. J. (1976), *The Culture of Professionalism: The Middle Class and the Development of Higher Education in America*, W. W. Norton & Co., New York: NY.

BPP (British Parliamentary Papers) (1849), *Minutes of Evidence*, Select Committee on the Audit of Railway Accounts, London.

BPP (British Parliamentary Papers) (1877), *Report and Minutes of Evidence, etc.*, Select Committee on the Companies Acts 1862 and 1867, London.

BPP (British Parliamentary Papers) (1910), *Minutes of Evidence*, Departmental Committee on Railway Accounts and Statistical Returns, London.

BPP (British Parliamentary Papers) (1925), *Minutes of Evidence*, Company Law Amendment Committee, London.

BPP (British Parliamentary Papers) (1926), *Report*, Company Law Amendment Committee, London.

BPP (British Parliamentary Papers) (1945), *Report*, Committee on Company Law Amendment, London.

Boockholdt, J. L. (1983), "A Historical Perspective on the Auditor's Role: The Early Experience of the American Railroads," *The Accounting Historians Journal*, Spring, pp.69-86.

Bourn, J. (1993), "Value For Money in the United Kingdom's Marine Industries," *Journal of The Royal Society of Arts*, Vol.CXLI, No.5444, pp.803-7.

Boyd, E. (1905a), "Ancient Systems of Accounting," in Brown, R. (ed.), *A History of Accounting and Accountants*, T. C. and E. C. Jack, Edinburgh, pp.16-40.

Boyd, E. (1905b), "Early Forms of Accounts," in Brown, R. (ed.), *A History of Accounting and Accountants*, T. C. and E. C. Jack, Edinburgh, pp.41-73.

Boyd, E. (1905c), "The History of Auditing," in Brown, R. (ed.), *A History of Accounting and Accountants*, T. C. and E. C. Jack, Edinburgh, pp.74-92.

Boyd, E. (1905d), "Early Italian Accountants," in Brown, R. (ed.), *A History of Accounting and Accountants*, T. C. and E. C. Jack, Edinburgh, pp.173-180.

Brady, N. (1991), "ASB Off-Balance Sheet Initiative Runs Into Trouble," *The Accountant*, 2 December, p.19.

Braverman, H. (1974), *Labour and Monopoly Capital*, Monthly Review Press, New York: NY.

Bricker, R. J. and Previts, G. J. (1990), "The Sociology of Accountancy: A Study of Academic and Practice Community Schisms," *Accounting Horizons*, March, pp.1-14.

Brief, R. P. (Ed.), (1986), *Corporate Financial Reporting and Analysis in the Early 1900s*, Garland Publishing, New York: NY.

Briloff, A. J. (1990), "Accountancy and Society: A Covenant Desecrated," *Critical Perspectives on Accounting*, March, pp.5-30.

Brink, H. L. (1992), "A History of Philips' Accounting Policies on the Basis of Its Annual Reports," *European Accounting Review*, December, pp.255-75.

Bromwich, M. and Bhimani, A. (1989), *Management Accounting: Evolution Not Revolution*, The Chartered Institute of Management Accountants, London.

Bromwich, M. and Bhimani, A. (1991), "Strategic Investment Appraisal," *Management Accounting*, March, pp.45-8.

Bromwich, M. and Hopwood, A. (eds.) (1992a), *Accounting and the Law*, Prentice Hall, London.

Bromwich, M. and Hopwood, A. (1992b), "The Intertwining of Accounting and Law," in Bromwich, M. and Hopwood, A. (eds.) *Accounting And The Law*, Prentice Hall, London, pp.1-14.

Brown, R. (1905a), "Scotland - Before the Charters," in Brown, R. (ed.), *A History of Accounting and Accountants*, T. C. and E. C. Jack, Edinburgh, pp.181-202.

Brown, R. (1905b), "Scottish Chartered Accountants," in Brown, R. (ed.), *A History of Accounting and Accountants*, T. C. and E. C. Jack, Edinburgh, pp.203-31.

Brown, R. (1905c), "England and Ireland," in Brown, R. (ed.), *A History of Accounting and Accountants*, T. C. and E. C. Jack, Edinburgh, pp.232-52.

Brown, R. (1905d), "The United States of America," in Brown, R. (ed.), *A History of Accounting and Accountants*, T. C. and E. C. Jack, Edinburgh, pp.271-80.

Brown, R. (1905e), "Fiftieth Anniversary," in Brown, R. (ed.), *A History of Accounting and Accountants*, T. C. and E. C. Jack, Edinburgh, pp.401-49.

Brun, R. (1930), "A Fourteenth-Century Merchant of Italy," *Journal of Economic and Business History*, Vol.II(3), pp.451-66.

Bryer, R. A. (1993), "Double-Entry Bookkeeping and the Birth of Capitalism: Accounting for the Commercial Revolution in Medieval Northern Italy," *Critical Perspectives on Accounting*, June, pp.113-40.

Bunnell, C. (1911), *Cost Keeping for Manufacturing Plants*, D. Appleton and Company, New York: NY.

Burley, K. H. (1958), "Some Accounting Records of an Eighteenth Century Clothier," *Accounting Research*, January, pp.50-60.

Burnham, J. (1941), *The Managerial Revolution*, Pelican, Harmondsworth.

Burns, T. J. (1992), *US Accounting History 1965-1990*, Academy of Accounting Historians and The Ohio State University, Columbus: OH.

Byington, J. R. and Sutton, S. G. (1991), "The Self-Regulating Profession: An Analysis of the Political Monopoly Tendencies of the Audit Profession," *Critical Perspectives on Accounting*, December, pp.315-330.

Byrne, J. A. (1984), "The Cure That Kills," *Forbes*, 5 November, pp.210-11.

Byrne, J. A. (1993), "The Gravy Train Could Derail," *Business Week*, 15 March, p.31.

Cairns, D. (1993), "The IASC - 20 More Years of Vision And Commitment?," *Accountancy*, July, pp.72-3.

Camfferman, K. and Zeff, S. A. (1994), "The Contributions of Th. Limperg Jr. (1879-1961) to Dutch Accounting and Auditing," in Edwards, J. R. (ed.), *Twentieth-Century Accounting Thinkers*, Routledge, London, pp.112-41.

Canziani, A. (1994), "Gino Zappa (1879-1960)," in Edwards, J. R. (ed.), *Twentieth-Century Accounting Thinkers*, Routledge, London, pp. 142-65.

Caplan, E. H. (1966), "Behavioural Assumptions of Management Accounting," *The Accounting Review*, July, pp.496-509.

Carey, J. L. (1969a), "The Origins of Modern Financial Reporting," *Journal of Accountancy*, September, pp.35-48.

Carey, J. L. (1969b), *The Rise of the Accountancy Profession: From Technician to Professional 1896-1936*, American Institute of Certified Public Accountants, New York: NY.

Carey, J. L. (1970), *The Rise of the Accountancy Profession: To Responsibility and Authority 1937-1969*, American Institute of Certified Public Accountants, New York: NY.

Carmona, S. and Gutierrez, F. (1992), "Monopoly and Cost Management: The Case of the Royal Tobacco Factory (1773)," in Tsuji, A. (ed.), *Collected Papers of the Sixth World Congress of Accounting Historians*, Accounting History Association, Japan, Vol.II, pp.641-74.

Carr-Saunders, A. and Wilson, P. A. (1933), *The Professions*, Oxford University Press, Oxford.

Carsberg, B., Hope, A. and Scapens, R. W. (1974), "The Objectives of Published Accounting Reports," *Accounting and Business Research*, Summer, pp.162-73.

Chambers, R. J. (1965), "Financial Information and the Securities Market," *Abacus*, September, pp.3-30.

Chandler, A. D. (1977), *The Visible Hand: The Managerial Revolution in American Business*, Harvard University Press, Cambridge: MA.

Chandler, A. D. and Daems, H. (1979), "Administrative Co-ordination, Allocation and Monitoring: A Comparative Analysis of The Emergence of Accounting and Organisation in the USA and Europe," *Accounting, Organisations and Society*, Vol.1(2), pp.3-20.

Chandler, R. A. and Edwards, J. R. (1994) *Recurring Issues in Auditing*, Garland Publishing, New York: NY.

Chapman, L. J. and Chapman, J. P. (1967), "Genesis of Popular but Erroneous Psychodiagnostic Observations," *Journal of Abnormal Psychology*, No.72, pp.193-204.

Chatfield, M. (1977), *A History of Accounting Thought*, Robert E. Krieger Publishing Co., Huntington: NY.

Checkland, P. (1981), *Systems Thinking, Systems Practice*, John Wiley, Chichester.

Chen, R. S. (1975), "Social and Financial Stewardship," *The Accounting Review*, July, pp.533-43.

Cheney, G. A. (1994), "Stock Option Quest Sparks Questions About FASB's Future," *Accounting Today*, 10 October, pp.10 and 12.

Chiba, J. (1994), "Kiyoshi Kurosawa (1902-90): An Intellectual Portrait," in Edwards, J. R. (ed.), *Twentieth-Century Accounting Thinkers*, Routledge, London pp.181-97.

Choi, F. O. S. and Hiramatsu, K. (1987), *Accounting and Financial Reporting in Japan*, Van Nostrand Reinhold, London.

Chua, W. F. (1986), "Radical Developments in Accounting Thought," *The Accounting Review*, October, pp.601-32.

Church, A. H. (1901), "The Proper Distribution of Establishment Charges," *The Engineering Magazine*, Vol.XXI, pp.508-17, 725-34 and 904-12; and Vol.XXII, pp.31-40, 231-40 and 367-76.

Clanchy, M. (1975), "*Moderni* in Education and Government in England," *Speculum*, pp.671-88.

Clanchy, M. (1979), *From Memory to Written Record: England 1066-1307*, Edward Arnold, London.

Clark, J. M. (1923), *Studies in the Economics of Overhead Costs*, University of Chicago Press, Chicago: IL.

Clarke, F. L. and Dean, G. W. (1992), "The Views of Limperg and Schmidt: Discovering Patterns and Identifying Differences from a Chaotic Literature," *The International Journal of Accounting*, Vol.27(4) pp.288-309.

Clegg, S. (1975), *The Theory of Power and Organisation*, Routledge and Kegan Paul, London.

Coenenberg, A. G. and Schoenfeld, H. M. W. (1990), "The Development of Managerial Accounting in Germany: A Historical Analysis," *The Accounting Historians Journal*, December, pp.95-112.

Cohen, J. and Hansel, C. E. M. (1958), "The Nature of Decision in Gambling," *Acta Psychologica*, No.13, pp.357-70.

Cohen, J., Chesnick, E. I. and Haren, D. (1972), "A Confirmation of the Internal-Psi Effect in Sequential Choice and Decision," *British Journal of Psychology*, No.63, pp.41-6.

Colasse, B. and Durand, R. (1994), "French Accounting Theorists of the Twentieth Century," in Edwards, J. R. (ed.), *Twentieth-Century Accounting Thinkers*, Routledge, London, pp.41-59.

Cole, R. C., and Hales, H. L. (1991), *CIM Justification in the Process Industry: A Case Study*, National Association of Accountants, Montvale: NJ.

Cole, W. M. (1908), *Accounts: Their Construction and Interpretation*, Houghton Mifflin, New York.

Connon, H. (1992), "Still Too Much Rope," *Chartered Accountant*, February, p.52.

Cook, M. J., Freedman, E. M., Groves, R. J., Madonna, J. C., O'Malley, S. F. and Weinbach, L. A. (1992), "The Liability Crisis in the United States: Impact on the Accounting Profession," *Journal of Accounting*, November, pp.18-23.

Cooke, T. (1985), "SSAP 22 and 23: Do They Lack Clear Directives?," *Accountancy*, August, pp.101-4.

Cooper, R. and Kaplan, R. S. (1988), "How Cost Accounting Distorts Product Costs," *Management Accounting*, April, pp.20-7.

Costouros, G. J. (1979), "Early Greek Accounting on Estates (Fourth Century B.C.)," in Coffman, E. F. (ed.), *Working Paper 21, Working Paper Series Volume 2*, Academy of Accounting Historians, Richmond, pp.1-6.

Costouros, G. J. and Stull, J. B. (1989), "The Development of Letters and Numbers as Tools of Accounting," in Toudkar, R. H. and Coffman, E. N. (eds.), *Working Paper 1, Working Paper Series Volume 4*, Academy of Accounting Historians, Richmond, pp.160-69.

CPA Journal (1993), "In the Public Interest - *The CPA Journal* Symposium," *CPA Journal*, October, pp.30-8.

Cram, D. (1961), *Explaining Teaching Machines and Programming*, Fearon, San Francisco: CA.

Crichton, J. (1991), "Consolidated Accounts: Interpreting the Act," *Accountancy*, March, p.30.

Crivelli, P. (1924), *Double-Entry Book-Keeping: Fra Luca Pacioli* (an original translation) for the Institute of Book-Keepers (reprinted 1966).

Croizé, A. and Croizé, H. (1907), *De l'Inventaire Commercial*, Librairie Comptable Pigier, Paris.

Cronhelm, F.W. (1818), *Double-Entry by Single: A New Method of Bookkeeping*, Arno Press, New York: NY (reprinted 1978).

Daley, L. A., and Tranter, T. (1990), "Limitations on the Value of the Conceptual Framework in Evaluating Extant Accounting Standards," *Accounting Horizons*, March, pp.15-24.

Davidson, S. and Anderson, G. D. (1987), "The Development of Accounting and Auditing Standards," *Journal of Accountancy*, May, pp.110-27.

Davis, H. Z. and Strawser, J. A. (1993), "The Accounting Profession: Expert Witness and/or Advocate?," *Critical Perspectives on Accounting*, June, pp.141-54.

De Cazaux, L. F. G. (1824), *De la Comptabilité dans une Enterprise Industrielle et Spécialement dans une Exploitation Rurale*, J. M. Douladoure, Toulouse.

Defliese, P. L. (1981), "British Standards in a World Setting," in Leach, R. and Stamp, E. (eds.), *British Accounting Standards: The First Ten Years*, Woodhead-Faulkner, Cambridge, pp.105-18.

De Groote, L. H. V. (1978), "Two Sixteenth Century Accountants," in Yamey, B. S. (ed.), *The Historical Development of Accounting: A Selection of Papers*, Arno Press, New York: NY.

DeLuzio, M. C. (1993), "Management Accounting in a Just-in-Time Environment," *Journal of Cost Management*, Winter, pp.6-15.

Demski, J. S. (1967), "An Accounting System Structured on a Linear Programming Model," *The Accounting Review*, October, pp.701-12.

Demski, J. S. (1973), "The Nature of Management Accounting Research: A Comment," in Dopuch, N. and Revsine, L. (eds.), *Accounting Research 1960-1970: A Critical Evaluation*, University of Illinois Press, Urbana: IL, pp.69-78.

De Roover, R. (1938), "Characteristics of Bookkeeping Before Paciolo," *The Accounting Review*, June, pp.144-49.

De Roover, R. (1941), "A Florentine Firm of Cloth Manufacturers," *Speculum*, Vol.XVI(1), pp.3-33.

De Roover, R. (1956), "The Development of Accounting Prior to Luca Pacioli According to the Account Books of Medieval Merchants," in Littleton, A. C. and Yamey, B. S. (eds.), *Studies in the History of Accounting*, Sweet and Maxwell, London, pp.114-74.

de Ste. Croix, G. E. M. (1956), "Greek and Roman Accounting," in Littleton, A. C. and Yamey, B. S. (eds.), *Studies in the History of Accounting*, Sweet and Maxwell, London, pp.14-74.

Dickinson, A. L. (1924), "Publicity in Industrial Accounts: With a Comparison of English and American Methods," *The Accountant*, 4 October, pp.469-90.

Dicksee, L. R. (1892), *Auditing: A Practical Manual for Auditors*, Arno Press, New York: NY (reprinted 1976).

Dicksee, L. R. (1903), *Advanced Accounting*, Arno Press, New York: NY (reprinted 1976).

Dicksee, L. R. (1911), *Advanced Accounting*, Gee and Company, London.

Dicksee, L. R. (1927), *Published Balance Sheets and Window Dressing*, Arno Press, New York: NY (reprinted 1980).

Diemer, H. (1900), "The Commercial Organisation of the Machine Shop," *The Engineering Magazine*, Vol.XIX(3), pp.342-7; (4), pp.511-7; (5), pp.705-11; and (6), pp.892-8.

Dodson, J. (1750), *The Accountant or the Method of Book-keeping*, J. Norse, London.

Dopuch, N., Birnberg, J. G. and Demski, J. S. (1967), "An Extension of Standard Cost Variance Analysis," *The Accounting Review*, July, pp.526-36.

Dopuch, N. and Revsine, L. (eds.) (1973), *Accounting Research 1960-1970: A Critical Evaluation*, University of Illinois Press, Urbana: IL.

Drucker, P. F. (1963), "Managing for Business Effectiveness," *Harvard Business Review*, May-June, pp.53-60.

Drucker, P. F. (1993) "The Five Deadly Business Sins," *Wall Street Journal*, 21 October, p.A18.

Drury, C., and Braund, S. (1990), "The Leasing Decision: A Comparison of Theory And Practice," *Accounting and Business Research*, Summer, pp. 179-91.

Durham, J. W. (1992), "The Introduction of `Arabic' Numerals in European Accounting," *The Accounting Historians Journal*, December, pp.25-55.

Dyckman, T. R. (1973), "Some Fruitful Directions for Research in Management Accounting: Some Comments," in Dopuch, N. and Revsine, L. (eds.), *Accounting Research 1960-1970: A Critical Evaluation*, University of Illinois Press, Urbana: IL, pp.79-88.

Dyckman, T. R. (1974), "Public Accounting: Guild or Profession?," in Sterling R. R. (ed.), *Institutional Issues in Public Accounting*, Scholars Book Co., Houston: TX.

Economist (1991), "Bean-Counters Fight Back," *Economist*, 14 December, pp.85-6.

Economist (1992), "The Nine Lives of Creative Accounting," *Economist*, 28 November, p.91.

Economist (1993), "British Accounting Standards: Crunch Time," *Economist*, 19 April, pp.89-90.

Eden, C., Jones, S. and Sims, D. (1983), *Messing About in Problems*, Pergamon Press, Oxford.

Edey, H. C. (1989), "True Substance and Fair Reporting," in Macdonald, G. and Rutherford, B. A. (eds.), *Accounts, Accounting and Accountability*, Van Nostrand Reinhold, London, pp.61-70.

Edey, H. C. and Panitpakdi, P. (1956), "British Company Accounting and the Law 1844-1900," in Littleton, A. C. and Yamey, B. S. (eds.), *Studies in the History of Accounting*, Sweet and Maxwell, London, pp.356-79.

Edler, F. (1937), "Cost Accounting in the Sixteenth Century," *The Accounting Review*, July, pp.226-37.

Edwards, J. R. (1976), "The Accounting Profession and Disclosure in Published Reports, 1925-1935," *Accounting and Business Research*, Autumn, pp.289-303.

Edwards, J. R. (1981), *Company Legislation and Changing Patterns of Disclosure in British Company Accounts, 1900-1940*, The Institute of Chartered Accountants in England and Wales, London.

Edwards, J. R. (1985), "The Origins and Evolution of the Double Account System: An Example of Accounting Innovation," *Abacus*, March, pp.19-43.

Edwards, J. R. (ed.), (1986), *Legal Regulation of British Company Accounts 1836-1900*, Volumes I and II, Garland Publishing, New York: NY.

Edwards, J. R. (1989a), *A History of Financial Accounting*, Routledge, London & New York.

Edwards, J. R. (1989b), "Industrial Cost Accounting Developments in Britain to 1830: A Review Article," *Accounting and Business Research*, Autumn, pp.305-17.

Edwards, J. R. (ed.), (1994), *Twentieth-Century Accounting Thinkers*, Routledge, London.

Edwards, J. R. and Boyns, T. (1992), "Industrial Organisation and Accounting Innovation: Charcoal Ironmaking in England 1690-1783," *Management Accounting Research*, No.3, pp.151-69.

Edwards, J. R. and Boyns, T. (1994), "Accounting Practice and Business Finance. Case Studies from the Iron and Coal Industry 1865-1914," *Journal of Business Finance and Accounting*, December, pp.1151-78.

Edwards, J. R. and Newell, E. (1991), "The Development of Industrial Cost and Management Accounting Before 1850: A Survey of the Evidence," *Business History*, Vol.33(1), pp.35-57.

Edwards, J. R., and Webb, K. M. (1984), "The Development of Group Accounting in the United Kingdom to 1933," *The Accounting Historians Journal*, Spring, pp.31-62.

Edwards, R. S. (1937a), *A Survey of the French Contributions to the Study of Cost Accounting During the Nineteenth Century*, Gee and Company, London.

Edwards, R. S. (1937b), "Some Notes on the Early Literature and Development of Cost Accounting in Great Britain," *The Accountant*, Vol.XCVII, pp.193-5, 225-31, 253-5 and 283-7.

Einhorn, H. J. and Hogarth, R. M. (1978), "Confidence in Judgement: Persistence of the Illusion of Validity," *Psychological Review*, No.5, pp.395-416.

Eisenstein, E. L. (1979), *The Printing Press as an Agent of Social Change: Communications and Cultural Transformations in Early-Modern Europe*, Cambridge University Press, Cambridge.

Emerson, H. (1908-9), "Efficiency as a Basis for Operation and Wages," *The Engineering Magazine*, Vols.XXXV and XXXVI.

Employee Benefit Plan Review (1993), "FAS 106: Firms Wait, Costs to Rise," *Employee Benefit Plan Review*, January, pp.50-1.

Evans, G. (1977), "From Abacus to Algorism: Theories and Practice in Medieval Arithmetic," *British Journal for the History of Science*, pp.114-31.

Evans, R. (1993), "Tweedie Rewrites the Rules," *Global Finance*, June 1993, pp.2-3.

Ewen, S. (1988), *Consuming Images: the Politics of Style in Contemporary Culture*, Basic Books, New York: NY.

Ezzamel, M., Hoskin, K. and Macve, R. (1990), "Managing It All By Numbers: A Review of Johnson & Kaplan's *Relevance Lost*," *Accounting and Business Research*, Spring, pp.153-66.

FASB (1978), "Objectives of Financial Reporting by Business Enterprises," *Statement of Financial Accounting Concepts 1*, Financial Accounting Standards Board, Stamford: CT.

FASB (1985), "Employers' Accounting For Pensions," *Statement of Financial Accounting Standards 87*, Financial Accounting Standards Board, Stamford: CT.

FASB (1991), *Financial Accounting Series Status Report*, 27 December, p.4.

Featherstone, M. (1991), *Consumer Culture and Postmodernism*, Sage Publications, London.

Fennell, E. A. (1994), *Figures in Proportion: Art, Science and the Business Renaissance*, Institute of Chartered Accountants in England and Wales, London.

Financial Reporting Council (FRC) (1992), *The State of Financial Reporting: Second Annual Review*, November, Financial Reporting Council, London.

Financial Reporting Council (FRC) (1993), *The State of Financial Reporting: Third Annual Review*, November, Financial Reporting Council, London.

Fisher, L. (1992), "Industry and ASB on Collision Course?," *Accountancy*, June, p.23.

Fitzgerald, A. (1993), "Benefits for the Professional, Not the Punter," *Accountancy*, April, p.95.

Fitzgerald, N. (1993), "Crucial to the Design," *CA Magazine*, August, pp.6-8.

Fleischman, R. K., Hoskin, K. W., and Macve, R. H. (1995), "The Crux of Alternative Approaches to Accounting History: The Boulton & Watt Case," *Accounting and Business Research,* forthcoming.

Fleischman, R. K. and Parker, L. D. (1990), "Managerial Accounting Early in the British Industrial Revolution: The Carron Company, A Case Study," *Accounting and Business Research*, Summer, pp.211-21.

Fleischman, R. K. and Parker, L. D. (1991), "British Entrepreneurs and Pre-Industrial Revolution Evidence of Cost Management," *The Accounting Review*, April, pp.361-75.

Fleischman, R. K. and Parker, L. D. (1992), "The Cost-Accounting Environment in the British Industrial Revolution Iron Industry," *Accounting, Business and Financial History*, September, pp.141-60.

Fleischman, R. K., Parker, L. D. and Vamplew, W. (1991), "New Cost Accounting Perspectives on Technological Change in the British Industrial Revolution," in Graves, F. O. (ed.), *The Costing Heritage*, Academy of Accounting Historians, Harrisonburg: VA, pp.11-24.

Fleischman, R. K. and Tyson, T. N. (1993), "Cost Accounting During the Industrial Revolution: The Present State of Historical Knowledge," *Economic History Review*, Vol.XLVI(3), pp. 503-17.

Flinn, M. W. (ed.) (1957), *The Law Book of the Crowley Ironworks*, Andrews & Co., Durham.

Flinn, M. W. (1962), *Men of Iron: The Crowleys in the Early Iron Industry*, Edinburgh University Press, Edinburgh.

Flood, R. L. and Carson, E. R. (1988), *Dealing with Complexity: An Introduction to the Theory and Application of Systems Science*, Plenum Press, London.

Flower, J. (1992), "The Verdict on FRED 1, Room for Improvement," *Accountancy*, March, pp.32-3.

Fogarty, T. J., Heian, J. B. and Knutson, D. L. (1991), "The Rationality of Doing `Nothing': Responses to Legal Liability in an Institutionalised Environment," *Critical Perspectives on Accounting*, September, pp.201-26.

Fogarty, T. J., Kirch, D. P., Zucca, L. J. and Meonske, N. (1993), "Institutional Theory, the Regulation of Accountant Competence, and the Board That Did Not Act: A Critical Assessment," *Unpublished Paper*, Third Critical Perspectives on Accounting Symposium, New York: NY.

Fogo, J. R. (1905), "History of Bookkeeping," in Brown, R. (ed.), *A History of Accounting and Accountants*, T. C. and E. C. Jack, Edinburgh, pp.93-170.

Forrester, D. (1980), "Early Canal Company Accounts: Financial and Accounting Aspects of the Forth and Clyde Navigation, 1768-1816," *Accounting and Business Research*, Special Issue, pp.109-23.

Foucault, M. (1980), *Power/Knowledge: Selected Interviews and Other Writings*, Pantheon Books, New York: NY.

Foucault, M. (1981), "The Order of Discourse," in Young, R. (ed.), *Untying the Text*, Routledge & Kegan Paul, London, pp.48-78.

Freedman, J. and Power, M. (eds.) (1992), *Law and Accountancy: Conflict and Cooperation in the 1990s*, Paul Chapman Publishing, London.

Freidson, E. (1986), *Professional Powers: A Study of the Institutionalisation of Formal Knowledge*, University of Chicago Press, Chicago: IL.

Freedman, J. and Power, M. (1992), "Law and Accounting: Transition and Transformation," in Freedman, J. and Power, M. (eds.) *Law and Accountancy - Conflict and Cooperation in the 1990s*, Paul Chapman Publishing, London, pp.1-23.

Fu, P. (1971) "Governmental Accounting in China During the Chow Dynasty," *Journal of Accounting Research*, Spring, pp.40-51.

Gaffikin, M. (1994), "Determined Seeker of Truth and Fairness: Raymond Chambers (1917-)," in Edwards, J. R. (ed.), *Twentieth-Century Accounting Thinkers*, Routledge, London, pp.1-18.

Garbutt, D. (1984), "The Significance of Ancient Mesopotamia in Accounting History," *The Accounting Historians Journal*, Spring, pp.83-101.

Garcke, E. and Fells, J. M. (1887), *Factory Accounts, Their Principle and Practice*, Arno Press, New York: NY (reprinted 1976).

Gardella, R. (1992), "Squaring Accounts: Commercial Bookkeeping Methods and Capitalist Rationalism in Late Qing and Republican China," *Journal of Asian Studies*, Vol.51(2), pp.317-39.

Gardner, M. (1983), *Logic Machines and Diagrams*, Harvester Press, Brighton.

Garner, S. P. (1954), *Evolution of Cost Accounting to 1925*, University of Alabama Press, Tuscaloosa: AL.

Garnsey, G. (1923), "Holding Companies and Their Published Accounts," *The Accountant*, 6 January, pp.13-26 and 13 and January, pp.53-68.

Garnsey, G. (1931), *Holding Companies and Their Published Accounts*, Gee & Co., London.

Garrett, A. A. (1961), *History of The Society of Incorporated Accountants 1885-1957*, printed by Oxford University Press, Oxford.

Gavens, J. J. (1990), "An Historical Perspective of Integration of the Australian Accounting Profession," in Parker, R. H. (ed.), *Accounting in Australia*, Garland Publishing, New York: NY, pp.381-434.

Gavens, J. J. and Gibson, R. W. (1992), "An Australian Attempt to Internationalise Accounting Professional Organisations," *The Accounting Historians Journal*, December, pp.79-102.

Geach, P. T. (1981), *Logic Matters*, Basil Blackwell, Oxford.

Gee, P. (1993), "The Off Balance Sheet Finance Solution," *Accountancy*, March, pp.82-3.

Geijsbeeck, J. B. (1914), *Ancient Double-Entry Bookkeeping*, Scholars Book Co., Houston: TX (reprinted 1974).

George, F. (1980), "Testrologic," *Computer Age*, October, pp.62-2 and November, pp.64-5.

Ghosh, J. (1993), "Conflicts, Resolutions and Enforcement," *Accountancy*, April, pp.90-1.

Gilmore, C. and Willmott, H. (1992), "Company Law and Financial Reporting: A Sociological History of the UK Experience," in Bromwich, M. and Hopwood, A. (eds.), *Accounting and the Law*, Prentice Hall, London, pp.159-90.

Godard, M. (1827), *Traité Général et Sommaire de la Comptabilité Commerciale*, Librairie du Commerce, Paris.

Goodhead, C. and Eilbeck, D. (1992), "Goodbye to Single Performance Indicators," *Accountancy*, December, pp.116-17.

Graese, C. E. (1964), "Responsibility Reporting to Management," *The Accounting Review*, April, pp.387-91.

Greer, H. C. (1954), "Managerial Accounting - Twenty Years from Now," *The Accounting Review*, April, pp.175-85.

Griffiths, I. (1986), *Creative Accounting*, Sidgwick & Jackson, London, 1986.

Guo, D. (1982), *Zhongguo Kuaiji Shigao*, Vol.I, Wuhan.

Guo, D. (1988a), *Zhongguo Kuaiji Shigao*, Vol.II, Beijing.

Guo, D. (1988b), "The Historical Contributions of Chinese Accounting," in Craswell, A. T. (ed.), *Collected Papers of the Fifth World Congress of Accounting Historians*, University of Sydney, Sydney, pp. 1-8.

Gwilliam, D. and Russell, T. (1991a), "Polly Peck: Where Were the Analysts?," *Accountancy*, January, pp.25-6.

Gwilliam, D. and Russell, T. (1991b), "Compliance With the Letter But Not the Spirit," *Accountancy*, April, p.35.

Gynther, R. S. (1966), *Accounting for Price-Level Changes: Theory and Procedures*, Pergamon, London.

Habermas, J. (1987), *The Philosophical Discourse of Modernity*, MIT Press, Cambridge: MA.

Hacking, I. (1990), *The Taming of Chance*, Cambridge University Press, Cambridge.

Hadden, T. and Boyd, D. (1992), "The Legal Control of Accounting Standards: A Critical View," in Bromwich, M. and Hopwood, A. (eds.), *Accounting and the Law*, Prentice Hall, Hemel Hempstead, pp.55-75.

Hain, H. P. (1966), "Accounting Control in the Zenon Papyri," *The Accounting Review*, October, pp.699-703.

Hall, H. L. C. (1904), *Manufacturing Costs*, The Bookkeeper Publishing Company, Detroit: MI.

Hamilton, R. (1777), *An Introduction to Merchandise*, privately printed, Edinburgh.

Hanson, F. A. (1993), *Testing Testing: Social Consequences of the Examined Life*, University of California Press, Berkeley: CA.

Harmon, R. L. (1992), *Reinventing the Factory II*, The Free Press, New York: NY.

Harrison, G. C. (1918-19), "Cost Accounting to Aid Production," *Industrial Management*, Vol.LVI(4), pp.273-82, (5), pp.391-8, and (6), pp.456-63; and Vol.LVII(1), pp.49-55, (2), pp.131-8, (3), pp.218-24, (4), pp.314-7, (5), pp.400-3, and (6), pp.483-7.

Harvey, D. (1989), *The Condition of Postmodernity*, Basil Blackwell, Oxford.

Hatfield, H. R. (1909), *Modern Accounting: Its Principles and Some of Its Problems*, Appleton, New York: NY (reprinted 1976).

Hatfield, H. R. (1966), "Some Variations in Accounting Practice in England, France, Germany and the United States," *Journal of Accounting Research*, Autumn, pp.169-82.

Heath, L. C. (1978), "Financial Reporting and the Evolution of Solvency," *Accounting Research Monograph 3*, American Institute of Certified Public Accountants, New York: NY.

Hein, L. W. (1963), "The Auditor and the British Companies Acts," *The Accounting Review*, July, pp.508-20.

Hein, L. W. (1978), *The British Companies Acts and the Practice of Accountancy: 1844-1962*, Arno Press, New York: NY.

Hernandez Esteve, E. (1994), "Luca Pacioli's Treatise *De Computis et Scripturis*: A Composite or a Unified Work?," in Yamey, B. S. and Edwards, J. R. (eds.), "From Clay Tokens to Fukushiki-Boki: Record Keeping over Ten Millennia," *Accounting, Business and Financial History*, March, pp.67-82.

Hess, H. (1903), "Manufacturing: Capital, Costs, Profits and Dividends," *The Engineering Magazine*, Vol.XXVI, pp.367-79.

Hines, R. D. (1989), "Financial Accounting Knowledge, Conceptual Framework Projects and the Social Construction of the Accounting Profession," *Accounting, Auditing and Accountability Journal,* Vol.2(2), pp.72-92.

Hiromoto, T. (1988) "Another Hidden Edge - Japanese Management Accounting," *Harvard Business Review*, July-August, pp.22-6.

Hodges, A. (1983), *Alan Turing: The Enigma of Intelligence*, Unwin, London.

Hofstede, G. (1978), "The Poverty of Management Control Philosophy," *Academy of Management Review*, Vol.4(3), pp.450-61.

Holgate, P. (1991), "A Hearty Welcome to the ASB - Mostly," *Accountancy*, April, p.33.

Holmes, G. (1970), "The Pergamon Story: The Historical Background," *Accountancy*, October, pp.697-705.

Holzer, H. P. and Rogers, W. (1990), "The Origins and Developments of French Costing Systems," *The Accounting Historians Journal,* December, pp.57-71.

Hooks, K. L. (1992), "Professionalism and Self-Interest: A Critical View of the Expectations Gap," *Critical Perspectives on Accounting*, June, pp.109-36.

Hope, A. and Briggs, J. (1982), "Accounting Policy Making - Some Lessons from the Deferred Tax Debate," *Accounting and Business Research*, Spring, pp.83-96.

Hope, A. and Gray, R. (1982), "Power and Policy Making - The Development of an R and D Standard," *Journal of Business Finance and Accounting*, Winter, pp.531-58.

Hopper, T. M. and Armstrong, P. (1991), "Cost Accounting, Controlling Labour and the Rise of Conglomerates," *Accounting, Organisations and Society*, Vol.16(5/6), pp.405-38.

Hopwood, A. G. (1972), "An Empirical Study of the Role of Accounting Data in Performance Evaluation," *Empirical Research in Accounting Supplement to the Journal of Accounting Research*, pp.156-82.

Hopwood, A. G. (1989), "International Pressure for Accounting Change: An Introduction," in Hopwood, A. G. (ed.), *International Pressure for Accounting Change*, Prentice Hall, Hemel Hempstead, pp.1-6.

Horngren, C. T. (1989), "Cost and Management Accounting: Yesterday and Today," *Journal of Management Accounting Research*, Fall, pp.21-32.

Hoskin, K. W. and Macve, R. H. (1986), "Accounting and the Examination: A Genealogy of Disciplinary Power," *Accounting, Organisations and Society*, Vol.11(2), pp.105-36.

Hoskin, K. W. and Macve, R. H. (1988), "The Genesis of Accountability: The West Point Connection," *Accounting, Organisations and Society*, Vol.13(1), pp.37-74.

Hoskin, K. W. and Macve, R. H. (1994), "Reappraising the Genesis of Managerialism: A Re-Examination of the Role of Accounting at the Springfield Armoury, 1815-1845," *Accounting, Auditing and Accountability Journal*, Vol.7(2), pp.4-29.

Howell, R. (1988), "After Product Costing: New Frontiers for Management Accounting," *Unpublished Paper*, NAA Third Annual Cost Conference, St. Louis: MO, 15 September.

Howitt, H. (1966), *The History of The Institute of Chartered Accountants in England and Wales 1880-1965 and of Its Founder Accountancy Bodies 1870-1880*, Heinemann, London.

Hudson, P. (1977), "Some Aspects of Nineteenth-Century Accounting Development in the West Riding Textile Industry," reprinted in Parker, R. H. and Yamey, B. S. (eds.) (1994), *Accounting History: Some British Contributions*, Clarendon Press, Oxford, pp.434-49.

Hughes, M. (1991), "A Challenging Task Ahead for All," *Accountancy*, December, p.33.

Humphrey, C., Moizer, P. and Turley, S. (1992), "The Audit Expectations Gap - Plus Ça Change, Plus C'est la Même Chose?," *Critical Perspectives on Accounting*, June, pp.137-62.

Humphrey, C., Turley, S. and Moizer, P. (1993), "Protecting Against Detection: The Case of Auditors and Fraud?," *Accounting, Auditing and Accountability Journal*, Vol.6(1), pp.39-62.

IASC (1988), *Framework for the Preparation and Presentation of Financial Statements*, International Accounting Standards Committee, London.

IASC (1994), *Reporting Financial Information By Segment*, International Accounting Standards Committee, London.

IASC Insight (1994), "A Tribute to David Cairns, Ten Years at IASC...," *IASC Insight*, December, pp. 4-5.

ICAEW (1969), "Statement of Intent on Accounting Standards in the 1970s," *Accountancy*, January (1970), pp.2-3.

Jacobsen, L. E. (1983), "Use of Knotted String Accounting Records in Old Hawaii and Ancient China," *The Accounting Historians Journal*, Fall, pp.53-61.

Jaques, E. (1982), *The Form of Time*, Heinemann, London.

Johnson, H. T. (1972), "Early Cost Accounting for Internal Management Control: Lyman Mills in the 1850s," *Business History Review*, Vol.46(4), pp.466-74.

Johnson, H. T. (1981), "Toward a New Understanding of Nineteenth Century Cost Accounting," *The Accounting Review*, July, pp.510-18.

Johnson, H. T. (1984), *The Role of History in the Education of Prospective Accountants*, University of Glasgow, Glasgow.

Johnson, H. T. (1986), *A New Approach to Management Accounting History*, Garland Publishing, New York: NY.

Johnson, H. T. (1991), "Managing by Remote Control," in Temin, P. (ed.), *Inside the Business Enterprise: Historical Perspectives on the Use of Information*, University of Chicago Press, Chicago: IL, pp.41-65.

Johnson, H. T. (1992a), *Relevance Regained: From Top-Down Control to Bottom-up Empowerment*, The Free Press, New York: NY.

Johnson, H. T. (1992b), "It's Time to Stop Overselling Activity-Based Concepts," *Management Accounting*, Vol.74(3), pp.26-35.

Johnson, H. T. and Kaplan, R. S. (1987a), *Relevance Lost: The Rise and Fall of Management Accounting*, Harvard Business School Press, Boston: MA.

Johnson, H. T. and Kaplan, R. S. (1987b), "The Rise and Fall of Management Accounting," *Management Accounting*, Vol.68(7), pp.22-30.

Johnson, R. T. (1993), "A History of Accounting for Income Taxes," in Coffman, E. N., Tondkar, R. T., and Previts, G. J. (eds.) *Historical Perspectives of Selected Financial Accounting Topics*, Irwin, Homewood: IL, pp.271-85.

Johnson, T. J. (1972), *Professions and Power*, Macmillan, London.

Johnson-Laird, P. N. (1983), *Mental Models: Towards a Cognitive Science of Language, Inference and Consciousness*, Cambridge University Press, Cambridge.

Jones, H. (1985), *Accounting, Costing and Cost Estimation, Welsh Industry: 1700-1830*, University of Wales Press, Cardiff.

Jones, M. J. (1992), "Accounting Revolution at Oxford in 1882: The Case of a Governmental `Deus ex Machina'," *Accounting and Business Research*, Spring, pp.125-32.

Journal of Accountancy (1994), "IASC Completes Comparability Project, Receives IOSCO Endorsement," *Journal of Accountancy*, January, p.23.

Kahneman, D., Slovic, P. and Tversky, A. (1982), *Judgment Under Uncertainty: Heuristics and Biases*, Cambridge University Press, New York: NY.

Kantar, R. (1984), *The Change Masters*, John Wiley, New York: NY.

Kaplan, R. S. (1984), "The Evolution of Management Accounting," *The Accounting Review*, July, pp.390-418.

Kedslie, M. J. M. (1990), *Firm Foundations: The Development of Professional Accounting in Scotland 1850-1900*, University of Hull Press, Hull.

Keister, O. R. (1963), "Commercial Record-Keeping in Ancient Mesopotamia," *The Accounting Review*, April, pp.371-6.

Keister, O. R. (1970), "The Influence of Mesopotamian Record-Keeping," *Abacus*, December, pp.169-81.

Keister, O. R. (1986), "Accounting 101 Four Thousand Years Ago," *The Accounting Historians Notebook*, Fall, pp.28-31.

Khalaf, R. (1993), "If It Ain't Broken," *Forbes*, April, p.100.

Kimizuka, Y. (1991), "The Evolution of Japanese Cost Accounting to 1945," in Graves, F. O. (ed.), *The Costing Heritage*, Academy of Accounting Historians, Harrisonburg: VA, pp.74-88.

Kimizuka, Y. (1992), "Cost Accounting in the Meiji Era (1868-1912)," *Sakushin Business Review*, No.1, pp.13-42.

Kitchen, J. (1982), "Auditing: Past Development and Current Practice," in Hopwood, A. G., Bromwich, M. and Shaw, J. (eds.), *Auditing Research: Issues and Opportunities*, Pitman Books, London, pp.25-51.

Kitchen, J. and Parker, R. H. (1980), *Accounting Thought and Education: Six English Pioneers*, The Institute of Chartered Accountants in England and Wales, London.

Kitchen, J. and Parker, R. H. (1994a), "Lawrence Robert Dicksee (1864-1932)," in Edwards, J. R. (ed.), *Twentieth-Century Accounting Thinkers*, Routledge, London, pp.206-44.

Kitchen, J. and Parker, R. H. (1994b), "Frederic Rudolph Mackley de Paula (1882-1954)," in Edwards, J. R. (ed.), *Twentieth-Century Accounting Thinkers*, Routledge, London, pp.225-51.

Knights, D. (1990), "Subjectivity, Power and the Labour Process," in Knights, D. and Willmott, H. (eds.), *Labour Process Theory*, Macmillan, London, pp.297-335.

Krause, E. A. (1971), *The Sociology of Occupations*, Little, Brown and Company, New York: NY.

Lane, F. C. (1977), "Double-Entry Bookkeeping and Resident √ Merchants," *The Journal of European Economic History*, Spring, pp.177-91.

Lane, H. M. (1897), "A Method of Determining Selling Price," *Transactions of the American Society of Mechanical Engineers*, pp.221-7.

Langenderfer, H. Q. (1987), "Accounting Education's History: a 100-Year Search for Identity," *Journal of Accountancy*, May, pp.302-31.

Larson, M. S. (1977), *The Rise of Professionalism: A Sociological Analysis*, University of California Press, Berkeley: CA.

Law, J. (1986), "On the Methods of Long-Distance Control: Vessels, Navigation and the Portuguese Route to India," *Sociological Review Monograph 32*, pp.235-63.

Leach, R. G. (1969), "The President Answers Back," *Accountancy*, October, pp.725-7.

Leach, R. G. (1981), "The Birth of British Accounting Standards," in Leach, R. G. and Stamp, E. (eds.), *British Accounting Standards the First 10 Years*, Woodhead-Faulkner, Cambridge, pp.3-11.

Lee, G. A. (1977), "The Coming of Age of Double-Entry: The Giovanni Farolfi Ledger of 1299-1300," *Accounting Historians Journal*, Fall, pp.77-95.

Lee, T. A. (1971), "The Historical Development of Internal Control From the Earliest Times to the End of the Seventeenth Century," *Journal of Accounting Research*, Spring, pp.150-57.

Lee, T. A. (1979), "The Evolution and Revolution of Financial Accounting: A Review Article," *Accounting and Business Research*, Autumn, pp.209-16.

Lee, T. A. (1989), "Education, Practice and Research in Accounting: Gaps, Closed Loops, Bridges and Magic Accounting," *Accounting and Business Research*, Summer, pp.237-53.

Lee, T. A. (1992), "The Audit Liability Crisis: They Protest Too Much!," *Accountancy*, December, p.102.

Lee, T. A. (1993), "Financial Reporting Quality Labels: The Social Construction of the Audit Profession and the Expectations Gap," *Accounting, Auditing and Accountability Journal*, Vol.7(2), pp.30-49.

Lee, T. A., (1995) "Shaping the US Academic Accounting Research Profession: The American Accounting Association and the Social Construction of a Professional Elite," *Critical Perspectives on Accounting*, forthcoming.

Lemarchand, Y. (1994), "Double-Entry Versus Charge and Discharge Accounting in Eighteenth-Century France," *Accounting, Business and Financial History*, March, pp.119-45.

Lennard, A. (1993), "Debt, Equity, or Something Else?," *Accountancy*, February, p.87.

Letwin, W. (1963), *The Origins of Scientific Economics*, Methuen, London.

Lewin, K. (1952), *Field Theory in the Social Sciences: Selected Theoretical Papers*, Associated Book Publishers, London.

Lilley, S. (1993), "Discourse and Sociotechnical Transformation," *PhD Thesis*, University of Edinburgh, Edinburgh.

Lin, Z. J. (1992), "Chinese Double-Entry Bookkeeping Before the Nineteenth Century," *The Accounting Historians Journal*, December, pp.103-22.

Lindblom, C. (1959), "The Science of Muddling Through," *Public Administration Review*, No.19, pp.79-88.

Littler, C. R. (1986), *The Development of the Labour Process in Capitalist Societies*, Gower Publishing, Aldershot.

Littleton, A. C. (1933), *Accounting Evolution to 1900*, American Institute Publishing Co., New York: NY. ✓

Lodge, D. (1975), *Changing Places*, Martin, Secker & Warburg, London.

Loehlin, J. C. (1968), *Computer Models of Personality*, Random House, New York: NY.

Loft, A. (1986), "Towards a Critical Understanding of Accounting: The Case of Cost Accounting in the UK, 1914-1925," *Accounting, Organisations and Society*, Vol.11(2), pp.137-70.

Loft, A. (1990), *Coming Into the Light*, Chartered Institute of Management Accountants, London.

Lopez, R. S. (1962), "Hard Times and Investment in Culture," *The Renaissance: Six Essays*, New York: NY.

Lowe, D. J., and Pany, K. (1993), "Expectations of the Audit Function," *The CPA Journal*, August, pp.58-9.

Lukka, K. and Pihlanto, P. (1994), "Martti Saario (1906-88): The Developer of Finnish Accounting Theory," in Edwards, J. R. (ed.), *Twentieth-Century Accounting Thinkers*, Routledge, London, pp.60-78.

MacDonald, G. (1992), "Substance, Form and Equity in Taxation and Accounting," in Freedman, J. and Power, M. (eds.), *Law and Accountancy - Conflict and Cooperation in the 1990s*, Paul Chapman Publishing, London, pp.62-79.

Macdonald, K. M. (1985), "Social Closure and Occupational Registration," *Sociology*, November, pp.541-56.

Macdonald, K. M. (1989), "Building Respectability," *Sociology*, February, pp.55-80.

MacNaughton, J. (1899), *Factory Bookkeeping for Paper Mills*, Wood Pulp, London.

MacNeal, K. (1939), *Truth in Accounting*, University of Pennsylvania Press, Pennsylvania: PA.

Macve, R. H. (1985), "Some Glosses on `Greek and Roman Accounting,'" *History of Political Thought*, pp.233-64.

Macve, R. H. (1989a), "Solomons Guidelines: Where Do They Lead?," *Accountancy*, March, pp.20-1.

Macve, R. H. (1989b), "Questioning the Wisdom of Solomons," *Accountancy*, April, pp.26-7.

Mann, J. (1903), "Oncost," *The Encyclopaedia of Accounting*, William Green and Sons, London.

Marple, R. P. (ed.) (1965), *National Association of Accountants on Direct Costing*, Ronald Press Co., New York: NY.

Marquette, R. P. and Fleischman, R. K. (1992), "Government/Business Synergy: Early American Innovations in Budgeting and Cost Accounting," *The Accounting Historians Journal*, December, pp.123-45.

Marshall, G. (1980), *Presbyteries and Profits*, Clarendon Press, Oxford.

Martinelli, A. (1983), "The Ledger of Cristianus Lomellinus and Dominicus De Garibaldo, Stewards of the City of Genoa (1340-41)," *Abacus*, December, pp.83-118. √

Mattessich, R. (1987), "Prehistoric Accounting and the Problem of Representation: On Recent Archaeological Evidence of the Middle-East From 8000 BC to 3000 BC," *The Accounting Historians Journal*, Fall, pp.71-91.

Mattessich, R. (1992), "On the History of Normative Accounting Theory: Paradigm Lost, Paradigm Regained?," *Accounting, Business and Financial History*, September, pp.181-98.

Matthews, J. (1993a), "Study Warns of Options Rule Impact," *Washington Post*, 12 May, p.F3.

Matthews, J. (1993b), "Congress Enters the Fray Over Executive Stock Option Rule," *Washington Post*, 13 August, p.G1.

Matz, A., Curry, O. J. and Frank, G. W. (1957), *Cost Accounting*, South-Western, Cincinnati: OH.

McBarnet, D. and Whelan, C. (1992a), "Regulating Accounting: Limits in the Law," in Bromwich, M. and Hopwood, A.(eds.) *Accounting and the Law*, Prentice Hall, Hemel Hempstead, pp.99-111.

McBarnet, D. and Whelan, C. (1992b), "The Elusive Spirit Of The Law: Formalism and the Struggle for Legal Control," in Freedman, J. and Power, M. (eds.), *Law and Accountancy - Conflict and Cooperation in the 1990s*, Paul Chapman Publishing, London, pp.80-105.

McCulloch W. (1970), *Embodiments of Mind*, MIT Press, Cambridge: MA.

McGee, A. (1992), "The 'True and Fair View' Debate: A Study in the Legal Regulation of Accounting," in Freedman, J. and Power, M. (eds.), *Law and Accountancy - Conflict and Cooperation in the 1990s*, Paul Chapman Publishing, London, pp.106-20.

McInnes, W. (ed.) (1993), *Auditing into the Twenty-First Century*, Institute of Chartered Accountants of Scotland, Edinburgh.

McKendrick, N. (1970), "Josiah Wedgwood and Cost Accounting in the Industrial Revolution," *Economic History Review*, Vol.XXIII(1), pp.45-67.

McKinnon, S. M. and Bruns, W. J. (1992), *The Information Mosaic*, Harvard Business School Press, Boston: MA.

McKinsey, J. O. (1922), *Budgetary Control*, Ronald Press Co., New York: NY.

McLuhan, M. (1964), *Understanding Media*, Routledge, London.

McMickle, P. L. and Vangermeersch, R. G. (eds.) (1987), *The Origins of a Great Profession*, The Academy of Accounting Historians, Memphis: TN.

McMonnies, P. N. (ed.) (1988), *Making Corporate Reports Valuable*, Kogan Page, London.

Measalle, R. L. (1993), "Market Value Accounting," *Arthur Andersen Paper*, CATO Institute, March, Chicago: IL.

Megill, A. (1979), "Foucault, Structuralism and the Ends of History," *Journal of Modern History*, pp.451-503.

Melis, F. (1950), *Storia Della Ragioneria*, Dott, Cesare Zuffi, Bologna.

Mepham, M. (1987), "A Conceptual Model for Data Base Accounting," *Working Paper*, British Accounting Association Conference, Glasgow.

Mepham, M. J. (1988), *Accounting in Eighteenth Century Scotland*, Garland Publishing, New York: NY.

Mepham, M. J. and Stone, W. E. (1977), "John Mair, M. A.: Author of the First Classic Bookkeeping Series," *Accounting and Business Research*, Spring, pp.128-34.

Merino, B. D. (1975), "The Professionalisation of Public Accounting in America: A Comparative Analysis of the Contributions of Selected Practitioners 1900-1925," *PhD Dissertation*, University of Alabama, Tuscaloosa: AL.

Metcalfe, H. (1885), *The Cost of Manufactures*, John Wiley & Sons, New York: NY.

Miller, P. (1987), *Domination and Power*, Routledge & Kegan Paul, New York: NY.

Miller, P., Hopper, T. M. and Laughlin, R. C. (1991), "The New Accounting History: An Introduction," *Accounting, Organisations and Society*, Vol.16(5/6), pp.395-403.

Miller, P. and Napier, C. (1993), "Genealogies of Calculation," *Accounting, Organisations and Society*, Vol.18(7/8), pp.631-47.

Miller, P. and O'Leary, T. (1987), "Accounting and the Construction of the Governable Person," *Accounting, Organisations and Society*, Vol.12(3), pp.235-65.

Miller, P. and Power, M. (1992), "Accounting, Law and Economic Calculation," in Bromwich, M. and Hopwood, A. (eds.) *Accounting and the Law*, Prentice Hall: Hemel Hempstead, pp.230-53.

Miller, P. B. W., Redding, R. J. and Bahnson, P. R. (1994), *The FASB - The People, the Process, and the Politics*, Irwin, Burr Ridge: IL.

Mills, P. A. (1994), "Henry Rand Hatfield (1866-1945): Life and Humour in the Dust of Ledgers," in Edwards, J. R. (ed.), *Twentieth-Century Accounting Thinkers*, Routledge, London, pp.293-308.

Mintzberg, H. (1973), *The Nature of Managerial Work*, Harper and Row, New York: NY.

Mintzberg, H. (1975), *Impediments to the Use of Management Information*, National Association of Accountants and The Society of Management Accountants of Canada, New York: NY.

Miranti, P. J. (1990), *Accountancy Comes of Age: The Development of an American Profession*, The University of North Carolina Press, Chapel Hill: NC.

Mitchell, A. (1990), "Bankruptcies Raise Questions Over Auditors," *Financial Times*, 6 December, p.13.

Mitchell, A. and Sikka, P. (1993), "Accounting for Change: The Institutions of Accounting," *Critical Perspectives on Accounting*, March, pp.29-52.

Mitchell, A., Puxty, A., Sikka, P. and Willmott, H. (1991), "Accounting for Change: Proposals for Reform of Audit and Accounting," *Discussion Paper 7*, Fabian Society, London.

Monden, Y. and Hamada, K. (1991), "Target Costing and Kaizen Costing in Japanese Automobile Companies," *Journal of Management Accounting Research*, Fall, pp.16-34.

Motyl, K. (1992a), "ASB Takes a Firm Stand on Securitised Loans," *Accountancy Age*, 26 November, p.11.

Motyl, K. (1992b), "Goodwill Wrangle to Reopen," *Accountancy Age*, 15 October, p.3.

Motyl, K. (1993a), "ASB Sets Sights on Off Balance Sheet Financing," *Accountancy Age*, 25 February, p.9.

Motyl, K. (1993b), "ASB to Outlaw `Hidden Liabilities,'" *Accountancy Age*, 18 February, p.1.

Motyl, K. (1993c), "Law Forces ASB to Think Again," *Accountancy Age*, 11 February, p.10.

Motyl, K. (1993d), "ASB New Rigour on Acquisitions," *Accountancy Age*," 8 April, p.12.

Motyl, K. (1993e), "Balance Sheet Reform Plans Come Under Fire," *Accountancy Age*, 8 July, p.3.

Mumford, M. (1979), "The End of a Familiar Inflation Accounting Cycle," *Accounting and Business Research*, Spring, pp.98-104.

Mumford, M. (1994), "Edward Stamp (1928-86): A Crusader for Standards," in Edwards, J. R. (ed.), *Twentieth-Century Accounting Thinkers*, Routledge, London, pp.274-92.

Murray, A. (1978), *Reason and Society in the Middle Ages*, Clarendon Press: Oxford.

NAA (1983), "Definition of Management Accounting," *Statement on Management Accounting 1A*, National Association of Accountants, New York: NY.

NACA (1922), *Proceedings of the International Cost Conference*, National Association of Accountants, New York: NY.

NACA (1958), *How Standard Costs Are Being Used*, National Association of Cost Accountants, New York: NY.

NACA (1968), "The Uses and Classifications of Costs," in Solomons, D. (ed.), *Studies in Cost Analysis*, Irwin, Homewood: IL, pp.105-17.

Nailor, H. (1994), "Towards Fairness in Acquisition Accounting," *Accountancy*, January, p.82.

Nakanishi, A. (1979), "On the Life of Luca Pacioli," *The Accounting Historians Journal*, Fall, pp.53-9.

Napier, C. J. (1991), "Secret Accounting in the P & O Group in the Inter-War Years," *Accounting, Business and Financial History*, September, pp.303-33.

Napier, C. and Noke, C. (1992a), "Accounting and the Law: An Historical Overview of an Uneasy Relationship," in Bromwich, M. and Hopwood, A. (eds.), *Accounting and the Law*, Prentice Hall, London, pp.30-54.

Napier, C. and Noke, C. (1992b), "Premiums and Pre-Acquisition Profits: The Legal and Accountancy Professions and Business Combinations," in Freedman, J. and Power, M. (eds.), *Law and Accountancy - Conflict and Cooperation in the 1990s*, Paul Chapman Publishing London, pp.42-61.

Neely, G. (1991), "The Spectre of a Predator's Charter," *Accountancy*, July, p.29.

Nicholson, J. L. (1909), *Factory Organisation and Costs*, Kohl Technical Publishing Co., New York: NY.

Nikitin, M. (1990), "Setting Up an Industrial Accounting System at Saint-Gobain (1820-1880)," *The Accounting Historians Journal*, December, pp.73-93.

Nobes, C. W. (1979), "Pacioli - the First Academic Accountant," *Accountancy*, September, pp.66-8.

Nobes, C. W. (1982), "The Gallerani Account Book of 1305-1308," *The Accounting Review*, April, pp.303-10.

Nobes, C. W. (1991), "Cycles in UK Standard Setting," *Accounting and Business Research*, Summer, pp.265-74.

Nobes, C. W. and Parker, R. H. (1984), "The Development of Company Financial Reporting in Great Britain 1844-1977," in Lee, T. A. and Parker, R. H. (eds.), *The Evolution of Corporate Financial Reporting*, Garland Publishing, New York: NY, pp.197-207.

Nobes, C. W. and Parker, R. H. (eds.), (1991), *Comparative International Accounting*, Prentice Hall, Hemel Hempstead.

Noke, C. (1981), "Accounting for Bailiffship in Thirteenth Century England," *Accounting and Business Research*, Spring, pp.137-52.

Norton, G. P. (1889), *Textile Manufacturers' Bookkeeping for the Counting House, Mill and Warehouse*, Simpkin, Marshall, Hamilton & Kent: London.

O'Bryan, D. O. (1989), "An Historical Development of Statement of Financial Accounting Standards Number 95: A New Era of Solvency Reporting," in Tondkar, R. H. and Coffman, E. N. (eds.) *The Academy of Accounting Historians Working Paper Series Volume 4*, Academy of Accounting Historians, Harrisonburg: VA, pp.312-26.

Olson, W. E. (1982), *The Accountancy Profession: Years of Trial: 1969-1980*, American Institute of Certified Public Accountants, New York: NY.

Orton, I. (1991), "ASB Begins to Rewrite Accounting Rule Book," *Corporate Accounting International*, 15 February, pp.6-7.

Ouchi, W. (1981), *Theory Z: How American Business Can Meet the Japanese Challenge*, Addison-Wesley, Reading: MA.

Pacioli, L. (1494), *Summa de Arithmetica, Geometria, Proportioni et Proportionalita*, Paganino de Paganini, Venice (reprinted *Paganino de Paganini*, Toscolano, 1523).

Pacioli Society (1990), *Luca Pacioli: Unsung Hero of the Renaissance*, Pacioli Society/ South-Western (video), Cincinnati: OH.

Paciolo, L. (1494), "Particularis de Computis et Scripturis," Brown, R. G. and Johnson, K. S., *Paciolo on Accounting*, McGraw-Hill, New York: NY.

Page, M. (1991), "Now Is the Time to be More Critical," *Accountancy*, October, p.31.

Pare, T. P. (1993), "A New Tool for Managing Costs," *Fortune*, 14 June, pp.124-29.

Parker, L. D. (1993), "Professional Accounting Body Ethics: In Search of the Private Interest," *Working Paper*, University of Alabama, Tuscaloosa: AL.

Parker, L. D., Ferris, K. R. and Otley, D.T. (1989), *Accounting for the Human Factor*, Prentice Hall of Australia: Sydney.

Parker, R. H. (1969), *Management Accounting: An Historical Perspective*, Augustus Kelley Publishers, New York: NY.

Parker, R. H. (1986), "The Development of the Accountancy Profession in Britain in the Early Twentieth Century," *Monograph 5*, The Academy of Accounting Historians, San Antonio: TX.

Parker, R. H. (1989), "How Accountants Invented Counting and Writing," *The Accountant's Magazine*, January, pp.26-7.

Parker, R. H. (ed.) (1990), *Accounting in Australia*, Garland Publishing, New York: NY.

Parker, R. H. (1991), *Macmillan Dictionary of Accounting*, Macmillan, London.

Pask, G. (1960), *An Approach to Cybernetics*, Hutchinson, London.

Pask, G. (1964), "A Discussion of Artificial Intelligence and Self-Organisation," *Advances in Computers*, Vol.5, p.109.

Patient, M. (1992), "The Relationship between Accounting and the Law from the Professional Accountant's Perspective," in Bromwich, M. and Hopwood, A. (eds.), *Accounting and the Law*, Prentice Hall, Hemel Hempstead, pp.15-29.

Paton, W. A. and Littleton, A. C. (1940), *An Introduction to Corporate Accounting Standards*, American Accounting Association, Evanston: IL.

Payen, A. (1817), *Essai sur la Tenue des Livres d'un Manufacturer*, Chez A. Johanneau, Paris.

Pears, S. (1929), "The Companies Act 1928," *The Accountant*, 2 February, pp.149-54.

Peasnell, K. V. (1982), "The Function of a Conceptual Framework for Corporate Financial Reporting," *Accounting and Business Research*, Autumn, pp.243-56.

Peasnell, K. V. and Yaansah, R. (1988), "Off Balance Sheet Financing," *ACCA Certified Research Report 10*, Certified Accounting Publications, London.

Perks, B. and Georgiou, G. (1992), "Financial Reporting Standard 1: A Fresh Start?," *Management Accounting*, February, pp.39 and 54.

Peterson, C. R., Schneider, R. J. and Miller, A. J. (1965), "Sample Size and the Revision of Subjective Probability," *Journal of Experimental Psychology*, Vol. XX, pp.522-27.

Pfeffer, J. (1977), "Power and Resources Allocation in Organisations," in Staw, B. and Salancik, G. (eds.), *New Directions in Organisational Behaviour*, St. Clair Press, Chicago: IL.

Pimm, D. (1990), "Off Balance Sheet Vehicles Survive Redefinition," *Accountancy*, June, pp.88-91.

Pollard, S. (1965), *The Genesis of Modern Management*, Harvard University Press, Cambridge: MA.

Pollins, H. (1956), "Aspects of Railway Accounting Before 1868," in Littleton, A. C. and Yamey, B. S. (eds.), *Studies in the History of Accounting*, Sweet & Maxwell, London, pp.332-55.

Pope, P. and Puxty, A. (1992), "What Is Equity?: New Financial Instruments in the Interstices between the Law, Accounting and Economics," in Freedman, J. and Power, M. (eds.) *Law and Accountancy - Conflict and Cooperation in the 1990s*, Paul Chapman Publishing, London, pp.121-43.

Porter, D. M. (1980), "The Waltham System and Early American Textile Cost Accounting 1813-1848," *The Accounting Historians Journal*, Spring, pp.1-15.

Potthoff, E. and Sieben, G. (1994), "Eugen Schmalenbach (1873-1955)," in Edwards, J. R. (ed.), *Twentieth-Century Accounting Thinkers*, Routledge, London, pp.79-94.

Power, M. (1993a), "Auditing and the Politics of Regulatory Control in the UK Financial Services Sector," in Picciotto, S., McCahery, J. and Scott, C. (eds.), *Corporate Control and Accountability*, Oxford University Press, Oxford, pp.187-202.

Power, M. (1993b), "The Politics of Financial Auditing," *The Political Quarterly*, July-September, pp.272-84.

Pratten, (1991), *Company Failure*, Institute of Chartered Accountants in England and Wales, London.

Previts, G. J. and Merino, B. D. (1979), *A History of Accounting in America: A Historical Interpretation of the Cultural Significance of Accounting*, Ronald Press, New York: NY.

Previts, G. J., Parker, L. D. and Coffman, E. N. (1990), "An Accounting Histiography: Subject Matter and Methodology," *Abacus*, September, pp.136-58.

Previts, G. J. and Robinson, T. R. (1994), "William A. Paton (1889-1991): Theorist and Educator," in Edwards, J. R. (ed.), *Twentieth-Century Accounting Thinkers*, Routledge, London, pp.309-18.

Raphael, B. (1976), *The Thinking Computer*, Freeman, San Francisco: CA.

Rayburn, F. R. and Powers, O. S. (1991), "A History of Pooling of Interests Accounting for Business Combinations in the United States," *The Accounting Historians Journal*, December, pp.155-92.

Rayer, K. (1992), "Bridging the GAP - American Style," *Accountancy*, June, pp.27-8.

Renshall, M. (1984), "A Short Survey of the Accounting Profession," in Carsberg, B. and Hope, A. (eds.), *Current Issues in Accounting*, Philip Allan Publishers, Oxford, pp.23-45.

Rhodes, R. (1990), "Goodwill - Are We Really Making Progress?" *Accountancy*, October, p.23.

Richardson, A. J. (1988), "Accounting Knowledge and Professional Privilege," *Accounting, Organisations and Society*, Vol.13(4), pp.381-96.

Robb, F. F. (1979), "The Dynamics of Opinion Change From a Systems Theoretic Viewpoint," *PhD Thesis*, Brunel University, London.

Robb, F. F. (1984), "Cybernetics in Management Thinking," *Systems Research*, Vol.1(1), pp.5-24.

Robb, F. F. (1986), "Alternative Ways of Managing the Development of I.T. Applications," *The Accountant's Magazine*, March, pp.45-8.

Robb, F. F. (1987), "Systems, Cybernetics and Managerial Information Systems," in Rose, J. (ed.), *Cybernetics and Systems: The Way Ahead*, Thales Publications, Margate, pp.735-40.

Robb, F. F. (1993a), "Suprahuman Systems and Management: Steering in Jeopardy?," in Stowell, F. A., West, D. and Howell, J. G. (eds.), *Systems Science: Addressing Global Issues*, Plenum Press, New York: NY, pp.97-107.

Robb, F. F. (1993b), "Human Conversations in Organisations- A Degraded Endosymbiosis?," in Lasker, G. E. (ed.) *Advances in Systems Studies*, International Institute for Advanced Studies in Systems Research and Cybernetics: Windsor, Ontario, pp.93-8.

Robertson, T. (1970), *A Pitman's Notebook: The Diary of Edward Smith, Houghton Colliery Viewer 1749*, Frank Graham, Newcastle-Upon-Tyne.

Robertson, T. (1984), "A Scottish Farmer and His Accounts: 1822-23," *The Accountant's Magazine*, January, pp.21-4.

Robnett, R. H., Hill, T. M. and Beckett, J. A. (1951), *Accounting: A Management Approach*, Irwin, Chicago: IL.

Rohan, T. M. (1990), "Sneak a Peek," *Industry Week*, Vol.239(2), 22 January, p.44.

Roll, E. (1930), *An Early Experiment in Industrial Organisation*, Augustus Kelley Publishers, New York: NY (reprinted 1968).

Rouse, R. and Rouse, M. (1979), *Preachers, Florilegia and Sermons*, Pontifical Institute of Medieval Studies, Toronto.

Runciman, W. G. (1978), *Weber: Selections in Translation*, Cambridge University Press, Cambridge.

Sadhwani, A. T. and Tyson, T. (1990), *Financial Managers' Guide to Selecting and Implementing Bar Codes*, National Association of Accountants, Montvale: NJ.

Saenger, P. (1982), "Silent Reading: Its Impact on Late Medieval Script and Society," *Viator*, Vol.13, pp.367-414.

Samuel, H. B. (1933), *Shareholders' Money*, Pitman, London.

Sapori, A. (1932), *Una Compagnia di Calimala ai Primi del Trecento*, Olschki, Florence.

Sasaki, S. (1992), "The Development of the Japanese Railway Accounting System: The Japanising Process of the British System, 1885-1950," in Tsuji, A. (ed.), *Collected Papers of the Sixth World Congress of Accounting Historians*, Accounting History Association, Japan, Vol.I, pp.223-54.

Scapens, R. W. (1991), *Management Accounting: A Review of Recent Developments*, MacMillan, London.

Schachner, M. (1993), "Small Firms Can Learn Lessons From Others' FAS 106 Encounters," *Business Insurance*, 3 May, 1993, p.7.

Schemenner, R. W. (1988), "Escaping the Black Holes of Cost Accounting," *Business Horizons*, January-February, pp.66-72.

Scheuermann, L. (1929), *Die Fugger als Montanindustrielle in Tirol und Karnten*, Duncker and Humbolt, Munich.

Schmalenbach, E. (1899), "Buchfuehrung und Kalkulation in Fabrikgeschäft," *Deutsche Metallindustriezeitung*, Vol.15.

Schmalenbach, E. (1920), *Grundlagen dynamischer Bilanzlehre*, Leipzig.

Schmalenbach, E. (1948), *Pretiale Wirtschaftslenkung*, Vol.2, W. Dorn, Bremen-Horn.

Schnutenhaus, O. R. (1948), *Neue Grundlagen der "Feste" Kostenrechnung. Die Betriebstrukturkostenrechnung*, Deutscher Betriebswirte-Verlag, Berlin.

Schweitzer, M. (1992), "Eugen Schmalenbach as the Founder of Cost Accounting in the German-speaking World," in Tsuji, A. (ed.), *Collected Papers of the Sixth World Congress of Accounting Historians*, Accounting History Association, Japan, Vol.II, pp.393-418.

Seay, R. A. and Schoenfeldt, R. C. (1989), "H. K. Hathaway on Product Costing: Relevant Issues of Contemporary Concern," *The Accounting Historians Journal*, Spring, pp.111-24.

SEC (1992), "SEC Announces Three Part Initiative on Exec Compensation," *SEC Accounting Report*, 4 April, Securities Exchange Commission, Washington: DC.

Shank, J. K. (1989), "Strategic Cost Management: New Wine, or Just New Bottles?," *Journal of Management Accounting Research*, Fall, pp.47-65.

Shank, J. K. (1993), "How Safe Is Your Job?," *Journal of Accountancy*, October, pp.72-80.

Shank, J. K. and Govindarajan. V. (1989), *Strategic Cost Analysis: The Evolution from Managerial to Strategic Accounting*, Irwin, Homewood: IL.

Shank, J. K. and Govindarajan, V. (1992), "Strategic Cost Analysis of Technological Investments," *Sloan Management Review*, Fall, pp.39-51.

Shannon, C. E. and Weaver, W. (1963), *The Mathematical Theory of Communication*, University of Illinois Press, Chicago: IL.

Shillinglaw, G. (1989), "Managerial Cost Accounting: Present and Future," *Journal of Management Accounting Research*, Fall, pp.33-46.

Sikka, P., Puxty, A., Willmott, H. and Cooper, C. (1992), "Eliminating the Expectations Gap?," *Certified Research Report 28*, The Chartered Association of Certified Accountants, London.

Sikka, P., Willmott, H. and Lowe, T. (1989), "Guardians of Knowledge and Public Interest: Evidence and Issues of Accountability in the UK Accountancy Profession," *Accounting, Auditing and Accountability Journal*, Vol.2(2), pp.47-71.

Simon, F. N. (1832), *Methode Complete de la Tenue des Livres*.

Simon, H. A. (1957), *Administrative Behaviour*, Free Press, New York: NY.

Simon, H. A., Guetzkow, H., Kozmetsky, G. and Tyndall, G. (1954), *Centralisation vs Decentralisation in Organising the Controller's Department*, Controllership Foundation, New York: NY.

Singleton-Green, B. (1990), "The Rise and Fall of the ASC," *Accountancy*, August, pp.84-5.

Singleton-Green, B. (1993), "The ASB: Critics That Won't Be Pacified," *Accountancy*, November, p.26.

Slimmings, W. (1981) "The Scottish Contribution," in Leach, R. G. and Stamp, E. (eds.), *British Accounting Standards: The First Ten Years*, Woodhead-Faulkner, Cambridge, pp.12-26.

Smallpeice, B. (1949), "The Evolution of Industrial Accounting," *The Accountant*, 1 October, pp.350-55.

Smith, A. (1776), *The Wealth of Nations*, Cannan, A. (ed.), Methuen, London (1904 reprint).

Smith, T. (1992), *Accounting for Growth: Stripping the Camouflage from Company Accounts*, Century Business, London.

Smout, T. C. (1986), *A Century of the Scottish People: 1830-1950*, Collins, London.

Solomons, D. (1952), *Studies in Costing*, Sweet & Maxwell, London.

Solomons, D. (1983), "The Political Implication of Accounting and Accounting Standard Setting," *Accounting and Business Research*, Spring, pp.107-18.

Solomons, D. (1986), *Making Accounting Policy: The Quest for Credibility in Financial Reporting*, Oxford University Press, Oxford.

Solomons, D. (1989a), *Guidelines for Financial Reporting Standards*, Institute of Chartered Accountants in England and Wales, London.

Solomons, D. (1989b), "The Solomons Guidelines: A Reply to the Critics," *Accountancy*, August, pp.21-3.

Solomons, D. (1991a), "Accounting and Social Change: A Neutralist View," *Accounting, Organisations and Society*, Vol.16(3), pp.287-95.

Solomons, D. (1991b), "A Rejoinder," *Accounting, Organisations and Society*, Vol.16(3), pp.311-12.

Someya, K. (1989), "Accounting `Revolutions' in Japan," *The Accounting Historians Journal*, Spring, pp.75-86.

Sowell, E. M. (1973), *The Evolution of the Theories and Techniques of Standard Costs*, University of Alabama Press, Tuscaloosa: AL.

Spencer-Brown, G. (1969), *Laws of Form*, Allen Unwin, London.

Spicer, E. E., and Pegler, E. C. (1911), *Practical Auditing*, H. F. L. Publishers, London.

Stacy, G, and Tweedie, D. (1989), "Setting a Standard for the Value of Goodwill," *Financial Times*, 7 December, p.15.

Stamp, E. (1969), "The Public Accountant and the Public Interest," *Journal of Business Finance*, April, pp.32-42.

Stamp, E. (1980), *Corporate Reporting: Its Future Evolution*, Canadian Institute of Chartered Accountants, Toronto.

Stamp, E. (1981), "A View from Academe," in Leach, R. G. and Stamp, E. (eds.), *British Accounting Standards: The First Ten Years*, Woodhead-Faulkner, Cambridge, pp.231-47.

Stamp, E. and Marley, C. (1970), *Accounting Principles and the City Code: The Case for Reform*, Butterworths, London.

Standish, P. (1990), "Origins of the *Plan Comptable Général*: A Study in Cultural Intrusion and Reaction," *Accounting and Business Research*, Winter, pp.337-51.

Stevelinck, E. (1985), "Accounting in Ancient Times," *The Accounting Historians Journal*, Spring, pp.1-16.

Stewart, J. C. (1986), *Pioneers of a Profession*, Garland Publishing, New York.

Stewart, J. E. (1993), "The Financial Accounting Standards Board's Project on Financial Instruments and Off Balance Sheet Financing," in *Proceedings of Arthur Andersen Accounting and Auditing Symposium*, Arthur Andersen & Co., Chicago: IL.

Stone, W. E. (1969), "Antecedents of the Accounting Profession," *The Accounting Review*, April, pp.284-91.

Stone, W. E. (1973), "An Early English Cotton Mill Cost Accounting System: Charlton Mills, 1810-1889," *Accounting and Business Research*, Winter, pp.71-8.

Stone, W. E. (1975), "The Tally: An Ancient Accounting Instrument," *Abacus*, June, pp.49-57.

Storey, R. K. (1977), *The Search for Accounting Principles: Today's Problems in Perspective*, Scholars Book Co., Houston: TX.

Strachan, W. (1909), *Cost Accounts*, Stevens and Haynes, London.

Strait, M. A. and Bull, I. (1992), "Do Academic Traditions Undermine Teaching?," *Journal of Accountancy*, September, pp.69-73.

Swift, J. (1726), *Gulliver's Travels*, Part III, Chapter 5.

Sweeney, H. W. (1936), *Stabilised Accounting*, Harper, New York: NY.

Taylor, F. W. (1903), "Shop Management," *Transactions of the American Society of Mechanical Engineers*, Vol. XXIV(2), pp.1337-480.

Taylor, R. E. (1956), "Luca Pacioli," in Littleton, A. C. and Yamey, B. S. (eds.), *Studies in the History of Accounting*, Sweet and Maxwell, London, pp.175-84.

Taylor, P. and Turley, S. (1986), *The Regulation of Accounting*, Basil Blackwell, Oxford.

Thompson, G. (1991), "Is Accounting Rhetorical?: Methodology, Luca Pacioli and Printing," *Accounting, Organisations and Society*, Vol.16(5/6), pp.572-99.

Thompson, S. (1994), "Bringing Substance to Transactions," *Accountancy*, May, p.96.

Thompson, W. (1777), *The Accountant's Oracle*, N. Nickson, York.

Tinker, T. (1991), "The Accountant as Partisan," *Accounting, Organisations and Society*, Vol.16(3), pp.297-310.

Tinker, A., Merino, B. D. and Neimark, M. D. (1982), "The Normative Origins of Positive Theories: Ideology and Accounting Thought," *Accounting, Organisations and Society*, Vol.7(2), pp.167-200.

Tolkmitt, H. (1894), *Grundriss der Fabrik-Geschaeftsfuehrung*, Verlag von G.A. Gloeckner, Leipzig.

Towne, H. R. (1885-86), "The Engineer as an Economist," *Transactions of the American Society of Mechanical Engineers*, Vol.VII(2) pp.428-32.

Tse, N. S. (1993), "Applying Dynamical Systems Theory to the Understanding of Control Phenomena in Organisations," *PhD Thesis*, University of Edinburgh, Edinburgh.

Turley, S. (1992), "Developments in the Structure of Financial Reporting Regulation in the United Kingdom," *The European Accounting Review*, May, pp.105-22.

Tversky, A. and Kahneman, D. (1980), "Causal Schemas in Judgment Under Uncertainty," in Fishbein, M. (ed.), *Progress in Social Psychology*, Lawrence Erlbaum, Hillsdale: NJ, pp.49-72.

Tweedie, D. P. (1981), "Standards, Objectives and the Corporate Report," in Leach, R. and Stamp, E. (eds.), *British Accounting Standards: The First 10 Years*, Woodhead-Faulkner, Cambridge, pp.168-89.

Tweedie, D. P. (1983), "The ASC in Chains: Whither Self-Regulation Now?," *Accountancy*, March, pp.112-20.

Tweedie, D. P. (1986), *The Accountant: A Crusader or a Prisoner of the Past?*, Institute of Chartered Accountants of Scotland, Edinburgh.

Tweedie, D. P. (1993), "The Accounting Profession and Financial Reporting: Why Should They Believe Us?," *Research in Accounting Regulation*, Vol.7, pp.161-82.

Tweedie, D. P. and Kellas, J. (1987), "Off-Balance Sheet Financing," *Accountancy*, April, pp.91-4.

Tweedie, D. P. and Whittington, G. (1984), *The Debate on Inflation Accounting*, Cambridge University Press, Cambridge.

Tweedie, D. P. and Whittington, G. (1990), "Financial Reporting: Current Problems and Their Implications for Systematic Reform," *Accounting and Business Research*, Winter, pp.87-102.

Tyson, T. (1989), "Improving Data Collection Through Bar Coding," *Journal of Accounting and EDP*, Winter, pp.10-13.

Tyson, T. (1990), "Accounting for Labour in the Early Nineteenth Century: the US Arms Making Experience," *The Accounting Historians Journal*, Spring, pp.47-59.

Tyson, T. (1992), "The Nature and Environment of Cost Management Among Early Nineteenth Century US Textile Manufacturers," *The Accounting Historians Journal*, Fall, pp.1-24.

Tyson, T. (1993), "Keeping the Record Straight: Foucauldian Revisionism and 19th Century US Cost Accounting History," *Accounting, Auditing and Accountability Journal*, Vol.6(2), pp.4-16.

Vatter, W. (1950), *Managerial Accounting*, Prentice Hall, New York: NY.

Volmer, F. G. (1994), "Lucia Pacioli: The Perfect Accountant," in *The Flaming Torch*, Institute of Chartered Accountants of Scotland, Edinburgh, pp.1-18.

von Gebsattel, A. (1994), *Luca Pacioli's Exposition of Double-Entry Bookkeeping: Venice 1494*, Albrizzi Editore, Venice, pp.35-94 (English translation).

Walker, R. G. (1978), *Consolidated Statements: A History and Analysis*, Arno Press, New York: NY.

Walker, S. P. (1988), *The Society of Accountants in Edinburgh 1854-1914. A Study of Recruitment to a New Profession*, Garland Publishing, New York: NY.

Walker, S. P. (1991), "The Defence of Professional Monopoly: Scottish Chartered Accountants and `Satellites in the Accountancy Firmament' 1854-1914," *Accounting, Organisations and Society*, Vol.16(3), pp.257-83.

Walker, S. P. (1993), "Anatomy of a Scottish CA Practice: Lindsay, Jamieson & Haldane 1818-1921," *Accounting, Business and Financial History*, September, pp.127-54.

Walker, S. P. (1995), "The Genesis of Professionalisation in Scotland: A Contextual Analysis," *Accounting, Organizations and Society*, forthcoming.

Walsh, E. J. and Stewart, R. E. (1993), "Accounting and the Construction of Institutions: The Case of a Factory," *Accounting, Organisations and Society*, Vol.18 (7/8), pp.783-800.

Wason, P. C. (1960), "On the Failure to Eliminate Hypotheses in a Conceptual Task," *Quarterly Journal of Experimental Psychology*, No.12, pp.129-40.

Walton, S. (1988), "Beyond the Variance: Cost Accounting Challenges for the '90s," *Journal of Cost Management*, Winter, pp. 39-43.

Webb, S. (1993), "The Off Balance Sheet Finance Solution," *Accountancy*, March, pp.83-4.

Weber, C. M. (1992), "Harmonisation of International Accounting Standards: Process and Policy Steps," *The National Public Accountant*, October, pp. 40-2.

Weick, K. E. (1979), *The Social Psychology of Organising*, Random House, New York: NY.

Wells, M. C. (1977), "Some Influences on the Development of Cost Accounting," *The Accounting Historians Journal*, Fall, pp.47-61.

Whitmore, J. (1908), "Shoe Factory Cost Accounts," *Journal of Accountancy*, January, pp.12-25.

Whittington, G. (1989), "Accounting Standard Setting in the UK After 20 Years: A Critique of the Dearing and Solomons Reports," *Accounting and Business Research*, Summer, pp.195-205.

Whittington, G. (1991), "Good Stewardship and the ASB's Objectives," *Accountancy*, November, p.33.

Wiener, N. (1948), *Cybernetics: or Control and Communication in the Animal and in the Machine*, MIT Press, Cambridge: MA.

Wiener, N. (1954), *The Human Use of Human Beings: Cybernetics and Society*, Houghton Mifflin, Boston: MA.

Wilkinson, J. W. (1986), *Accounting and Information Systems*, John Wiley and Son, New York: NY.

Williams, J., Stanga, K. and Holder W. (1989), *Intermediate Accounting*, Harcourt Brace Jovanovich, New York: NY.

Willmott, H. (1990), "Serving the Public Interest? A Critical Analysis of a Professional Claim," in Cooper, D. J. and Hopper, T. M. (eds.), *Critical Accounts*, Macmillan, London, pp.315-31.

Wise, T. A. (1982), *Peat, Marwick, Mitchell & Co.: 85 Years*, Peat, Marwick Mitchell & Co., New York: NY.

Wood, R. (1993a), "Securitisation - The View from the Sharp End," *Accountancy*, January, pp.74-5.

Wood, R. (1993b), "A View from the Boardroom," *Accountancy*, July, pp.96-7.

Woolf, E. (1990), "Arguments in the Goodwill Debate," *Accountancy*, May, pp.92-3.

Wootton, C. W. and Wolk, C. M. (1992), "The Development of `The Big Eight' Accounting Firms in the United States, 1900 to 1990," *The Accounting Historians Journal*, June, pp.1-27.

World Accounting Report (1991), "UK Earnings: Nothing to Escape Below the Line," *World Accounting Report*, May, pp.1-2.

World Accounting Report (1992a), "Who's a Fred (of the Big Bad Wolf?)," *World Accounting Report*, January, p.7.

World Accounting Report (1992b), "Hard Line Means Hard Luck For Hybrids," *World Accounting Report*, January, p.7.

World Accounting Report (1992c), "Consolidation Standard Issued," *World Accounting Report*, October, p.9.

World Accounting Report (1992d), "UITF Closes Goodwill Loophole," *World Accounting Report*, February, p.11.

World Accounting Report (1992e), "ASB Report on Goodwill," *World Accounting Report*, March, p.9.

World Accounting Report (1992f), "Post-Retirement Benefits to Follow US Lead," *World Accounting Report*, December, pp.10-11.

World Accounting Report (1992g), "New Proposals on Securitisation," *World Accounting Report*, December, p.10.

World Accounting Report (1993a), "Straightening Out the Hidden Finance," *World Accounting Report*, March, p.1.

World Accounting Report (1993b), "ASB Claims Legal Status for its Rulings," *World Accounting Report*, July, pp.9-10.

World Accounting Report (1994), "No Consensus on Goodwill," *World Accounting Report*, February, p.11.

Wright, D. W. (1990), "Accounting Pedagogy Based on Extant Authoritative Rules Versus Decision-Oriented Analysis: The Case of Other Post Employment Benefits," *Journal of Accounting Education*, Vol.8., pp.183-205.

Wyatt, A. R. (1988), "Professionalism in Standard Setting," *CPA Journal*, July, pp.20-32.

Yamey, B. S. (1947), "Notes on the Origin of Double-Entry Bookkeeping," *The Accounting Review*, July, pp.263-72.

Yamey. B. S. (1949), "Scientific Bookkeeping and the Rise of Capitalism," *The Economic History Review*, Vol.I(2&3), pp.99-113.

Yamey, B. S. (1956), "Introduction," in Littleton, A. C. and Yamey, B. S. (eds.), *Studies in the History of Accounting*, Sweet & Maxwell, London, pp.1-13.

Yamey, B. S. (1960), "The Development of Company Accounting Conventions," *Three Banks Review*, September, pp.3-18.

Yamey, B. S. (1964), "Accounting and the Rise of Capitalism: Further Notes on a Theme by Sombart," *Journal of Acoounting Research*, Autumn, pp.117-36.

Yamey, B. S. (1967), "Fifteenth and Sixteenth Century Manuscripts on the Art of Bookkeeping," *Journal of Accounting Research*, Spring, pp.51-76.

Yamey, B. S. (1974a), "Luca Pacioli's *"Scuola Perfetta"*: A Bibliographical Puzzle," *Gutenberg-Jahrbuch*, Mainz, Germany, pp. 110-16.

Yamey, B. S. (1974b), "Pious Inscriptions; Confused Accounts; Classification of Accounts: Three Historical Notes," in Edey, H. and Yamey, B. S. (eds.), *Debits, Credits, Finance and Profits*, Sweet & Maxwell, London, pp.143-60.

Yamey, B. S. (1975a), "Four Centuries of Books on Bookkeeping and Accounting," *Historical Accounting Literature*, London, pp. xvii-xxvi.

Yamey, B. S. (1975b)," Notes on Double-Entry Bookkeeping and Economic Progress," *Journal of European Economic History*, Winter, pp. 717-23.

Yamey, B. S. (1975c), "The Authorship and Sources of the `Niewe Instructie,'" in Kojima, O. and Yamey, B. S. (eds.), *Ympyn's A Notable and Very Excellente Woorke, 1547*, Kyoto, pp. 60-73.

Yamey, B. S. (1976), "Two Typographical Ambiguities in Pacioli's "*Summa*" and The Difficulties of its Translators," *Gutenberg-Jahrbuch*, Mainz, Germany, pp. 156-61.

Yamey, B. S. (1977), "Some Topics in the History of Financial Accounting in England, 1500-1900," in Baxter, W. T. and Davidson, S. (eds.), *Studies in Accounting*, Institute of Chartered Accountants in England and Wales, London, pp.11-34.

Yamey, B. S. (1978), "Pacioli's Pioneering Exposition of Double-Entry Bookkeeping: A Belated Review," in *Studi in Memoria di Frederigo Melis*, Vol.III, Giannini Editore, Naples, pp.569-80.

Yamey, B. S. (1980), "Early Views on the Origins and Development of Bookkeeping and Accounting," *Accounting and Business Research Special Issue*, pp.81-91.

Yamey, B. S. (1981), "Some Reflections on the Writing of a General History of Accounting," *Accounting and Business Research*, Spring, pp.127-35.

Yamey, B. S. (1989), "Business Accounts, 1200-1800: Double-Entry Bookkeeping," *Working Paper*, London School of Economics, London.

Yamey, B. S. (1991), "The Earliest Book on Industrial Accounting," in Graves, F. O. (ed.), *The Costing Heritage*, Academy of Accounting Historians, Harrisonburg: VA, pp.122-7.

Yamey, B. S. (1994a), "Preface," "Luca Pacioli, the *Summa* and *De Scripturis*," "Commentary on Pacioli's *De Computis et Scripturis*," in *Luca Pacioli's Exposition of Double-Entry Bookkeeping: Venice 1494*, Albrizzi Editore, Venice, pp.9, 11-33 and 95-171.

Yamey, B. S. (1994b), "Benedetto Cotrugli on Bookkeeping (1458)," *Accounting, Business and Financial History*, March, pp.43-50.

Yamey, B. S. (1994c), "Notes on Pacioli's First Chapter," *Accounting, Business and Financial History*, March, pp.51-66.

Young, W. A. (1923-24), "Works Organisation in the 17th Century: Some Accounts of Ambrose and John Crowley," *Transactions of the Newcomen Society*, Vol.IV, pp.73-101.

Zeff, S. A. (1972), *Forging Accounting Principles in Five Countries: A History and an Analysis of Trends*, Stipes, Champaign: IL.

Zeff, S. A. (1978), "The Rise of Economic Consequences," *Journal of Accountancy*, December, pp.56-63.

Zeff, S. A. (1982a), *Accounting Principles Through the Years*, Garland Publishing, New York: NY.

Zeff, S. A. (1982b), *The Accounting Postulates and Principles Controversy of the 1960s*, Garland Publishing, New York: NY.

Zeff, S. A. (1982c), "*Truth in Accounting:* The Ordeal of Kenneth MacNeal", *The Accounting Review*, July, pp. 528-53.

Zeff, S. A. (1984), "Significant Developments in the Establishment of Accounting Principles in the United States, 1926-1978," in Lee, T. A. and Parker, R. H. (eds.), *The Evolution of Corporate Financial Reporting*, Garland Publishing, New York: NY, pp.208-21.

Zeff, S. A. (1987), "Does the CPA Belong to a Profession?," *Accounting Horizons*, June, pp.65-8.

Zeff, S. A. (1989), "Recent Trends in Accounting Education and Research in the USA: Some Implications for UK Academics," *The British Accounting Review*, June, pp.159-76.